CHRISTIAN MIN[...]
CHIEFTAINCY

PROPOSING CHAPLAINCY AS AN INNOVATIVE MISSIONAL WAY TO ENGAGE THE INSTITUTION OF CHIEFTAINCY

GABRIEL N. YIDANA

Gabriel Yidana's book invites us to reimagine the contextualisation of the Christian message and ministry to reach the very core of African culture – the institution of chieftaincy. By reflecting on Pentecostal engagement with indigenous chiefs and their systems, Yidana reignites one of the most important questions in African Christianity: How can Christianity become truly African? His suggestion of chaplaincy as a missional strategy points us in the right direction. Anyone deeply interested in contextualisation in Africa will find this book helpful.

Dr Harvey C. Kwiyani
Lecturer: African Christianity and Theology, Liverpool Hope University, Liverpool, UK

Gabriel Yidana has addressed the need for a missional approach to serve the Chieftains, Christian and non-Christian of his home nation, Ghana. Derived from his doctoral studies, he argues for the need for Pentecostals to use a non-Denominationally neutral term of Chaplain, to serve Chieftains. This has a missional application as he describes the history and context and reasons to provide this ministry across Ghana. Every minister should consider this approach for their own local ministries with the Institution of Chieftaincy.

Dr Anne E Dyer
Research Centre Manager for the Library and Donald Gee Archives and Lecturer / Doctoral supervisions. Mattersey Hall, UK

In this blurb, two key words are underscored to situate this "must read book" in context. These words are *Christianity* and *Chieftaincy*. The subject of Chieftaincy as an Institution provides a very broad spectrum of thoughts that may be impossible to fully explore. It is interesting to note that in this book, the subject of Chieftaincy Institution has been situated within a major "complementary" domain which is Christianity, but often times the former is seen by many as "rival" because it is presumed to be suffused with conflicting spiritualties. I am very delighted to say that this book has breathed fresh breath into this debate. And, in this debate the question of which institution is influencing the other comes up. I believe it is not one-way directional engagement which one institution is dominating the other. Rather, as beautifully crafted by the author, it is a mutually beneficial two-way engagement which each institution is influencing the other for the betterment of society. It is against this backdrop that I consider this book to be a very useful contribution to developmental knowledge and must be read. Indeed, the book is on a journey to comprehend the relatively little constructive missionary engagements between Christianity and Chieftaincy. Adopting the model of Chaplaincy as a key missional, the author is set to fill the gap that exists between Christianity and the Institution of Chieftaincy, and provide opportunities in fulfilling God's mission.

Prof. Paul Sarfo-Mensah
(Nana Kwasi Anim Sarfo Kantanka II, Chief of Kwadaso Anoo)
Senior Research Fellow/Development Consultant, KNUST, Kumasi,
Ghana

CHRISTIAN MINISTRY TO CHIEFTAINCY IN GHANA

CHRISTIAN MINISTRY TO CHIEFTAINCY IN GHANA

Proposing Chaplaincy as an Innovative Missional Way to
Engage the Institution of Chieftaincy

GABRIEL N. YIDANA

ISBN: 9798490953029

Missio Africanus
Liverpool, UK
info@missioafricanus.com
www.missioafricanus.com

Author Contact Details
Email address: gyidana75@gmail.com

Cover Photo by Retlaw Snellac Photography on flickr.

Contents

Foreword

Rev. Prof. Paul Frimpong-Manso

The work of the ministry has oftentimes been narrowed to church dogmas, sizes of congregations and the influence of ministers. This book expounds beyond such borders and brings on board the contemporary and theological significance of ministry work and how it impacts the Institution of Chieftaincy (IoC) in Ghana, West Africa. It shows how a carefully and prayerfully aligned ministry can touch Chieftaincy and move their concerns beyond dynasties and successions.

In this nine-chapter book, we find a positive correlation between and among Christianity, the ministry of chaplaincy and the institution of chieftaincy. The author gives us a broad plethora of examples with respect to how Christianity has positively changed and modernized structures governing the Institution of Chieftaincy. A classic example of this is seen in his assertion that, "… it is noteworthy that King Prempeh I converted to Christianity whilst in exile in the Seychelles. His conversion to Christianity had a great influence on the royal family and some culture and customs of Asanteman over the years." Christianity in Africa, no doubt, has been influenced by certain aspects of African cultures and traditions. However, the author points out that this influence is minimal; and that sometimes the adjustments became intractable.

The author extends the treatise to the Akan and Mamprusi Chieftaincy, and makes the point that all of these traditional set-ups were largely altered by Christianity. We have been informed in this all-encompassing book, about the manifesting contentions, criticisms and crisis that nearly jeopardized the co-existence of Christianity and the IoC. The author then calls for *chaplaincy involvement in transforming the IoC.*

We have been given exclusives to chew on in this large scale book, and I recommend it to all church and traditional leaders.

Rev. Prof. Paul Frimpong-Manso
General Superintendent, Assemblies of God, Ghana

Acknowledgments

This book comes out of my Doctoral study that was undertaken at Mattersey Hall Bible College in the UK but validated by the University of Chester. The study that informs the thesis could not have been possible without the support and assistance of the many marvellous people the Lord has brought into my life. First, I am very grateful to God and our Lord Jesus Christ for granting me the grace to pursue this study. Second, I wish to express my sincere gratitude to Dr Anne E. Dyer, Dr Harvey C. Kwiyani and Dr Robin Routledge for their support, timely insightful comments and constructive criticism of this work. To the Principals and staff of Mattersey Hall UK, ForMission College UK, the Presidents of West African Advanced School of Theology Togo and Assemblies of God Graduate School of Theology Ghana, I extend my sincere thanks for your support during this study. A special thanks to Dr Mary Ballenger, Rev Solomon Gomnah Nyabah, Rev James Abdulai, Rev Dr David Akonsi, Rev John K Boachie, Apostle Eric Nyamekye and Dr Ebenezer Owusu-Addo for all their help during my research in West Africa.

I would also like to thank Rev Prof Paul Frimpong-Manso and the entire leadership of the Assemblies of God Ghana (AoGG), as well as the leadership of the Church of Pentecost for their encouragement to pursue this study. I am grateful to Naa Prof. John Sebiyam Nabila (Wulugu Naba and Ex-President of National House of Chiefs, Ghana), Prof. Paul Sarfo-Mensah (Nana kwasi Anim II), Dr David Mensah (Mo/Deg *Gyasehene*), all participant Christian and traditional leaders for their invaluable support and contribution for this study.

Without the support and prayers of friends and family, this study would not have succeeded. I would forever be grateful to my parents Mary and Yidana Mankutui, whose support, prayer and wise counsel have brought me this far in my education and Christian faith. My sincere thanks to Maranatha Charismatic Centre – Tamale, Ghana and Good Shepherd Church – Leeds, UK for your prayers and financial support in my education. Finally, thanks to my lovely wife Joana, and four children for their love, support and encouragement during this study.

Abbreviations

AoG: Assemblies of God

AoGG: Assemblies of God, Ghana

ASRCL: Ashanti Region Christian Leader

ASRTL: Ashanti Region Traditional Leader

ATR: African Traditional Religion

CAC: Christ Apostolic Church

CoP: Church of Pentecost

IoC: Institution of Chieftaincy

NRCL: Northern Region Christian Leader

NRTL: Northern Region Traditional Leader

ONE

General Introduction

1.0 Introduction

F rom the 1960s, Pentecostalism in Ghana has been concerned
with growth and development of Christians in the country.
This period has witnessed the emergence of many impressive
congregations that attract young people and develop ministries
with programs that may affect the future of older churches.[1]
Instead of establishing programs to evaluate the efficiency of
missional engagement with the people and their culture, the church
is preoccupied in developing 'power' and 'prosperity' ministries to
sustain the growth experienced in the past decades. Failure to
address the shortcomings of engaging with groups such as the
Institution of Chieftaincy (IoC), considered to be deeply embedded
in the fabric of the Ghanaian society[2] has produced a gap between
Christianity and the IoC.

Some concerned members of the Assemblies of God Ghana (AoGG)
along with myself, have become aware of this lack of engagement
between Christianity and the IoC. This led the researcher to ask
questions about how Pentecostals can have a sustained engagement

with IoC. What are the cultural and theological concerns affecting any form of engagement? What mode of ministry would facilitate sustained engagement for the purpose of fulfilling the Church's mission? The question of why such lack of engagement between Christianity and the IoC existed was further heightened when the author realised that Pentecostal missionaries and indigenous Christians made attempts to convert people associated with chieftaincy in obedience to the Great Commission. The issue of lack of sustained engagement after earlier attempts require explanation and will not be resolved satisfactorily by using the available primary and secondary sources on Ghanaian Pentecostalism and the IoC. An exploration of potential reasons regarding the neglect of sustained engagement between Pentecostals and chieftaincy became the basis the author wanted to pose in his research. The purpose of this chapter is to provide the background and rationale of the study, aims and objectives, a survey of the theoretical literature used and methodology.

1.1 Background to the Development of Christianity, Chaplaincy and Chieftaincy in Ghana and Rational of Study

Ghana has been the recipient of Christianity from Western missionaries since the 15th Century. Today we see how the current growth in the church is highly evident in the African continent[3] which is the opposite of the situation c.1900. Christianity in Ghana has developed along Western ecclesiastical denominational lines as well as having some African Indigenous Churches with about 71.2% of the population being 'Christians',[4] whether Catholic, Anglicans, Presbyterian, Methodist or Pentecostal and others. Among the different ecclesiastical traditions, Pentecostals and Charismatics appeal to the Ghanaian society due to the pneumatic emphasis of Christianity. The missional drive of the church has enabled the formation of different strategies of outreach to fulfil God's mission. One such strategy is chaplaincy, which 'provides religious and spiritual care within an organisational setting,'[5] but in the context of the IoC is non-existent from Pentecostals. According to Andrew Todd who has programmes for training chaplains, Christian chaplains serve and live the gospel in different social domains like, prisons, hospitals, military, sport, theatre and many more.[6] Similarly, Ben Ryan who is a researcher at Theos identifies fresh chaplaincy models in commercial and retail workplace, city centres, targeting specific age groups and social groups that allow chaplains to engage with significantly diverse social settings.[7] This is evident to me that chaplaincy has moved beyond its traditional setting to engaging the broader society.

The IoC on the other hand, developed from the leadership of early community settlers until its present state. Stephen A. Brobbey states that these community leaders or chiefs were responsible for social stability, order and governance.[8] By the time missionary activities began in Ghana, the IoC was present in every tribal group with structures of leadership that developed into states and kingdoms. Brobbey acknowledged that Britain made use of the indigenous institution found on the ground to facilitate their rule and when democratic rule was introduced the importance of indigenous traditional systems of local government continued to be recognised.[9] However, the church seems to have neglected these indigenous political structures due to their link to African Traditional Religion. It is also evident in current literature that no detailed account has been documented on Christian involvement with chieftaincy. Despite useful contributions of some writers on Christianity and chieftaincy, these have generally not explained how Christianity has influenced or not influenced chieftaincy. The lack of extensive research on this subject is quite disturbing because missiological and other interest groups would not have any reference sources by which to determine gains and challenges encountered over time amongst both institutions.

During my pilgrimage as a Christian and minister of the Gospel in Ghana, I have observed that Pentecostals do not have sustained Christian witness within the IoC. I have observed from my own role

as a minister that ministry to the palaces are not sufficiently represented. For instance, converted Christian chiefs do not have the
privilege of readily accessing spiritual services of ministers. In addition, non-Christian chiefs, elders and all who are associated with
chieftaincy are denied Christian witness due to the insufficient
representation. Therefore, I wanted through this thesis to explore
the need for missional engagement through the lived experiences of
Christian and traditional leaders. Both Christianity and chieftaincy
claim divine connections. Whilst Christian leaders believe that they
are commanded by God to fulfil the Great Commission through
preaching salvation to all people on earth, chiefs are of the view that
God has placed them as leaders to serve the people (Matt. 28:18-20;
Mark 16:15-18; Luke 24:46-49; Acts 1:8; Rom. 13:1, 5 -6). This dissertation seeks to explore the role of chaplaincy in facilitating Pentecostal missional engagement with the IoC. The dissertation plots
the availability of ministry opportunities for chaplaincy within the
IoC. I argue that the proposal of chaplaincy as a missional model for
chieftaincy will fill the gap that exists between Christianity and the
IoC and provide ministry opportunities in fulfilling God's mission.
Although the word 'chaplaincy' has diverse meanings as argued in
chapter five and may be considered western, it is a familiar word
and ministry among Christian and traditional leaders in Ghana.[10]
Chaplaincy is taught in institutions in Africa.[11] The reason that I
chose chaplaincy is within the context of ministry, where spiritual
services are offered outside the structures of sacred places.[12]

The writer has been well and truly challenged by Emmanuel
Natogma, in the Conclusion of his 2008 PhD thesis where he states,
'African cultures dovetail the teachings of the Bible... African
church leaders, especially those with backgrounds of royalty
[should] explore the vast riches of their cultures.'[13] Similarly, Paul
Frimpong-Manso called for the need to teach chieftaincy issues at
our Bible colleges[14] whilst Kwame Opuni-Frimpong recounted
traditional leaders' desire to become "practicing and professing

Christians" as indicated by Nene Mate Kole.[15] The realization of these calls and aspirations would be achieved if the church's mission to chieftaincy is intentional. It is possible that the missional model of chaplaincy can be used as a strategy for Pentecostals to engage with the IoC. This, in essence, is the focus of my dissertation.

1.1.1 Research Question and Aims

The research question that justifies this thesis is: *How would chaplaincy enable Pentecostal denominational involvement with the Institution of Chieftaincy?*

The primary aim of this study is to provide an empirical foundation for how Christian chaplaincy would facilitate missional engagement with the IoC. To achieve this aim, the thesis has the following objectives:

1. To explore the historical account of chieftaincy, early Christian witness and engagement with the IoC
2. To narrate chiefly responsibilities and examine how missionaries and Christian leaders were criticising the IoC and why that impacts today's understanding of Pentecostals relating to Chiefs.
3. To examine the role of chaplaincy as a missional model for chieftaincy and assess the possibilities of chieftaincy cultural transformation through chaplaincy involvement in Christian witness with the IoC.

The study anticipates that achieving these objectives will provide practical guidelines and strategic insight for church leaders to develop mission policies. The findings from this study will provide reference for current and future generations to be informed of how the church bridged the gap between Christianity and the IoC. In addition, this work can serve as a resource for instructing Christians and training future leaders called to serve with the IoC and other institutions.

1.1.2 Thesis Structure

This thesis is divided into nine chapters. Chapter one provides the background to the study, its aims and objectives. It reviews relevant literature that covers the work of writers in Ghanaian Pentecostalism, chieftaincy and chaplaincy. Here I also discuss how and why my methodology was planned, the process of data collection and how data will be analysed and presented. It details the scope and limitations of the research and issues relating to the researcher's identity and flexibility. Chapter two explores the historical accounts of chieftaincy and early Christian engagement with the IoC. Chapter three accounts for the institutional setting of chieftaincy, narrates chiefly rituals and responsibilities just as sustained contact with missionaries and Christianity increased. It examines what missionaries and Christian leaders were criticising the IoC and why? The chapter closes with an assessment of the current relationship between the IoC and Christianity.

Chapter four looks at the ecclesial, contemporary cultural and institutional context of chaplaincy ministry. How existing chaplains operate in denominations other than Pentecostals and the role of the traditional priest to chieftaincy are covered in chapter five. This is followed by stating the theory, theology and practice of chaplaincy and the proposal of chaplaincy as a missional model to chieftaincy, highlighting its purpose and potential to conclude the chapter. Chapter six briefly explores the development and growth of major Pentecostal denominations, and it is here that the lack of Pentecostal chaplaincy to chieftaincy is revealed. The chapter also captures the formation of the Christian chiefs' associations and their call for Christian involvement in chieftaincy.

Chapter seven contains data analysis and results which identified key themes of participants' perceptions of the IoC. These themes, which include the role of chaplaincy in transforming chieftaincy culture and calls for chaplaincy involvement in the IoC, are captured in chapter eight. Chapter nine provides a summary, conclusions and recommendations.

1.2 Literature Review

The need to find relevant materials to the thesis led me to libraries across the UK, USA, Ghana and Togo. The search for recent scholarship was done through ATLA Religion Database and e-libraries of research institutions, using keywords such as; 'Pentecostals', 'Chieftaincy', 'Chaplaincy', 'Christianity', and 'Missional'. The subject 'Pentecostal chaplaincy ministry with the IoC' was only found in the few materials discovered in relation to the research.

To seek assistance for the research, I visited the headquarters of AoG, CoP and National House of Chiefs in Ghana. I met with Rev Prof Paul Frimpong Manso (General Superintendent of AoGG), Apostle Alexander Nana Yaw Kumi-Larbi (General Secretary of CoP) and Naa Prof John Sebiyam Nabila (Wulugunaba and Former President of National House of Chiefs) to request information relating to the thesis. At the Centre for Arts and Culture situated in Kumasi, I had access to archives of primary data in relation to the Ashanti King and the kingdoms' early contact with Christianity. The information applicable to the thesis I found is referred below.

The difficulty of finding existing scholarship seems to prevent conducting the research for this thesis within the field of current scholarship. However, scholarship in the area of chaplaincy in the West and Pentecostal history in particular, has been steadily growing. There is also a growing number of scholars in Ghana investigating Christianity and the IoC in general but not from the Pentecostal perspective that I am using. Since Pentecostalism has grown in imported and indigenous forms to a larger proportion of the population[16] than many mainline imported denominations, this has far more importance for the nation. The knowledge gained from these sources have contributed to the research. The following survey of existing scholarship seeks to gain understanding of Pentecostal denominational engagement with the IoC and to demonstrate the need for further research in this area.

1.2.1 Sources on African and Ghanaian Pentecostalism

Allan Heaton Anderson is a leading expert in the field of Pentecostal studies. His work, *An Introduction to Pentecostalism,* has provided an overview of contemporary global Pentecostal history.[17] He acknowledges how Pentecostalism is fast becoming a leading form of Christianity in Africa, comprising African initiated churches (CIA) and those from the 'classical' Pentecostal origin. He referred to the growth and development of African Pentecostalism as an 'African Reformation' which is inclined 'to adapt to and fulfil religious aspirations and offer practical solutions to felt needs.'[18] Anderson, in a follow up to his work *To the Ends of the Earth* explores the origin, organization, theology, mission, ministry and impact of global Pentecostalism.[19] Cornelis van der Laan summarises Anderson's contribution to Pentecostalism, with which I agree, as focusing on 'the global nature of the movement right from the start, speaking of a metaculture brought into existence through periodicals and missionary networks in its early stage'.[20] Whilst Anderson has significantly contributed to the understanding of global Pentecostalism and its impact on church growth in Africa, this thesis concentrates on chaplaincy as a missional model for Ghanaian Pentecostal denominational engagement with the IoC.

Ogbu Kalu's book, *African Pentecostalism: An Introduction,*[21] particularly outlines indigenous African Pentecostal experiences and 'classical' Pentecostal missionaries works of the AoG USA in Burkina Faso and Ghana from the late 19th to early 20th century. He wrote on Pentecostal theological emphasis on wealth creation, their engagement in African public space in ceremonies, deities, politics, other faiths and the reverse flow of immigrant Africans in the West. Paul Gifford *Ghana's New Christianity: Pentecostalism in a Globalizing African Economy*[22] examined recent developments in African Christianity. Gifford emphasised the independent Pentecostal/Charismatics doctrine and practices among megachurches in the Greater Accra region of Ghana. Emmanuel Kingsley Larbi's *Pentecostalism: The Eddies of Ghanaian Christianity*[23] explores the origins and development of the Pentecostal and charismatic Christianity in Ghana with particular interest in the concept of salvation through the worldview of the Akan peoples. Larbi acknowledges the appeal of Pentecostalism to Ghanaians and argues that unless a proper theological and practical response is made by the leadership of mainline churches, they run the risk of being swept aside by the wave of Pentecostal-Charismatic Christianity. Although chieftaincy, politics, deities and cultural ceremonies are mentioned in these writings, such references are minor to the main emphasis on Pentecostalism. This thesis redresses the neglected role of Pentecostal missional engagement with the IoC. By the end of this dissertation the researcher will have argued that Pentecostals should appoint chaplains to the IoC in order to facilitate furtherance of God's kingdom principles in their kingly responsibilities.

Johnson Kwabena Asamoah-Gyadu's *Contemporary Pentecostal Christianity*[24] and Joseph Quayesi-Amakye's *Christology and Evil in Ghana: Towards a Pentecostal Public Theology*[25] examine the contribution of Pentecostalism and its distinctive pneumatology to interpret key theological and missiological themes in reshaping African Christian spirituality. Asamoah-Gyadu argues that the Pentecostal plant of Ghana is not an imported tree, but a homegrown body.[26] He considers the growth of Ghanaian Pentecostalism to be linked to indigenous African beliefs and their encounter with Western Christianity and globalization. Similarly, Quayesi-Amakye explores the beliefs of members and leaders of CoP songs and sermons on Christology and evil, to discuss their fear of evil and finding security in the power of Jesus. Although Asamoah-Gyadu presents African Pentecostalism as a movement for the reinvention of the traditions of ATR and cultures and Christianity, he did not discuss how the 'reinventions' are implemented. Chapters seven and eight of this research examines the ministry opportunities for chaplaincy in ceremonies, festivals and traditions of chieftaincy cultures to enable cultural transformation within the IoC. Quayesi-Amakye on his part, has developed a 'theology of the public domain' in which he calls on the church to make a difference through its services and the establishment of educational institutions. In chapter seven of this thesis, participants identified education as one of the roles of chaplaincy ministry to facilitate cultural transformation of the IoC.

David Vespa[27] includes one chapter in his book entitled: 'Favor with the Kumbungu Chief', which described kind acts and how he and another missionary killed a Cape Buffalo (bush cow) that terrorised the people at Kumbungu. Vespa did not comment on the church's role of engaging with the IoC or what attempts were made to have Christians involved with chieftaincy. His work lacked empirical data on Christianity and chieftaincy. However, he narrated the steps they took to gain trustworthiness and wanted Jesus to shine through all their dealings with the chief and his people. This narration is significant to the research and, in my view, reveals the need for the church's continual engagement with chieftaincy for gospel witness. Natogma's[28] research study enabled him to describe and analyse the leadership styles of AoG Bible Colleges and Ministers in West Africa. Natogma noted the conflict between most African cultural practices and biblical principles of servant leadership. His analysis of the relationship between Pastoral leadership and chieftaincy is important to this thesis.

Ghanaian Pentecostal scholar, Paul Frimpong-Manso, provides the history of AoGG in his PhD thesis.[29] His objectives were to examine and explore constitutional developments, assess the extent to which AoGG has grown over the years since the 1930s, assess AoGG changes in character and style over time and to investigate how the church influenced the social, educational and political development of Ghana.[30] He narrates how chiefs received missionaries that enabled the establishments of churches in their communities. His discussion on AoGG influence in politics as one of his objectives was limited to democratic governance and admitted that the church as a religious organisation does not engage in politics but has encouraged individual members to be active in politics.[31] This is in line with what Burgess has said is 'the shift to Pentecostal political engagement and the increasing political influence of Pentecostal churches and leaders'[32] in Africa. Frimpong-Manso prioritised the internal AoGG history and did not focus on how the church influenced the IoC, which has been the indigenous Ghanaian political structure. Nevertheless, his research is still relevant to this study and his views as one of the respondents are captured in chapters six, seven and eight.

1.2.2 Sources on the Institution of Chieftaincy

The retired Ghanaian Supreme Court judge Brobbey, who worked as a legal consultant to the Government of Zimbabwe from 1981 to 1986 and seconded as the Chief Justice of the Gambia between 2004 to 2006, wrote *The Law of Chieftaincy in Ghana*.[33] In this book, Brobbey provides the constitutional and legal bases for chieftaincy in Ghana. He traces the origins, categories, installation processes and functions of chiefs. He states that the constitution 'takes away the power of the government or Parliament to control chiefs or reduce the dignity or honour of chiefs.'[34] This is significant in that it affirms the importance of the IoC in Ghana. Whilst painstakingly and systematically providing a useful general perspective to the study of chieftaincy in Ghana, Brobbey provided scanty information on chieftaincy and Christianity. He briefly mentioned chieftaincy's relation to religion and spiritism where he asked: 'Can a good Christian or Muslim be a good chief, or vice versa?'[35] Since Brobbey was writing on chieftaincy, he did not give much attention to their relations with Christianity, neither did he answer the question of whether good Christians can become chiefs. He simply explains how chieftaincy cultural practices raises issues with religion and spiritualism. This thesis explores chieftaincy cultural practices and argues that they are ministry opportunities for Pentecostal engagement through chaplaincy with the IoC.

Oseadeeyo Addo Dankwa III (*Okuapehene*) *The Institution of Chieftaincy in Ghana – the Future*,[36] Osei Safo-Kantanka *Can a Christian Become a Chief? An examination of Ghanaian ancestral practices in the light of the Bible*[37] Michelle Gilbert,[38] Gillian Feeley-Harnik,[39] Birgit Meyer,[40] Nauja Kleist,[41] Wyatt MacGaffey,[42] Pashington Obeng,[43] David C. Davis,[44] Kwabena J. Darkwa Amanor[45] and Peter Kwasi Sarpong,[46] all provide some historical perspective of Christianity and the IoC. Dankwa and Kleist throw some light on the roles of chiefs in Ghanaian social settings which include dealing with maintenance of law and order. Gilbert, Sarpong, Meyer, Amanor and Safo-Kantanka reveal the tensions that exist between Christianity and the IoC. These tensions are as a result of differences in the belief systems of Christianity and ATR associated with the IoC. For this reason, there is the need to find solutions to ease the tensions in areas relating to chieftaincy culture and beliefs in ATR. Safo-Kantanka particularly argues that commitment to the Christian faith does not necessarily mean cultural alienation. 'On the contrary Christianity must purify and heighten the ethnic experience of African people in light of the definitive and radical self-revelation of God in Jesus Christ.'[47] This is relevant to this thesis as it proposes chaplaincy as a missional model for Pentecostals to engage with the IoC in chapter 5.

Suzan Drucker-Brown's scholarly works[48] record Mamprusi chieftaincy culture, traditions and rituals in northern Ghana. Drucker-Brown outlines detailed analysis of the essential nature of the office of a chief (*naam*) and the role of the Female Chiefs, Chief Priests and Elders who share in certain aspects of ritual power with the *Nayiri* (King of Mamprugu). Drucker-Brown's works are social research documents and mainly descriptive of relevant information. Likewise, J. H. Kwabena Nketia,[49] Ernestina Afriyie[50] and Robert Addo-Fening[51] provide papers on Christianity and chieftaincy. Afriyie calls for the need for Christians to engage the religious beliefs and practices of the people but did not show how the engagement should be. Addo-Fening narrates the power of the gospel in transforming a traditionalist to a Christian evangelist. Whilst Nketia looks at the possibility of remodeling tradition in Christianity and African culture. However, none considered the role of chaplaincy in their discussion. Nevertheless, they are valuable to this research which looks at chaplaincy ministry opportunities in chieftaincy cultural practices, rituals, ceremonies and festivals within the IoC.

The Presbyterian scholar Kwabena Opuni-Frimpong's book *Indigenous Knowledge & Christian Missions: Perspectives of Akan Leadership Formation on Christian Leadership* examines the Akan pre-missionary leadership institutions, in order to use the wisdom and resources available for the construction of relevant Akan Christian leadership theology.[52] He observed the challenges, problems and concerns of indigenous Christian scholars and Western missionary interpretation of the Akan indigenous systems. Opuni-Frimpong acknowledges a paradigm shift in Christian mission that calls for reconciliation between African grass-root theologies and Christian mission theologies. His work is essentially helpful and by way of distinction, he calls for active participation of Christianity with culture and indigenous social groups such as the IoC. For Opuni-Frimpong, the denial of indigenous theologies in missionary enterprise has proved to be unhelpful, creates cultural tensions and makes Christian conversion superficial.[53] I agree. The empirical data of this present study supports the issues that Opuni-Frimpong identified with regard to cultural tensions and a new face of Christian mission in Ghana. That is why there is the need to consider hybridity as one way of resolving the tensions through chaplaincy in facilitating cultural transformation with the IoC. Daniel Shaw points out that hybridity is a more neutral term that reflects the reality of doing mission today.[54] He argues that hybridity represents the new thing that emerges because other entities came together, having two sides of the same coin, both of which are necessary.[55] Notwithstanding the criticism of 'hybridity',[56] I argue in this study that chieftaincy culture is one necessary side of the coin that should be handled by traditional elders alongside the provision of spiritual care to Christian chiefs through chaplaincy. Consequently, it is possible that the chaplaincy ministry would provide one of these necessary sides of the coin for missional engagement with the IoC.

1.2.3 Biblical (Theological) Understanding of Chieftaincy

For the Pentecostals, chieftaincy or kingship was ordained by God.[57] Both Christian and traditional leaders interviewed for this research acknowledged the divine connection of chieftaincy with God. They emphasised that chiefs as community leaders, occupy stools or skins which have been established by God and used the biblical Israelite kingship to buttress their stance. For them, God has not only ordained chieftaincy, but he also gives chiefs the wisdom to rule.[58] In the Old Testament, God gave Israel their first king in the person of Saul, as Samuel performed the ceremonial rituals.[59] Following king Saul, Israel continued to have kings up until the exile to Babylon. During the exilic period, faithful Jews like Daniel and Nehemiah served in kings' courts and God referred to kings such as Cyrus as his servants.[60] Opuni-Frimpong states that there are several traditional leaders who have benefited from Christian values of leadership formation from mission schools.[61] I agree because such leaders insist on the relevance of Christian leadership formation to their functions as traditional leaders.[62]

In the New Testament, the Gospels indicate that Jesus' disciples would be brought before governors and kings as witnesses to the gentiles.[63] Elsewhere in the New Testament, Paul is chosen to preach Christ to the Gentiles and kings.[64] Christians are asked to pray for kings and those in authority.[65] There is also a reference of the kings of the earth bringing their splendour before the Lord.[66] Safo-Kantanka comments and I agree that, the beauty of the New Jerusalem is not just an end-time reality, but through evangelism, cultures would be transformed, people-groups won for the Lord and chieftaincy must be brought under the Lordship of Jesus Christ.[67]

Elaine Graham, Heather Walton and Frances Ward's work reveal diverse models for *Theological Reflection Methods*, where 'Theology in the Vernacular': Contextual Theologies[68] is relevant to this study as this model gives 'attention to *culture* as a multidimensional lived reality that shapes the reception and transmission of the Christian faith'.[69] Reflecting from history, Graham, Walton and Ward argue that the day of Pentecost proved the global importance of Christianity as the early church dealt with the relationships between Jewish and Gentile cultures. Subsequently, the method was realized in the second Vatican Council and the evangelization of cultures and Donovan's ministry among the Masai to produce 'An African Creed'.[70] It is possible that the missional model of chaplaincy proposed in this study would enable Pentecostals to theologically reflect on the cultural practices through sustained ministry with the IoC.

1.2.4 Sources on Chaplaincy

The works cited here are on the missional and transformational approach of chaplaincy mostly drawn from western writers due to limited literature from the Ghanaian context relating to this dissertation. Although this is the case, the theory, theology and practice of chaplaincy from Western literature relevant to this study can be very much applicable to Christian mission in Ghana. Victoria Slater, in her 2013 thesis regarding the surge of chaplaincy in Church of England context, states that there is 'no literature relating to the theological, ecclesiological or cultural significance of the current re-emergence of interest in chaplaincy in community contexts'.[71] If there is insufficient literature in the UK context with regard to the development of chaplaincy in the contemporary setting, how much more is that true for Africa and within a Ghanaian context? Nevertheless, the following western literature on chaplaincy provides the theological bases in the context of God's mission in support of the proposal of chaplaincy to chieftaincy in Ghana. The biblical basis of chaplaincy in fulfilling God's mission and its broader outreach to diverse social settings is the reason why I am proposing it as a missional model for Pentecostals to engage with the IoC.

Gabriel Amoateng-Boahen, a certified professional staff chaplain at the University of Chicago Hospital, has written some proposals about engagement with health services and care in the Asante context.[72] He examined the Western and traditional approaches to Pastoral Care and discussed the African sense of spirituality relating to patients' emotional problems associated with fear of evil spirits. In as much as he has achieved his aim for writing his book, his view of chaplaincy as spiritual care providers has led him to consider traditional healers as 'Pastoral-Care Givers' and has not emphasised the missional role of chaplaincy in health services. On the contrary, Swift argues for an urgent need for theological re-engagement in an atmosphere of conflicting signals and statements on the professional identity of health care chaplaincy.[73] This is where a specifically Pentecostal chaplain may contribute due to their understanding of the holistic worldview. David N. A. Kpobi,[74] in Ogbu Kalu's *African Christianity: An African story*, provides a useful chapter on 'African chaplains.' Kpobi states that the chaplaincy institution sustained Christian Mission presence during European slave trading with nations. 'It was a policy of the Portuguese to place a priest on board all their ships, whose primary task was to keep spiritual oversight over the sailors.'[75] These chaplains were also responsible for evangelizing the local Africans. Kpobi revealed the role of notable men of African descent, trained as chaplains to evangelize West Africa.[76]

The missional model of chaplaincy proposed in chapter five in this study is based on the understanding that mission is fundamentally drawn from God's character as the source of mission and motivates Christians to fulfil the *missio Dei* (God's mission).[77] In the missional model of chaplaincy, Christian chaplains minister in the market-place and provide different forms of spiritual care to people outside the church walls.[78] Paget and McCormack, who are certified with the Association of Professional Chaplains, note that many religious groups provide chaplaincy ministry as an extension of their services to fill vital needs of spiritual care in the community.[79] The missional model of chaplaincy in this study goes beyond filling vital needs of spiritual care to include advising, evangelising and expecting transformation towards Christian values. According to Slater who spent several years as a Healthcare chaplain with CoE, 'chaplaincy is central to the mission of today's church.'[80] She came to this conclusion based on a qualitative case study research on the developments of chaplaincy roles. Similarly, Walters and Bradley argue that whilst evangelism should be seen as one aspect of the chaplain's ministry, chaplains should view their role as leading others in mission.[81] Caperon, who has been involved with school chaplaincy, notes that part of the necessary outward movement of mission is the ability of chaplaincy to continually discern the trans-forming purposes of God in diverse social situations and people.[82] These writers' contributions are relevant to this study, as they argue for the role of chaplaincy in the mission of the church.

Paterson who is a healthcare chaplain and lead trainer with NHS Scotland states, 'While informational learning can happen in solitude, transformational learning requires relationship.'[83] The transforma-tional approach requires the need to provide resources to inspire indi-vidual spiritual growth to attain maturity in Christ. In this context, in order to facilitate transformational learning, the presence of chaplains with chiefs builds relationships and gives assurances to the IoC. It is for this reason that the emergence of cultural competencies[84] required for chaplains ministering in multicultural societies would be an addi-tional value to help relationship building. The transformational approach would first of all enable chaplains to facilitate the spiritual growth of Christians within the IoC. Secondly, this approach would facilitate cultural transformation by introducing changes relevant in place of outmoded cultures in the IoC. The transformational approach of chaplaincy is relevant to this study because as Tienou observed, customs are considered pagan, 'but we have rarely provided appropriate substitutes for the cultural elements we ask people to discard'.[85] He goes on to say that there is nothing like a 'de-culturalised Gospel' and that there is the 'need to examine African culture very closely to see what elements are compatible or incompatible with the Gospel message'.[86] The empirical data revealed that Christians' active participation with chieftaincy would enable chaplaincy to provide the education and counsel needed to facilitate spiritual growth of individuals and cultural transformation in the IoC.

For the purpose of this dissertation, Threlfall-Homes' five theological models of chaplaincy[87] are important. First, the missionary model sees their task of sending the gospel to the unchurched in ways that suit their context. Second, the pastor model shares God's love and cares for the people. Third, the incarnational or sacramental model speaks of a ministry of presence or being not doing. Fourth, the historical parish model allows the chaplain to be present and engage with the people all the time. Fifth, the prophetic or challenging model enables the chaplain to question the status quo and speak prophetically to unjust or ungodly structures. Each of these models applies to either the missional or transformational approach of chaplaincy argued for in chapter five.

The above literature reveals that there is a limited work related to Pentecostal denominational engagement with the IoC. On the one hand, the existing works indicate lack of Pentecostal involvement and demonstrates tensions that exist between Christianity and chieftaincy. On the other hand, there is a growing interest in co-operation in interfaith relations between Christianity and the IoC which previously were not considered. This thesis argues and proposes for chaplaincy as a missional model for Pentecostal denominational engagement with the IoC to facilitate the growing interest in interfaith relationships. The thesis seeks to create the awareness of chaplaincy being able to offer spiritual care in places not often considered traditional Christian places of worship especially by Pentecostals. This call is for Pentecostals to revalue their heritage and let the incarnation of Jesus Christ be seen in the cultural practices of the IoC.

1.3 Methodology

The research was based on a qualitative methodology using a phenomenological approach through semi-structured interviews, group discussions and participant observation to enable an in-depth study of the views of participants. Phenomenological qualitative study focuses on providing rich textual descriptions and interpretations of the lived experiences of individuals through their 'life-world' stories.[88]

Corbin and Strauss observe that one of the virtues of qualitative research is that there are many alternative sources of data for the researcher to use, depending on the problem to be investigated.[89] As such, I considered other research designs like grounded theory and ethnography within the qualitative field that share a number of similarities with phenomenological, but have different emphases.[90] The differences are in how the research question may be asked, sample selected and the data collected analyzed.[91] For instance, grounded theory can introduce new information to an emerging narrative, by revising them while gathering data and following emerging leads focusing the methods.[92] Grounded theory is often used to produce or create the theory grounded in the data, while ethnography is basically interested in analyzing and developing meanings relating to cultures and social groups. In this case, neither grounded theory nor ethnography seemed suitable for this type of enquiry, other than phenomenological approach. The research is designed to inform Pentecostals of chaplaincy ministry opportunities that exist in the IoC. This study describes cultural practices associated with the IoC and respondents' perspectives of Christianity and chieftainship. It also determines if there were any challenges and solutions offered to facilitate engagement among both institutions.

1.3.1 Why a Phenomenological approach?

The choice of a phenomenological approach was informed by the aims of the study and the extant literature on the need to ensure methodological congruence in religious studies of this nature. Nelson notes that in religious studies, phenomenology is a central qualitative design that is often adopted due to its inherent ability to explore people's lived experiences and religious contradictions compared to other qualitative designs such as constructionism and grounded theory.[93] Cox, for example, argues that phenomenology has played an important role in shaping religious studies as an academic field.[94] More importantly, as the research aims to explore how Pentecostals can engage with the IoC, there was the need to adopt a qualitative design, which on theoretical grounds requires the researcher setting aside prejudices, withholding judgment and bracketing any prior assumptions. Some scholars have argued that the key ingredients in phenomenological studies include bracketing out prior assumptions, employing a fully empathetic approach, identifying typologies, and interpreting meaning.[95] Similarly, Kristensen observes that the use of phenomenology allows the researcher to get at the shared "meaning" or "religious significance" of practices evident in various traditions.[96] This makes the choice of a phenomenological design appropriate in this study as the study sits at the intersection of unearthing the shared "meaning" of the Christian religion and how this can inform the practices of chieftaincy in terms of facilitating missional engagement with the IoC through chaplaincy.

In line with the phenomenological approach, the study also adopted the insider's research approach or emic ethnography, within the context of data collection procedure. Social scientists have greatly explored the insider-outsider status of research.[97] This approach is used because, according to Andre Droogers although insiders might be apologetic because of their experience, outsiders might have potentially a bigger problem of facing difficulties in understanding the lived experiential reality of issues considered.[98] Insider researchers are considered as those who share similar characteristics, roles, or experiences with participants, and outsiders as those who are 'not seen as similar to their participants.'[99]

As the researcher, I am aware of researching from the emic perspective. I come from the royal family of the Mamprusi tribe in northern Ghana. My birthplace, Wulugu, is one of the divisional areas of the Mamprugu Traditional Council whose capital seat is at Nalerigu where the *Nayiri* (King of Mamprugu) resides. The Mamprusi subscribe to the 'Great Man' theory of leadership where leaders are both born and made.[100] I was born and raised a Christian and have been involved with AoGG activities as a minister for the past 28 years after completing ministry training from 1990 to 1992. During these years, I have been privileged to teach at the Northern AoGG Bible College and the ForMission College UK. In addition, I have served in leadership roles with AoG in Ghana and England. The experience derived from being an insider of chieftaincy and Christianity has provided me with a strength of cultural affinity.[101] This enabled the participants to demonstrate a level of openness, trust and acceptance, which they perhaps would not have done otherwise.[102] In narrating their experiences, chieftaincy participants used the term 'gone to the village', a cultural phrase commonly used without offering interpretation when referring to the death of a chief among the Akan peoples. Although the participants felt that I understood, it could be problematic if based on such an assumption an insider researcher does not investigate further or seek clarity.[103]

Nevertheless, I am aware of the outsider perspective that frees me from potential biases of research findings.[104] On one hand, arguments in favour of outsider researchers assert that they are 'more objective as they do not have loyalties to the culture being studied,'[105] and have the 'ability to observe behaviours without distorting their meanings.'[106] On the other hand, those against outsider researchers claim that they cannot understand a phenomenon if they have not experienced it. However, one does not have to be an insider to recognize and adequately represent the experience of participants being studied.[107] In view of this, there was cognisance of how my perspective as an insider might influence the data collection and interpretation of the data. I therefore adopted a series of pragmatic measures during the data collection including management of personal views about the role of chaplaincy in the IoC, to remove any potential barriers between me, as the interviewer and the study participants. Further, being mindful of the researcher's power in shaping and interpreting the data, the following measures were adopted to ensure trustworthiness: making memos to document hunches and decisions made and member checking (e.g., seeking clarifications from participants during interviews). The adoption of these measures was also essential in enhancing the rigour, credibility and dependability of the study findings.[108]

1.3.2 Participants and Sample Size

The field work was carried out in two administrative regions (Northern and Ashanti) in Ghana using semi-structured interview guides.[109] Ghana covers a land surface area of 238,837 sq.km with population estimates as 24,658,823 conducted in 2010.[110] It has ten administrative regions as shown in Figure 1.1 with about 46 dialects[111] although the official language is English.

Figure1.1 Political map of Ghana as of 2018[112]

According to Flick and Liamputtong, one of the fundamental issues in qualitative research is the ability to select information rich cases that will make conclusions from the findings more meaningful.[113] This study used maximum variation purposive sampling to identify respondents who could serve as information rich cases to provide the best information that would achieve the objectives set out in the study.[114] The participants were Christian leaders drawn from the Pentecostal denominations of AoGG and CoP, and traditional leaders from the IoC. To ensure a reflection of the nation, participants for interviews were picked from Northern and Ashanti regions. These two regions largely represent other tribes of similar cultural traditions from the northern and southern sectors of Ghana.

A total of 50 participants (47 males and 3 females) aged forty-five to ninety years, drawn from 30 Christian leaders and 20 traditional leaders were involved in this study.[115] The sample size was determined by progress towards data saturation. That is, preliminary analysis was done after each interview and by the 50th interview, it was realised that data saturation had been achieved.[116] This sample size is considered adequate taking cognisance of the research aims and the chosen study design. John Creswell, for example, argues that in a phenomenological study, a sample size between five and 25 is adequate.[117] A content analysis by Mark Mason examining the sample sizes of 560 PhD theses using a qualitative approach found that the average sample size was 31 with the most common sample sizes being 20 and 30.[118]

Most of the Christian leaders have, in addition to being ministers of local congregations, served as officers at the district, regional and national level of AoG and CoP in Ghana. Among the Christian leaders, there were two foreign missionaries and 12 ministers who have lectured or are still lecturers at Bible colleges and have obtained a master's degree. Ten of the 30 Christian leaders were church deacons or have served in some leadership role as laymen,[119] whilst five had obtained doctoral degrees and four were doctoral candidates either in Missions, Biblical studies or Christian education. Three of the traditional leaders were Paramount chiefs, five divisional chiefs; the rest were chiefs or were in some capacity of traditional leadership. Some of these traditional leaders had obtained higher education and were serving as magistrates in the law-courts, executives in corporations, lecturers in the universities and public schools.

The research was conducted after applying for ethical approval to the Research Ethics Committee of the University of Chester through Prof Robert Warner, Dean of Humanities in March 2013. The application confirmed that participants would be adults who freely give their consent with no coercion or inducements, and that data collected guaranteed the anonymity of their identities. It also ensured that participants would not be physically or emotionally affected. David Silverman posits that participants must be protected from embarrassment, psychological harm, damage to career and endangerment to their personal and professional relationships.[120]

1.3.3 Data Collection and Analysis

I had no problem in obtaining information from most participants because English is the official language used in Ghana. However, I made provision to use a translator where necessary with traditional authorities that culture and customs demand that the chief, king, or elder speak in the tribal language or with persons unable to communicate in English. I ensured that the exact meaning of words from the questionnaires were conveyed to tribal speaking participants during interviews. Patton acknowledges the important role language plays in obtaining primary data from interviewees and states that 'Using words that make sense to the interviewee, words that are sensitive to the respondent's context and worldview, will improve the quality of data obtained during the interview'.[121] The participants were selected through expression of interest. I identified the potential participants and sent out letters to inform them about the research aims, objectives and expected outcomes. They were asked to volunteer to participate in the interviews and other data collection activities. Only those who expressed interest in participating and returned the expression of interest and signed consent forms were contacted.

Audio and video data recording modes of fidelity and structure were utilized to guide data collection. Fidelity is the researcher's ability to later 'reproduce exactly the data as they became evident to him or her in the field'[122] of research. In most effective fidelity data collection, audio and video recordings play a vital role in obtaining the data. Patton also comments that there is no substitute for raw data of the 'actual words spoken by interviewees.'[123] Field notes were taken in addition to audio and video recorded interviews; where recurring words, themes, concepts were noted during the interview to later transcribe for analysis.

Questionnaires

Arguably, knowledge and understanding between Pentecostals and the IoC is a complex phenomenon. The complexities are found in the attitudes, views and teachings held in both institutions. To get a better understanding and insight into these, four sets of question-naires[124] were given to ministers, chiefs, church lay workers and traditional elders on specific issues in relation to the subject. These questions probed their knowledge on the history of interactions between the two institutions and their opinion on how chaplaincy would facilitate engagement with each other. The questionnaire in section A captured participants' demographic information on gender, tribe, region and position and in section B revealed the lived experience in their respective roles as Christian or traditional leaders or both. The questionnaire added a new focus and depth to the research.[125]

Both Christian leaders (CL) and traditional leaders (TL) who consented to be interviewed, answered the questionnaires with enthusiasm and commented that the subject was highly overdue. One minister said the study was 100 years late. During the adminis-tration of the questionnaires, I uniformly applied an approach that ensured further clarification, explanation and justification of answers. This was necessary to establish authentication based on the principle of the coherence of the answers given by the respon-dents. All questions asked required specific responses as shown in Appendix 1. From the questionnaire, some were used to explore satisfaction and dissatisfaction with Pentecostals involvement with the IoC, first from a Christian leader's perspective, then from the traditional leader's perspective.

- Has the church been of any support to you and can you elaborate on ways in which the church has supported you as a TL?
- How would you ensure that the church plays an active role

in the ceremony preceding the enthroning of a Christian candidate as a chief?
- How satisfied are you with the current level of involvement of Christianity with the IoC?

a. Highly Satisfied
b. Satisfied
c. Not satisfied

- What changes would you want to see? (i.e., Do the changes include the presence of chaplaincy ministry with the IoC?)
- How has the church influenced the IoC?

Interviews

After securing participants' consent, interviews were conducted at homes, palaces, offices, and locations with flexible times suitable for the enquiry. The interviews were mostly carried out on a face-to-face conversational process with a few first contact telephone interviews or follow up telephone interviews for clarification. I got first-hand description of the phenomenon by asking suitable questions and giving participants' the opportunity to express their experiences at will. Phenomenological enquiry allows for disclosure and provides space for people to describe their lived experiences. According to Patton, standardized open-ended interviews help researchers obtain 'data that are systematic and thorough for each respondent'[126] and provide a framework within which participants can freely express their own opinions. Open-ended in-depth interviews are useful for 'getting beyond the surface appearances'[127] and for researching sensitive and hidden issues of lived experiences in a phenomenological investigation.[128] This standardized open-ended approach further assisted me in the organization and analysis of the data obtained.

Generally, interviews were conducted from January to March 2014 and lasted between forty-five minutes to one hour thirty minutes.

The cultural norms for chiefs require the services of linguists, acting as spokespersons for the chiefs. However, participating chiefs resorted to having a direct interview with the researcher. This was important to the researcher in accessing the validity, quality, relevance and meaningfulness of the responses provided, as well as safeguarding their anonymity. The interviews enabled me to observe participants' expressions and to get a sense of their experiences for gathering this type of data. Participants were given time to develop ideas, express themselves and describe their experiences in detail.[129] All face-to-face interviews were electronically recorded using a voice recorder in addition to notes taken. Participants felt comfortable to be recorded, though it is argued that recording during an interview could adversely affect the process.[130]

Immy Holloway and Stephanie Wheeler argued that steps should be taken to minimise power imbalance during research interviews.[131] It was obvious that some of the participants like chiefs were people who willed power. Despite the power disparity that existed between such participants and myself, it did not influence their willingness to share with me what was necessary. My role as a minister likely assured the chiefs a safe environment to express themselves as they perceive ministers to be 'God's mouthpiece'. Even so, I focused on my role as a researcher rather than a minister. Furthermore, I assured them that with gratitude, I was here as a listener, to document the knowledge that they were willing to share with me. It is possible that a different interviewer might not have received such depths of information from the participants or their narrations might have been told differently.

Participant Observation

Clark Moustakas described a heuristic process of phenomenological research to include immersion, where the researcher is involved in the world of the experience.[132] He acknowledged the importance of participant observation in phenomenological research where he summarised its value from Patton. They include the following:

observation of the situational context, conclusions of significance, inferences not disclosed to be investigated further, and personal interpretation of the data experienced to be checked out further.[133] Richards states that whatever means researchers use in gathering data, they are participating and observing.[134]

In keeping with this focus on participant observation, I attended two events organised by chiefs during the period of my field trip. The first event was the annual conference organised by the Northern Ghana Christian Chiefs Association.[135] I arrived at the conference venue late in the evening at Carpenter in the Brong Ahafo region of Ghana on 19th February 2014. The next day, I participated in all the activities with the traditional leaders programmed for the day. Some of the chiefs that I earlier inter-viewed attended the conference, but I also had the opportunity to interview more. Participating in that event offered me the opportu-nity to observe traditional leaders actively involved in the program of the conference that sought to empower their leadership skills with Christian values. It was important for me to know of their experience as traditional leaders being resourced through the conference on how this could impact their reign as chiefs but also what missional opportunity the church could offer.

The second event was the *Akwasidae* celebration held at the Palace ground of the Ashanti King at Kumasi on 23 February 2014. (See Appendix 5 for the photographic evidence). At this event, subordi-nate chiefs of the kingdom, heads of institutions, government and religious leaders and other dignitaries attend to pay homage to the Ashanti king. Representatives of leaders from Islam, the Roman Catholic church and the Anglican community attended the event but conspicuously absent were leaders of the Pentecostals. For me, the notable absence of Pentecostal leaders at this event was the issue of cultural identity which was also a major problem for the early church. Tertullian, who held the view of non-negotiable gospel demands asked, 'what has Athens to do with Jerusalem?... attributing the highest authority to the unbroken integrity of the apostolic witness.'[136] In contrast to Tertullian, Justin Martyr argued that Christian converts should not abandon cultural loyalties that are consistent with the gospel.[137] In view of all that have been mentioned so far, it is hoped that the proposal of chaplaincy as a missional model to the IoC would help address some of these issues.

Data Analysis

For data analysis, following the steps outlined by Virginia Braun, Victoria Clarke and Jennifer Attride-Stirling, thematic analysis was used to help identify relevant constructs, concepts and categories in the interview transcript.[138] The interviews were first transcribed verbatim by the researcher and followed by checking the transcripts against the audio recordings for accuracy.[139] The field notes taken by the researcher were added to the interview transcripts to provide a complete set for the analysis. The researcher read the combined transcripts several times to identify meaningful units of text at the familiarisation stage. To retain anonymity,[140] participants were assigned numbers with the region and institution initials. For example, Ashanti region Christian leader (ASRCL1, ASRCL2), Ashanti region traditional leader (ASRTL1, ASRTL2), Northern region Christian leader (NRCL1, NRCL2) and Northern region traditional leader (NRTL1, NRTL2). Codes were developed from the keywords in the transcript to ensure that the participants' voices were accurately captured to preserve the richness of the data and the context of the interviews. Coding provides the researcher a means to reflect on what the code represents and its meaning.[141] The transcribed interviews were imported into Nvivo 11 Software (QSR International) for data coding.[142] A total of forty codes were generated from coding the transcripts.

The codes were subsequently subjected to thematic network analysis[143] involving the grouping together of codes into basic themes.[144] The themes were developed inductively in order to stay close to the data required in qualitative description.[145] However, to organise and summarise the emerging patterns, an interpretive process was used to gain broader meanings. The themes were cross-checked with the transcript to ensure that they were coherent and consistent with the data to maximise their reliability.[146] Furthermore, I compared this finding against published literature in key sources to develop a clearer understanding in relation to the larger field of knowledge and practice[147] of how Pentecostals can use chaplaincy as a missional policy to engage with IoC.

1.4 Summary

This chapter has provided the general background to the thesis, aims and objectives, literature relevant to the study and methodology. The next chapter considers the origins and establishment of kingdoms in Ghana, missionary exploration and the early engagement of Christianity with chieftaincy.

---

1. Johnson Kwabena Asamoah-Gyadu, *Contemporary Pentecostal Christianity*, (Oxford: Regnum Books International, 2013), p. 15.
2. Oseadeeyo Addo Dankwa III, *The Institution of Chieftaincy in Ghana – The Future*, (Accra: Konrad Adenauer Foundation, 2004), p. 1.
3. Allan Heaton Anderson, *To the Ends of the Earth; Pentecostalism and the Transformation of World Christianity*, (Oxford: Oxford University Press, 2013), p. 2.
4. Ghana Statistical Service, *Population and Housing Census 2010*, (Accra, Ghana: Sankofa Press Limited, 2012).
5. Ben Ryan, *A Very Modern Ministry: Chaplaincy in the UK*, (London: Theos, 2015), p. 10.
6. Andrew Todd, 'A Theology of the World' in John Caperon, Andrew Todd and James Walters, (eds.), *A Christian Theology of Chaplaincy*, (London: Jessica Kingsley Publishers, 2018), p. 21.
7. Ben Ryan, *A Very Modern Ministry: Chaplaincy in the UK*, (London: Theos, 2015), pp. 14-16.
8. Stephen A. Brobbey, *The Law of Chieftaincy in Ghana*, (Accra: ALP, 2008), p. 2.
9. Brobbey, *The Law*, p. 3.
10. David N. A. Kpobi, 'African Chaplains in Seventeenth Century West Africa' in Ogbu Kalu, *African Christianity: An African story*, (Trenton, NJ: African World Press, 2007), pp. 140-71.
11. Ndungu J. B. Ikenye, 'Chaplaincy: African Theory and Practice of Clinical Pastoral Care and Cure of the Soul', (Nairobi, Kenya: St Paul's University, 2011).

12. Victoria Slater, *Chaplaincy Ministry and the Mission of the Church*, (London: SCM Press, 2015), p. xvii.
13. Emmanuel Abdulai. Natogma, 'Leadership Styles in Assemblies of God Colleges in West Africa: A Study of Perspectives of Alumni, Academic Deans and Presidents' *PhD Thesis*, (Ann Arbor, MI: ProQuest LLC, 2008), p. 122.
14. Paul Frimpong-Manso, 'Theological education of Assemblies of God, Ghana', in *JEPTA* 33.2 (2013), p. 173.
15. Kwabena Opuni-Frimpong, *Indigenous Knowledge & Christian Missions: Perspectives of Akan Leadership Formation on Christian Leadership Development*, (Accra: SonLife Press, 2012), p. 88.
16. The 2010 Population and Housing Census of Ghana reports that out of the 71.2% Christian population, Pentecostals have the highest membership (28.3%) of the entire Christian population. Ghana Statistical Service, Population, (Accra: SPL, 2012); Ghana Religions, <https://www.indexmundi.com/ghana/religions.html> (accessed 28 December 2018).
17. Allan H. Anderson, *An Introduction to Pentecostalism*, 2nd ed. (Cambridge: Cambridge University Press, 2014).
18. Anderson, *Pentecostalism*, pp. 134, 135.
19. Anderson, *To the Ends*, (2013).
20. Cornelis van der Laan, 'Historical Approaches' in Anderson, et al, (eds.), *Studying Global Pentecostalism: Theories and Methods*, (Los Angeles CA: University of California Press, 2010), p. 210.
21. Ogbu Kalu, *African Pentecostalism: An Introduction*, (Oxford: Oxford University Press, 2008).
22. Paul Gifford, *Ghana's New Christianity: Pentecostalism in a Globalizing Economy*, (Bloomington & Indianapolis: Indian University Press, 2004).
23. Emmanuel Kingsley Larbi, *Pentecostalism: The Eddies of Ghanaian Christianity*, (Accra: CPCS, 2001).
24. Asamoah-Gyadu, *Contemporary Pentecostal Christianity*, (Oxford: Regnum Books International, 2013).
25. Joseph Quayesi-Amakye, *Christology and Evil in Ghana: Towards a Pentecostal Public Theology*, (Amsterdam: Rodopi B. V., 2013).
26. Asamoah-Gyadu, *Contemporary Pentecostal Christianity*, p. xvii.
27. David C. Vespa, *To Africa by God's Design*, (East Lakeland, FL: n. p., 2015).
28. Natogma, 'Leadership Styles', (2008).
29. Paul Frimpong-Manso, 'The origins, growth, developments and influence of AOGG' *PhD Thesis*, (Glyndwr University, 2014). Frimpong-Manso is currently the General Superintendent of AoGG.
30. Frimpong-Manso, 'Origins', pp. 20-21.
31. Frimpong-Manso. 'Origins', pp. 192-200.
32. Richard Burgess, 'Pentecostalism and Democracy in Nigeria: Electoral Politics, Prophetic Practices and Cultural Reformation', *Nova Religio*, Vol. 18, Issue: 3, (ATLAS) pdf, pp. 38-62.
33. Brobbey, *The Law*, (2008).
34. Brobbey, *The Law*, p. 3.
35. Brobbey, *The Law*, pp. 166-85.
36. Dankwa, *Chieftaincy*, (2004).

37. Osei Safo-Kantanka, *Can a Christian Become a Chief? An Examination of Ghanaian Ancestral Practices in the Light of the Bible,* (Kumasi: Payless Publications, 1999).

38. Michelle Gilbert, 'The Christian Executioner: Christianity and Chieftaincy as Rivals', *Journal of Religion in Africa,* Vol. 25 (Nov. 1995), pp. 347-86.

39. Gillian Feeley-Harnik, 'Issues in Divine Kingship', *Annual Review of Anthropology,* Vol. 14 (1985), pp. 273-313.

40. Birgit Meyer, 'Make a Complete Break with the Past' Memory and Post-Colonial Modernity in Ghanaian Pentecostal Discourse', *Journal of Religion in Africa,* Vol. 28 (Aug. 1998), pp. 316-49.

41. Nauja Kleist, 'Modern Chiefs: Tradition, Development and Return among Traditional Authorities in Ghana', *African Affairs,* Vol. 110, No. 441 (Oct. 2011), pp. 629-47.

42. Wyatt MacGaffey, 'Death of a King, Death of a Kingdom? Social Pluralism and Succession to High Office in Dagbon, Northern Region', *The Journal of Modern African Studies,* Vol. 44, No. 1 (Mar. 2006), pp. 79-99.

43. Pashington Obeng, 'Re-Membering Through Oath: Installation of African Kings and Queens', *Journal of Black Studies,* Vol. 28, No. 3 (Jan. 1998), pp. 334-56.

44. David C. Davis, 'Then the White man Came with His Whitish Ideas...: The British and the Evolution of Traditional Government in Mamprugu', *The International Journal of African Historical Studies,* Vol. 20, No. 4 (1987), pp. 627-46.

45. Kwabena J. Darkwa Amanor, 'Pentecostal and Charismatic Churches in Ghana and African Culture: Confrontation or Compromise?' *Journal of Pentecostal Theology* 18 (2009) 123-140.

46. Peter Kwasi Sarpong, *The Sacred stools of the Akan,* (Accra: Ghana Publishing Corporation, 1971) and *Libation,* (Accra: Anansesem Publication, 1996).

47. Safo-Kantanka, *Christian* p. i.

48. Susan Drucker-Brown, 'Ritual Aspects of the Mamprusi Kingship', *African Studies Social Research Documents,* Vol. 8 (Cambridge: African Studies Centre, 1975), 'The Court and the Cola Nut: Wooing and Witnessing in Northern Ghana', *The Journal of the Royal Anthropological Institute,* Vol. 1 No. 1 (March, 1995), 'Mamprusi installation ritual and centralisation: a convection Model', *The Journal of Royal Anthropological Institute* (MAN) 24, No. 3, (University of Cambridge, 1989), 'Horse, dog, and donkey: the making of a Mamprusi king', *The Journal of Royal Anthropological Institute,* (MAN) 27, No.1, (University of Cambridge, 1992) and 'The Grandchildren's Play at the Mamprusi King's Funeral: Ritual Rebellion Revisited in Northern Ghana', *The Journal of the Royal Anthropological Institute,* Vol. 5, No. 2 (Jun., 1999), pp.181-92.

49. J. H. Kwabena Nketia, 'Christianity and African Culture: Remodelling Tradition', *JACT,* Vol. 13, No. 1, (Akropong- Akwapem: AITMC, June 2010), pp. 10-18.

50. Ernestina Afriyie, 'Christ our Perfect Sacrifice: The Odwira Festival and Christianity in Contemporary Ghana', *JACT,* Vol. 17, No. 1, (Akropong-Akwapem: AITMC, June 2014), pp. 26-33.

51. Robert Addo-Fening, 'From Traditionalist to Christian Evangelist and Teacher – The Religious Itinerary and Legacy of Emmanuel Yaw Boakye (1834-1914)', *JACT,* Vol. 7, No. 1, (Akropong-Akwapem: AITMC, June 2004), pp. 3-13.

52. Opuni-Frimpong, *Indigenous,* (2012).

53. Opuni-Frimpong, *Indigenous,* p. 207.

54. R. Daniel Shaw, 'Beyond Syncretism: A Dynamic Approach to Hybridity', *International Bulletin of Mission Research*, 2018 Vol. 42(1), p. 6.
55. Shaw, 'Beyond Syncretism', p. 8.
56. See Chapter 3.6; 8.3.1 and 9.2.3.
57. Quayesi-Amakye, *Christology*, pp. 220-25.
58. Prov. 8:15; King Solomon asked for wisdom to rule Israel and one of his ruling on a case was as a manifestation of wisdom (1 Kgs. 3:5-28; 2 Chr. 1:7-12).
59. 1 Sam. 8-10.
60. Dan. 1:1-21; Neh. 1:10; Isa. 45:1, 13; 2 Chr. 36:22-23; Ezra 1:1-2.
61. Opuni-Frimpong, *Indigenous*, p. 200.
62. See Appendix 4.
63. Matt. 10:18; Mark 13:9; Luke 21:12.
64. Acts 9:15.
65. 1 Tim. 2:2.
66. Rev. 21:24.
67. Safo-Kantanka, *Christian*, p. 61.
68. Elaine Graham, Heather Walton & Frances Ward, *Theological Reflection Methods*, 2nd ed. (London: SCM Press, 2019).
69. Graham, Walton & Ward, *Theological Reflection Methods*, p. 217.
70. Graham, Walton & Ward, *Theological Reflection Methods*, pp. 217-49.
71. Victoria Slater, 'The fresh significance of chaplaincy for the Mission and Ministry of the Church of England: Three case studies in community contexts', *Thesis*, (Anglia Ruskin University, 2013), pp. 4, 8-9.
72. Gabriel Amoateng-Boahen, *Integral Pastoral Care in Ghana*, (Amazon, GB: Xlibris, <www.Xlibris.com> 2016).
73. Chris Swift, 'How should Health Care Chaplaincy negotiate its Professional Identity?' in Francis Ward, Charles Hampton and James Woodward, (eds.), *Contact: The Interdisciplinary Journal of Pastoral Studies*, 144, (Oxford: Contact, 2004), pp. 4-13.
74. Kpobi, 'African Chaplains', pp. 140-71.
75. Kpobi, 'African Chaplains', p. 152.
76. Kpobi, 'African Chaplains', p. 170.
77. David Bosch, *Transforming Mission: Paradigm Shifts in Theology of Mission*, New ed. (Maryknoll, NY: Orbis Books, 1991); John G. Flett, *The Witness of God*, (Grand Rapids, Michigan: William B. Eerdmans Publishing Company, 2010); Mike Barnett and Robin Martin, (eds.), *Discovering the Mission of God*, (Downers Grove, Illinois: IVP Academic, 2012).
78. Naomi K. Paget and Janet R. McCormack, *The work of the chaplain*, (Valley Forge, PA: Judson Press, 2015), pp. iv-v.
79. Paget and McCormack, *Chaplain*, pp. 92-94.
80. Victoria Slater, *Chaplaincy Ministry and the Mission of the Church*, (London: SCM Press, 2015), p. xiii.
81. James Walters and Charlotte Bradley, 'Chaplaincy and Evangelism', in John Caperon, Andrew Todd and James Walter, (eds.), *A Christian Theology of Chaplaincy*, (London: JKP, 2018), pp. 143-57.
82. John Caperon, 'Introduction: The Age of Chaplaincy?', in John Caperon, Andrew Todd and James Walters, (eds.), *A Christian Theology of Chaplaincy*, (London: JKP, 2018), pp. 7-42.

83. Michael Paterson, 'Supervision, Support and Safe Practice', in Christopher Swift, Mark Cobb and Andrew Todd, (eds.), *A Handbook of Chaplaincy Studies*, (Farnham, Surrey UK: Ashgate, 2015), pp. 149-59.

84. Sr. Norma Gutierrez, 'Cultural Competencies', in Rabbi Stephen B. Roberts, (ed.), *Professional Spiritual & Pastoral Care*, (Woodstock, Vermont: Skylight Paths Publishing, 2016), pp. 407–20.

85. Tite Tienou, *The Theological Task of the Church in Africa: Theological Perspectives in Africa No. 1*, 2nd ed. (Achimota, Accra: ACP, 1990), p. 22.

86. Tienou, *Theological Task*, p. 23.

87. Miranda Threlfall-Holmes, 'Exploring models of chaplaincy', in Miranda Threlfall-Holmes and Mark Newitt, (eds.), *Being a Chaplain*, (London: SPCK, 2011), pp. 116 -26.

88. D. Langdridge, *Phenomenological psychology: theory, research and method* (Harlow: Pearson Prentice Hall, 2007).

89. J. Corbin, and A. Strauss, *A Basics of Qualitative Research*, 3rd ed. (Los Angeles: Sage, 2008), p. 27.

90. Sharan B. Merriam, *Qualitative Research: A Guide to Design and Implementation*, (San Francisco, CA: John Wiley and Sons, 2009), p. 22.

91. Merriam, *Qualitative Research*, p. 22.

92. B. Glaser and A. Strauss, *The Discovery of Grounded Theory: Strategies for Qualitative Research*, (New York: Aldine, 1967), p. 3; K. Charmaz, *Constructing Grounded Theory: A Practical Guide through Qualitative Analysis*, (London: Sage, 2006), p. 14.

93. J. M. Nelson, 'Phenomenological approaches to religion and spirituality', In J. M. Nelson, (ed.), *Psychology, Religion, and Spirituality*, (Springer, New York, NY: 2009), pp. 103-42.

94. J. L. Cox, *A Guide to the Phenomenology of Religion: Key Figures, Formative Influences and Subsequent Debates*, (London: T&T Clark, 2006); *An Introduction to Phenomenology of Religion*, (London: Bloomsbury, 2009).

95. N. Iqbal, A. Radulescu, A. Bains, S. Aleem, 'An Interpretative Phenomenological Analysis of a Religious Conversion', *Journal of Religion and Health*, 58: (2019), pp. 426–43; P. Liamputtong, *Qualitative Research Methods*, (Oxford: Oxford University Press, 2013); J. A. Smith, P. Flowers, M. Larkin, *Interpretative phenomenological analysis: Theory, method, and research*, (Los Angeles: SAGE, 2009).

96. W. B. Kristensen, *The Meaning of Religion: Lectures in the Phenomenology of Religion*, trans. John B. Carman, (The Hague: Martinus Nijhoff, 1960).

97. Sonya Corbin Dwyer and Jennifer L. Buckle, 'The Space Between: On Being an Insider-Outsider in Qualitative Research', *International Journal of Qualitative Methods*, 8 (2009), pp. 54-63.

98. Andre Droogers, 'Essentialist and Normative Approaches' in Allan Anderson, Michael Bergunder, Andre Droogers and Cornelis van der Laan, (eds.), *Studying Global Pentecostalism: Theories and Methods*, (London: UC Press, 2010), p. 31.

99. Dwyer and Buckle, 'The Space Between:', p. 90.

100. R. M. Stogdill and B. M. Bass, *Stogdill's handbook of leadership: A survey of theory and research*, (New York: Free Press, 1981), p. 26.

101. Corbin and Strauss, *Qualitative Research*, p. 27.

102. Dwyer and Buckle, 'The Space Between', p. 90.
103. Dwyer and Buckle, 'The Space Between', p. 58.
104. J. Heard, 'Re-evangelizing Britain? An Ethnographical Analysis and Theological Evaluation of the Alpha Course', *PhD Thesis*, (London: Kings College, 2008).
105. James A. Banks, 'The Lives and Values of Researchers: Implications for Educating Citizens in a Multicultural Society', *Educational Researcher*, 27 (1998), pp. 4-17 (p. 6).
106. Beverley Mullings, 'Insider or Outsider, Both or Neither: Some Dilemmas of Interviewing in a Cross-cultural Setting', *Geoforum*, 30 (1999), pp. 337-50 (p.340).
107. Dwyer and Buckle, 'The Space Between', p. 58.
108. M. Q. Patton, *Qualitative research and evaluation methods: integrating theory and practice,* 4th ed. (London: SAGE, 2015).
109. See Appendix 1.
110. Ghana Statistical Service, *Population,* (Accra: SPL, 2012).
111. Patrick Johnstone, Jason Mandryk and Robyn Johnstone, (eds.), *Operation World: 21st Century Edition,* (Milton Keynes: Authentic Media, 2005) p. 274. The Joshua Project identifies 100 people groups in Ghana.
112. Google images, 'Political Map of Ghana', <https://www.google.com/search?q=political+map+of+ghana> [accessed, 12 February 2018].
113. Uwe Flick, *An Introduction to Qualitative Research*, 3rd ed. (London: Sage, 2006), Liamputtong, *Qualitative Research Methods*, (2013).
114. R. Kumar, *Research Methodology,* (London: Sage, 1999).
115. The leadership roles of both institutions are mostly patriarchal in composition.
116. Mark Mason, 'Sample size and saturation in PhD studies using qualitative interviews', *Forum: Qualitative Social Research*, 11(3) Art. 8 (September, 2010), <http://nbn-resolving.de/urn:nbn:de:0114-fqs100387> [accessed 3 January 2019].
117. John. W. Creswell, *Qualitative inquiry and research design: choosing among five approaches*, 3rd ed. (Thousand Oaks, CA: Sage, 2013).
118. Mason, 'Sample size'.
119. Laymen is the term used to describe people who are serving in a church leadership role but are not trained Ministers.
120. David Silverman, *Qualitative Research: Issues in Theory, Methods and Practice,* 3rd ed. (Los Angeles, CA: Sage Publications, 2011), pp. 431-32.
121. M. Q. Patton, *How to Use Qualitative Methods in Evaluation,* (Newbury Park, CA: Sage Publications Inc., 1987), p. 124.
122. Y. Lincoln and E. Guba, *Naturalistic inquiry,* (Newbury Park, CA: Sage, 1985), p. 240.
123. Patton, *How to Use Qualitative Methods*, p. 137.
124. See Appendix 1.
125. Martyn Denscombe, *The Good Research Guide: For Small Scale Research Projects,* (Buckingham, Philadelphia: Open University Press, 1998), p. 112.
126. Patton, *How to Use Qualitative Methods*, p. 113.

127. Steinar Kvale and Svend Brinkmann, *Interviews: Learning the Craft of Qualitative Research Interviewing*, 2nd ed. (London: SAGE, 2009), p. 28.

128. Amedeo Giorgi, *The Descriptive Phenomelogical Method in Psychology: A Modified Husserlian Approach*, (Pittsburgh, PA: Duquesne University Press, 2009), p. 122.

129. Denscombe, *The Good Research Guide*, p. 113.

130. Bill Gillham, *Research Interviewing: The Range of Techniques*, (Maidenhead: Open University Press, 2005), p. 39.

131. Immy Holloway and Stephanie Wheeler, *Qualitative Research in Nursing and Healthcare*, 3rd ed. (Oxford, UK: Blackwell Publishing Company, 2002), p. 97.

132. Clark Moustakas, *Phenomenological Research Methods*, (London: SAGE Publications, 1994).

133. Moustakas, *Phenomenological*, pp. 3-4.

134. Richards, *Handling Qualitative Data*, p. 45.

135. See Chapter 6.2.

136. Graham, Walton & Ward, *Theological Reflection Methods*, p. 217.

137. Graham, Walton & Ward, *Theological Reflection Methods*, p. 218.

138. Virginia Braun, & Victoria Clarke, 'Using thematic analysis in psychology', *Qualitative Research in Psychology*, 3, (2006), pp. 77-101; Jennifer Attride-Stirling, 'Thematic networks: An analytical tool for qualitative research', *Qualitative Research*, vol. 1 (3), (2001), pp. 385-405.

139. A total of 130,505 words of unedited transcript of recorded interviews is available for records.

140. Heard, *Re-evangelizing Britain?* (London: Kings College, 2008).

141. Lyn Richards, Handling *Qualitative Data: A Practical Guide*, 3rd ed. (London: SAGE, 2015).

142. P. Bazeley, & K. Jackson, *Qualitative data analysis with NVivo*, 2nd ed. (London: SAGE, 2014) Nvivo software is a package which allows for importing and storing various kinds of qualitative data to aid data management and analysis. This software has been found to be useful in coding qualitative data for in-depth analysis.

143. Attride-Stirling, 'Thematic', pp. 385-405.

144. See Table 7.1. in Appendix 1.

145. Richards, *Handling*, pp. 126-36.

146. J. Fereday & E. Muir-Cochrane, 'Demonstrating rigor using thematic analysis: A hybrid approach of inductive and deductive coding and theme development', *International Journal of Qualitative Methods*, 5, pp. 1-11.

147. Merriam, *Qualitative Research*, pp. 215-16.

TWO

The Origins and Establishment of Kingdoms in Ghana, Missionary Exploration and the Early Engagement of Christianity with Chieftaincy

2.0 Introduction

The account of chieftaincy and establishment of kingdoms in Ghana is traceable from the history of the people in their tribal setting to the present. Communities had leaders who governed them, and life to some extent revolved around the leader. Following Brobbey's[1] understanding, community leaders were invariably individuals who founded settlements for the people to live and work in, led them into war for conquest and defended them against intruders.[2] He acknowledged that these leaders also saved their communities from a succession of calamities and sometimes distinguished themselves by some unique and outstanding achievements in their communities.[3] As such, these leaders were given the title "Chief", and were responsible for social stability and order in the community.

The purpose of this chapter is to trace a brief history of the origins of kingdoms in Ghana, missionary exploration and early engagement of Christianity with chieftaincy. It is an attempt to investigate

Christians' relationship with chieftaincy in their quest to evangelize the people and how that has developed over the years.

2.1 The Origins and Establishments of Kingdoms in Ghana

The earliest inhabitants of modern Ghana migrated from the ancient empire of Ghana which was situated around the southern borders of the Sahara Desert and was close to the north-west of the Niger but had been destroyed through wars in the 11th century.[4] Hundreds of years later and by linguistic evidence the Guan, Fante and Twi-speaking peoples of the Akan or Ntafo tribal group eventually settled at the forest region of the south and parts of the coastal plains[5] of Ghana. The Ga-Adangbes migrated from Nigeria and settled along the coast of the country in the Accra plains whilst the Ewes are believed to have also come from Nigeria or Benin to occupy over 90% of the Volta Region. Ghana has three main categories of languages, namely the Mande, the Kwa, and the Gur which are represented all over the country.[6] Some of these tribes cut across the borders of the country to neighbouring countries in West Africa.

2.1.1 The Northern Territories of Ghana

The northern territories now known as northern Ghana have the three main language groups represented as stated above, although the most dominant ones are the Dagombas, Mamprusis, Nanumbas and Mosis from the Gur language family and the Gonjas from the Guang group of the Kwa language family. They are considered the most dominant due to their population, land owned, and authority exercised over other tribes.[7] That is not the case today, as all tribes and citizenship rights are enshrined in the constitution of Ghana under democratic governance.

The first four larger tribes from the Gur language family (Dagombas, Mamprusis, Nanumbas and Mosis) who speak related languages and practise common traditions trace their ancestry back to a legendary warrior known as *Tohajie* (red hunter). Each of these tribes gives a different version of their ancestry to this mythical brave 'Red Hunter', although they all agree to have been founded by his grandson Naa Gbewa (Chief Gbewa). Baker 'placed the founding of the Mamprusi, Mossi, and Dagomba kingdoms in successive centuries, between 1250 and the early 1400s.'[8] Amenumey considers the Mamprugu and Dagbon as the first kingdoms to be created in the north through conquest and forcibly imposing authority on other language groups of people living there.[9]

2.1.2 States in Southern Ghana

The arrival of the Asantes into the country is placed around AD 1300 where they remained as separate states before they merged into a formidable kingdom around AD 1700.[10] It is believed that Kumasi was founded in the late 17th century by Asantehene Osei Tutu I and Okomfo Anokye, his priest.[11] The Asante kingdom is the largest of the Akan language group from the southern part of the country and made up of twenty-four different states whose leaders owe allegiance to the Asantehene (King of Asantes)[12] One of the reasons for uniting was to be able to mobilize warriors to defend themselves and to conquer their opponents. Growth of the Asante kingdom was due to the diplomatic skill, martial ardour and statesmanship displayed by King Osei Tutu I and subsequent able leadership of some of the kings. The kings immediately put in place institutions that enabled the rise and growth of the kingdom, one of which was through the assistance of Okonfo Anokye (the priest Anokye); a Golden Stool was provided to serve as a symbol of unity of all member states of the kingdom.[13] It is believed that this Golden Stool was supernaturally sent by the ancestors to confirm the chief of Kumasi as the custodian of the Stool and the recognised king of the Asante Kingdom.[14] The role of a fetish priest as a religious official for chieftaincy, equivalent to chaplaincy, would go on to become an integral part of the institution.

The origin of the Akwamu tribe is dated around AD1500. However, it was about the beginning of the 17th century that Otumfuo Asare led them to settle at Akyem Abuakwa and established the state of Akwamu.[15] Kwadwo states that the absence of strong neighbouring kingdoms to disturb the Akwamus' internal peaceful existence enabled them to consolidate the state, whilst trade with Europeans in gold also brought them to the limelight politically and economically.[16]

According to Amenumey, the Denkyira state was founded probably around AD 1600. Its first three rulers introduced a number of innovations that were later copied by other kingdoms. They divided the state among three-wing chiefs for administrative and military purposes, who later served as generals in times of war. They also introduced the state stool, the state sword and the executioner's knife as sacred state objects.[17] The height of their power was known when they became the most important inland state trading in gold and slaves with the West.[18]

2.1.3 States Along Coastal Ghana

Historians are not certain about the date of emergence of the Ga-Dangbe people into a kingdom along the coastal part of the country. Amenumey thinks the Ga state was created around the late 15th century which consisted of the Ga Mashi, Osu, La, Teshi, Nungua and Tema together with their surrounding villages.[19] At first, they did not have chiefs but were represented by family heads that looked after the welfare of the people. The traditional priest exercised real authority on the people, the most important of them being the 'Wulomo'. The 'Wulomo' is the priest responsible for the gods and offers sacrifices on behalf of the people of a given community. For the Ga's and most Ghanaian communities, the priest existed long before the establishment of chiefs. They later adopted some Akan political, social and military institutions for governance.[20]

The Fante state occupies the western coastal belt of the country. The Fantes migrated from the middle belt of the country to their current location around AD 1650. Their location offered them the benefit of trading with western merchants and monopolised the trade in firearms and were united as a state to resist any outside invasion. They had a council of Paramount chiefs or *amanhin* as supreme governing body of the Fanteland[21] which still exists today.

By the beginning of the 17th century, Eweland was made up of about 120 states. Some of these states include Anlo, Some, Dzodze, Ave, Abutia, Peki, Ho, Waya, Kpando, Taviefe and 13 Tongu states. Gadzekpo states that even though the Ewe's did not form one organized kingdom, they co-operated well in times of need. They had well defined roles for officers and political structures that contributed to their rise and growth. Religious beliefs played an important role in their growth as well. The *Mawu* (Supreme Being) is the most senior sky god, creator of the universe and humankind. Below *Mawu* were *trowo* (earthly gods) with priests serving at their shrines that promoted a common allegiance of the people to their gods.[22]

The political, administrative and religious structure of these states in addition to the role of traditional priests to chiefs provided opportunities that Christianity could relate with in their mission to convert the people. Paul acknowledged the religious passion of the people in Athens in the way they served many gods to the extent that a temple dedicated to the worship of the unknown god existed and used that opportunity to proclaim the one true God from the Christian perspective.[23] In my opinion, since chieftaincy played a primary role in the leadership and governance of the people prior to the arrival of Christianity, the church should have given greater consideration to engagement with the IoC and provided culturally accepted alternatives in practice as Ghanaian traditionalists converted to Christianity. This argument is supported by the empirical evidence analysed and discussed in chapters seven and eight.

2.2 Missionary Exploration and Missions in Ghana

In this section, missionary exploration and missions in Ghana is categorized as foreign missionary activities that led to the establishment of churches and indigenous Christian groups with foreign missionary assistance.

2.2.1 Foreign Missionary Activities in Ghana

It was during the late 15th century when Europeans made their way to Ghana. The Portuguese were the first from Europe to settle in the country and built their castle at Elmina, along the coast in 1482. Don Diego d'Azambuja led an expedition of six hundred men and they landed at Elmina, near Cape Coast in Ghana. Groves cites Major that a day before,

> ... [they] suspended the banner of Portugal from the bough of the lofty tree, at the foot of which they erected an altar, and the whole company assisted at the first mass that was celebrated in Guinea and prayed for the conversion of the natives from idolatry, and (sic) the perpetual prosperity of the church which they intended to erect upon the spot.[24]

Upon arrival, Diego d'Azambuja met with the chief of Elmina and told him about the Christian faith. It is not known whether the chief became a Christian at this point, but he gave the Portuguese a site on which a fort and a chapel were built. It thus goes further to suggest that one of the aims that Europeans had in coming to the coast of Ghana was the propagation of the Christian gospel.[25] It is worth noting that the first known missionary activity in the country included the raising of an altar for prayer and worship. Debruner writes that, 'the Portuguese understood their discovery of Africa as a divine commission in world history'.[26] Their mission was to convert the people of Western Africa to Christianity. For them these people that they had come to trade with 'were living under the dark shadow of paganism needed the light of Christianity.'[27]

However, it was not until the early 18th century that missionary societies made serious attempts to plant Christianity in the country.

Between the 1860s and 1870s, foreign missionary activities that led to the establishment of churches and denominations gathered momentum and covered most parts of the southern sector of the country, particularly when the Basel and Wesleyan Missions began to make more use of indigenes trained as catechists, ministers and agents.[28] I agree with Nukunya that the period between the 17th to the 18th century was not without activity either but the efforts of the Europeans were undermined by the reluctance of the Ghanaian people.[29] The missionaries showed bravery and determination to face the storms of antagonism, ill health and death upon arrival.[30] It would be fair to suggest that every mission agency had its fair share of the difficulties in pioneering missionary activity resulting in obvious lack of fulfilment and the grim prospect of failure staring at them each time.[31] Nevertheless, some of the evidence of the fruits of their missionary activities can be noted in the training of indigenous people for ministry. Philip Quarcoo (Kweku) stands out prominently in this regard. He was an Oxford-trained Ghanaian minister and teacher who later returned to Ghana and became the chaplain of Cape Coast Castle for nearly fifty years up to 1816.[32] Philip was an outstanding student among many which gave him the privilege to serve at that level and to be noted later by historians.

Missionary activities only took place along the coast and into the south of the country. The people in northern Ghana had to wait until the 1900s before mission stations were opened to evangelize them. The Roman Catholics opened a parish at Navrongo in 1906[33] whilst the Basel Mission also opened a station at Yendi in 1913 to work among the Dagombas. The ministry of Pentecostal missionaries will be examined in chapter six.

2.2.2 Indigenous Christian Groups With Foreign Missionary Assistance

The emergence of indigenous Christian groups in the country can be traced to the visit of Prophet William Wade Harris of Liberia along the coastal belt of South-western Ghana in 1914. His ministry led to the conversion of thousands from traditional religious practices to Christianity in the Nzema area. Richard Foli comments that William Wade Harris can be considered the African prophet of the twentieth century and has long been recognised as quite extraordinary in the effect of his ministry to various people groups along the West African coast.[34.] Like most other Pentecostal preachers of his days, Harris openly denounced the closed relationship of traditional priests with chiefs but did not have any formal chaplaincy role for himself or followers. One of his converts who later on was known as Prophet Samson Oppong led thousands including a number of chiefs to Christ in Ashanti region[35] but nothing is said of his chaplaincy role to chieftaincy either.

Indigenous Christian groups with foreign missionary assistance started with George Perfect of the Apostolic Church, UK as he led the pioneering missionary work of his denomination in Ghana in 1935.[36] He came under the invitation of Peter Anim's group of Faith Tabernacle brethren at Asamankese (an indigenous Pentecostal fellowship) with branches at Akim Akroso, Akim Manso, Winneba, Saltpond, Pepeadze, Bibiani, Korle Gonno, and many other areas, later on adopting the name 'Apostolic Church' after the Apostolic Church in Bradford upon embracing the teaching of the Church.[37]

2.3 Early Engagement of Christianity with Chiefs

The previous section has already outlined how Christianity came to the country under missionary exploration to propagate the gospel and plant churches. This section seeks to focus on Christian leaders having direct contact with the IoC in the communities. When missionaries arrived in Ghana, chiefs were often their first point of contact to announce their arrival and seek permission to preach and possibly settle for a period. It is not known whether the first contact with chiefs led to the conversion of some to Christianity or not, although this system of engagement existed amongst chiefs and missionaries subsequently.

However, Peel noted that in comparison to other West African cultures, such as the Yorubas, the Asante and other Akan groups were relatively hostile to Christianity and the rate of the uptake of this world religion in the Akan forest belt was notoriously slow.[38] In 1880, the then ruling Asantehene Mensa Bonsu welcomed Roman Catholic missionaries August Moreau and Eugene Murat to Kumasi. Muller cites a report from Moreau that:

> One day I expressed my desire to visit Kumasi. I asked him [prince Boakye] whether the king would agree to see me or order to have my head cut off. The prince answered: 'The king would be very glad to see you and be assured he will do you no harm.' This happened in the month of July 1881 and since then I have been waiting for the favourable moment to go to this Asante town.[39]

'This conversation' reveals the difficulty that missionaries had in reaching the Ashantis in particular and supports Peel's view of some tribal hostilities with missionaries. Such conditions of hostilities and uncertainties did not favour Christian leaders and chiefs' relationships in some parts of the country at that time.

John Mills, one of the missionaries of the Society for the Propagation of the Gospel, is however credited with taking the gospel to Kumasi. Mills held a service with the then ruling Asantehene Kwaku Duah I in 1839. But when his mission agency proposed to send someone to Kumasi for ministry in 1841, the Governor at Cape Coast vetoed the proposal on the ground that too many versions of the Christian faith would confuse the Asante.[40] This is another interesting development that revealed the challenge of missions during this period where political authority could influence the number of missionaries and mission agencies allowed at a given area. Relations amongst missionaries and the Asantes further worsened when the British ransacked the city of Kumasi in 1874 and later in 1896. This time, the Asantehene Agyeman Prempeh I was captured and taken to exile with others as political prisoners to Seychelles until 1924 where he converted to Christianity and after his release, returned to Asanteman.[41] The Basel Missionary Society (BMS) was refused permission to settle in Asante at this period and Ramseyer's presentation of the Twi Bible to the Asantehene later on was not well received as the King and people of Asanteman hardened their hearts although the BMS missionaries made occasional visits to them.[42]

However, it is noteworthy that King Prempeh I converted to Christianity whilst in exile in the Seychelles. His conversion to Christianity had a great influence on the royal family and some culture and customs of Asanteman over the years. A government official confirmed the conversion of Prempeh to Christianity in a letter. The letter revealed that the objection raised by the civil chaplain for Prempeh's confirmation was his relationship with the remaining concubine. When Prempeh was captured, three concubines accompanied him to the Seychelles for a period after which two of the concubines returned to Ghana. The governor noted in the letter, 'Prempeh has been converted to Christianity and is desirous of being confirmed...I think that Prempeh has the bona fide desire to lead a Christian and civilized life.'[43] Prempeh confirmed his conversion in a letter he wrote to his family and outlined the steps taken to formalize his faith.[44] Prempeh assumed the name Edward after his conversion and his brother took the name Albert. The exiled Ashanti royal family even at some point had one member, John Prempeh on a training trip as a Missionary with the Right Reverend the Lord Bishop of Mauritius and Seychelles.[45] It is also significant to note the role of a chaplain in the spiritual journey of Edward Prempeh as a Christian. It is possible that the introduction of chaplaincy to chiefs at the early years of Christianity in the country would have contributed positively to the gains of the church over the years. Prempeh's influence as a Christian was tested when he returned to Ghana after captivity. The manager of the Manhyia Palace museum attributed the abolition of human sacrifice that occurred during the death of Asantehene, as part of the funeral rites, to the conversion of Asantehene Prempeh I to Christianity. The King advocated that there was no need to take human life at the death of any king and that his faith as a baptized Anglican would not allow it. Instead, they should use animal sacrifice in place of human beings for those ceremonies, which has been so until today.[46]

At the Centre for Arts and Culture in Kumasi, archived documents revealed the strain in relations between Christian leaders, missionaries and some chiefs. These were issues relating to Christians and native customs, fetish days, festivals and the persecution of Christian converts who refuse to perform certain duties because of their faith. Waterworth who was the superintendent of Wesleyan Mission reported in a letter to the acting chief commissioner how a chief brutally punished some church members though he could not tell if their report was exaggerated or not, and that he was at a loss as to what the chief's motive was. Waterworth suggests that it may be that the chief feared that to become a Christian would mean the cessation of the subjects' loyalty to him. He then asked the commissioner to do him a favour and disillusion the chief on the point raised on subject loyalty.[47] The above report shows that relations between the minister and chief were not good. He missed the opportunity of following up the case himself to act as mediator for the members and facilitate cordial relations between community leaders and the members. There is no indication, at least from the report, that his life was also in danger. Moreover, why go to the police when you are not sure of your account which might be exaggerated? It is possible that a chaplain to chieftaincy would have handled the situation differently.

In another development, the mission reported to the police how the chief forced certain candidates for baptism to beat the drum.[48] It seems that these were Christian converts who used to play drums at the chief's palace, but had now refused to play the drums as they prepared for baptism.[49] In a reply to the case that the minister reported, the commissioner stated that the information supplied to the minister was incorrect and that the Christians failed to provide their certificates of baptism which he requested. He advised that the complainants should fulfil their duties towards the chief or else he would not hesitate to support the chief's demands to remove the complainants from his community owing to their obstinate refusal to serve him.[50]

There were also reports on Christians and native customs such as swearing oaths by fetish, the process of obtaining confession of adultery by native customs from Christians still married to unbelievers, observance of fetish days and festival days. The ministers' concern was that some of these customs were associated with ancestral worship, and in conflict with Christian principles. He therefore requested that Christians should be given the liberty to be exempted from festivals that occurred on Sundays so that believers may be able to attend public Christian worship on the Lord's day.[51] The police replied to the concerns raised and stated that it was true that the ideal for the country is to have Christian values, but that is not to say the missions should break up the ancient native customs which have been prevailing from time immemorial. He was of the opinion that it would be most inadvisable for the government to interfere but was a matter for the native authorities themselves to alter, 'as I have no doubt they will when the Missions have educated them sufficiently to the Christian ideal.'[52] The fact the church generally classified all native customs as fetish, idol worship or devilish all because traditional authorities supervised their observance in a community created the antagonistic reaction from some chiefs. I agree with Dickinson who was optimistic that if the church engaged with the chiefs some of these differences could be resolved which in my view, the role of Christian chaplaincy to chiefs would be ideally placed to facilitate.

Busia, a former Prime Minister of the Republic of Ghana from October 1969 to January 1972, made a close reflection in the early 1950s on the interaction of Akan converts with their indigenous cultural practices. He observed that the Akan converts kept distance from their cultural practices. The Akan converts were not encouraged to recognize their own indigenous leadership structures. Busia wanted a more integrative approach to the interaction between Christianity and African culture which is why he called for the ennoblement of the Akan culture.[53] Missionary presence did not function differently from their colonial authority in Akan society. Church leadership and the missionary headquarters became centres of authority for church members instead of traditional leaders and the palace.[54] Christians rejected activities which had little religious significance like communal labour or road construction just because it came from the traditional leaders. The traditional leadership became afraid of their own people because Christians could count on the support of church leadership and colonial influence against them as shown in some of the above reports to the Police Commissioner.

On the part of Pentecostal denominations and the AoG in particular from the early 1930s, chiefs were the first point of contact for Missionaries in the communities. Missionaries would most often preach the gospel near the grounds of the palace in what was often termed 'gospel crusade' so as to enable the chief to attend if he was available. Preaching the gospel near the chief's palace indicated that the chief welcomed Christian activities in the community. It also prevented a situation where some people could cause public disorder by attacking or disrupting the activity because no one dared cause trouble at the chief's palace. The chief provided security for the missionaries on certain occasions against those who might attempt physical assault for any reason whilst they were in the community. The chiefs also facilitated the release of land for

Mission stations and church buildings. Lehmann in an article on the history of AoG captures a picture of a chief and his elders with the description; 'The Tamale chief came to church every Sunday 1934'.[55] The researcher cannot state whether this particular chief died in his faith, but it was an opportunity for the church to consider outlining certain steps that one could take to maintain the faith as a Christian and still be a Chief. Subsequent years also saw the conversion of some chiefs to Christianity which the church tended to accept but would not accept a Christian taking up the role of being a chief. Some of these converted chiefs have narrated their stories during interviews conducted for this study which would be discussed in subsequent chapters. The church and its leadership nevertheless consider chiefs as leaders and are given the honour that they deserve as people of authority with divine recognition.[56]

2.4 Concluding Comments

This chapter has noted that the context of Christianity engaging with the IoC has been a challenging one. The greater challenge was the perception of traditional authorities about Christianity as a foreign religion, associated with colonial masters and concerned about the threat to existing social structures and culture. The attitudes of some Christian leaders and the actions they took to address conflicts between members and the traditional authorities did not help to build any good relation between the two institutions either, as government structures were often relied upon to the advantage of Christians over chiefs.

The key to resolving this challenge was for Christian leaders to understand the cultural and social structures of the people, analyse them, and produce relevant strategies to facilitate the mission of the church. Understanding culture does not imply compromise. Rather, it offers Christian leaders an opportunity to evaluate their theology and produce a more practical form of church life that positively represents Christ within the cultural context of the people. Instead, what prevailed in many parts of the nation showed that new Christian converts kept a distance from their culture. This method of keeping believers away from their culture was not peculiar to Ghana. Isichei stated that missionaries like their counterparts elsewhere in the late 19th century, 'tended to found Christian villages, in the belief that converts needed to live apart from traditional society if they were to develop a pure and fervent spiritual life.'[57] Hence, there is the need to treat cultural practices with respect and dignity in order to avoid a situation where the church would continue to look like an alien institution before the people.[58]

Civilization and modern enlightenment in education have to some extent facilitated to diffuse the tension that existed as both institutions acknowledge the benefits that would be derived in collaboration and partnership. Furthermore, the changing role of the chief in recent times from spiritual and military responsibilities to focusing on education, economic development, social integration and moral leadership of the community, offer the church ministry opportunities to facilitate this change and not to shun away from it. That is why I am proposing the introduction of Christian Chaplaincy as a missional strategy to the IoC from Pentecostals in particular.

The next chapter considers the political structure of chieftaincy, chiefly ritual and responsibilities just as sustained contact with missionaries and Christians increased.

---

1. See Ch.1.2.2.
2. Brobbey, *The Law*, p. 2.
3. Brobbey, *The Law*, p. 2.
4. Kwamina B. Dickson, and George Benneh, *A New Geography of Ghana*, Revised edn (Harlow, Essex: Longman Group UK Limited, 1995), p. 1.
5. Dickson and Benneh, *New Geography*, p. 2.
6. Peter Baker, *Peoples, Languages, and Religion in Northern Ghana – A Preliminary Report*, (Accra, Ghana: Evangelism Committee and Asempa Publishers, 1986), p. 19.
7. Dickson and Benneh, *New Geography*, p. 3.
8. Baker, *Peoples, Languages*, p. 120.

9. D. E. K. Amenumey, *Ghana A Concise History from Pre-Colonial Times to the 20th Century*, (Accra: Woeli Publishing Services, 2011), p. 23.

10. S. K. Gadzekpo, *History of Ghana*, (Accra: EPP Books Services, 2005), p. 30.

11. Gadzekpo, *History*, p. 15.

12. Gadzekpo, *History*, p. 32.

13. Gadzekpo, *History*, p. 37.

14. O. Kwadwo, *An Outline of Asante History*, (Kumasi: CITA press Ltd., 2009), p. 8.

15. Kwadwo, *Asante History*, p. 31.

16. Kwadwo, *Asante History*, p. 32.

17. Amenumey, *Ghana*, p. 30.

18. Amenumey, *Ghana*, pp. 30, 31.

19. Amenumey, *Ghana*, p. 49.

20. Gadzekpo, *History*, p. 40.

21. Gadzekpo, *History*, pp. 38, 39.

22. Gadzekpo, *History*, p. 42.

23. Acts 17:16-31

24. C. P. Groves, *The Planting of Christianity in Africa*, Vol. 1 (London: Lutterworth, 1954), p. 123, citing R. H., Major, *The Discoveries of Prince Henry the Navigator and their Results*, 1877, 2nd edn pp. 299-300.

25. Richard Foli, *Christianity in Ghana: A Comparative Church Growth Study*, (Accra: Trust Publications, 2006), p. 13.

26. W. Hans Debruner, *A History of Christianity in Ghana*, (Accra: Waterville Publishing House, 1967), p.14.

27. F. K. Buah, *West Africa since AD1000*, (Hong Kong: Macmillan Publishers, 1977), p.13.

28. Foli, *Christianity*, p. 14.

29. G. K. Nukunya, *Tradition and Change in Ghana: An Introduction to Sociology*, 2nd edn (Accra: Ghana University Press, 2003), p. 120.

30. W. Boyce, *Statistics of Protestant Missionary Society 1872-1873*, (London: W. Nicholas 1874), p. 127.

31. Foli, Christianity, p. 55.

32. A. Van Dantzig, *Forts and Castles of Ghana*, (Accra: Sedco Publishing, 1980), p. 71. Philip was born in 1741 and was one of the three Ghanaian children sent to England to be educated in 1754. He married Catherine Blunt – an educated English girl and returned to Ghana in 1766 as 'a Missionary Catechist and Schoolmaster to the Negroes...' till his death in 1816. <http://www.dacb.org> [accessed 4 June 2014].

33. Baker, *Peoples, Languages*, p. 40.

34. Foli, *Christianity*, p. 46.

35. Foli, *Christianity*, pp. 47-52.

36. See chapter six.

37. Foli, *Christianity*, p. 39.

38. D. J. Y., Peel, 'History, Culture and Comparative Method,' in *Comparative Anthropology*, ed. by L. Holy, (Oxford: Oxford University Press, 1987).

39. Louise, Muller, *Religion and Chieftaincy in Ghana*, (Zweigniederlassung Zürich: Lit Verlag GmbH & Co. KG Wien, 2013), p. 97.

40. S. G., Williamson, and J., Bardsley, *The Gold Coast: What of the Church?* (London: Edinburgh House Press, 1953).

41. Otumfuo Opoku Ware Jubilee Foundation, *A Guide to Manhyia Palace Museum*, (Kumasi: Gyabious Printing Press, 2003), p. 1.

42. D., Huppenbauer, 4th edn *Von Kyebi nach* (Kumasi: Basel, 1905), pp. 52-60.

43. Walter Edward Davidson, Governor, 'Correspondence, copy No. 449/1911', Government House, Seychelles, 3rd March, 1911.

44. Prempeh revealed in the letter that His Lordship the Bishop of Mauritius and Rev: Buswell accompanied by His Excellency Sir Eustace Fiennes paid a visit to our Camp and His Lordship told me that I am a midway Christian and so he is willing to confirm me and give me Holy Communion if I promise before him to get married to only one. I accepted His Lordship's good offer with pleasure; so did all my Ex Chiefs.' Edward Prempeh, (Ex-King of Ashanti) Le Rocher, Ashanti Camp, Seychelles, 13th December 1920.

45. Eustace Fiennes, Lt. Col. Bart, Governor, Registered No. D 367/20, Government House, Seychelles, 2nd February 1921.

46. Brobbey Justice, Interviewed at Manhyia Palace Museum, (Kumasi: 14 February 2014).

47. W. G. Waterworth, Rev. The Superintendent, Wesleyan Mission Society, Ashanti Mission, Coomassie, West Africa, to Arthur J. Philbrick, Acting Chief Commissioner, Ashanti, 11th September 1914.

48. Samuel Kwafo, Rev., to D C Juase, Chief Commissioner, Ashanti, (Mampong: Basel Mission, 11/09/1915).

49. Drumming has many roles in most communities. Some of which could be interpreted as calling ancestral spirits or praising the chief.

50. F. C. Fuller, Chief Commissioner, Ashanti, to The Revd. Samuel Kwafo, Basel Mission, Mampong 11/12/1915. In a follow up letter, the police reported that the drummers ran away to the Basel Mission and refused to beat the drums. He ordered them to beat the drums because he envisioned that the men wanted to get out of serving the chief. He explained to the Mission agent that they could not allow this kind of behaviour as it would lead to any man who does not want to serve their masters running away and saying they are Christians.

51. W. G. Watterworth, Acting General Superintendent, Wesleyan Methodist Missionary Society, Gold Coast District, West Africa, 20/07/1931.

52. J. R. Dickinson, District Commissioner, Eastern Province, Kumasi, 21/08/1931.

53. K. A Busia, *The Position of the Chief in the Modern Political System of Ashanti*, (Oxford: Oxford University Press, 1951), p.135.

54. Opuni-Frimpong, *Indigenous*, p. 60.

55. Lehmann, 'Story', p. 2.

56. 1 Tim. 2:1-4.

57. Elizabeth Isichei, *A History of Christianity in Africa: From Antiquity to the Present*, (London: Society for Promoting Christian Knowledge, 1995), p. 195.

58. Opuni-Frimpong, *Indigenous*, p. 63.

THREE

The Institution of Chieftaincy: Rituals and Responsibilities in the Mid 19th Century Just as Sustained Contact With Missionaries and Christians Increased

3.0 Introduction

The previous chapter narrated the origins and establishment of kingdoms in Ghana, which chieftaincy became the source of leadership responsible for governance in every community. It is certainly the case that good leadership structure is at the heart of every successful human endeavour. In order to appreciate the composition, style and importance of chieftaincy, there is the need to consider the organizational setting and cultural practices of chieftaincy.

The purpose of this chapter is to account for the institutional setting of chieftaincy, narrate chiefly rituals, responsibilities and examine what it was that missionaries and Christian leaders were criticising the IoC just as sustained Christianity increased and why?

3.1 The Institution of Chieftaincy, Culture and Cultural Traditions

We shall begin by considering "The Institution of Chieftaincy" after which we shall consider "Culture and Cultural Tradition."

3.1.1 The Institution of Chieftaincy

The term "Chieftaincy" is used to mean 'the institution through which the system of African traditional rule was conducted'.[1] As an institution, the chief is supported by elders, sectional leaders, linguists, and priests to rule.[2] Chieftaincy system of rule existed alongside colonialism and into democratic rule. The IoC gained constitutional recognition as stated in article 270 of the 1992 constitution of Ghana where it defines a chief as:

> A person, who, hailing from the appropriate family and lineage, has been validly nominated, elected or selected and enstooled, enskinned or installed as a chief or queen mother in accordance with the relevant customary law and usage.[3]

The IoC is thus political in nature and has the primary concern of governing Ghanaians then and now. Chieftaincy in modern Ghana is still highly relevant and plays important roles in community development.[4] It is the most effective system for preserving and promoting ethnic identity and solidarity in recent times for which the chief is the visible symbol of that identity and a focal point of mobilizing loyalty.[5]

His Royal Majesty Otumfuo Osei Tutu II outlined the role of modern traditional chiefs to include being active in dispute and conflict resolution in the community to ensure peaceful co-existence, to make laws and rules in consultation with his council of elders and the diverse representatives of the people in the community, have executive role – day-to-day running of the community, to act as spiritual leaders of the people and custodians of the numerous religious shrines and gods of the kingdom, to ensure and promote the welfare of the community by facilitating the development and execution of economic, educational, social and health related projects for the people.[6] Similarly, Kleist states that 'in addition to royalty and seniority, education and access to powerful networks have become central qualifications for chieftaincy elec-

tion.[7] I disagree because education and networks may be important, but not necessarily considered as key qualifications for
chieftaincy. Education and networks must be matched with special
qualities of unblemished character and boldness befitting the
respected status and dignity of chieftaincy.[8] The figure below illustrates the composition of the *Omanhene's* state sitting with 'ceremonial umbrellas showing sitting arrangements of chiefs. The
Omanhene's umbrella, Bisibiso, has a double canopy.'[9]

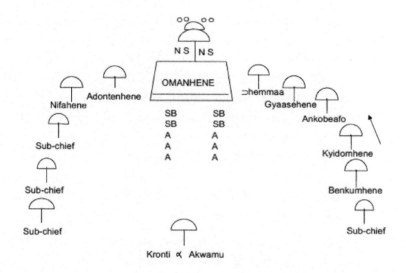

NS *Nkonguasoafo*, Stool bearer
SB *Mfoasoafo*, Sword bearer
OO *Fontomfrom*, Drum orchestra
A *Akyeamefo*, Line-up of state linguists

Figure 3.1: The *Omanhene* (Paramount chief) in state sitting.

The IoC organizational structure includes the National House of
Chiefs, composed of five paramount chiefs from the ten regions of
the country totalling 50 members. There are ten Regional Houses of
Chiefs and 275 Traditional Councils led by chiefs,[10] whose respon-

sibilities include the maintenance of culture and traditions of the people.

3.1.2 Culture and Cultural Tradition

Culture is the manifested lifestyle of a particular group of people or society. Culture is socially taught and learned and evolves for the purpose of living. According to Jean-Marc Ela and John Pairmain Brown, economic and socio-political factors play an important role in changing culture, and it is 'a way of living that is continually challenged by the critical events which shape a people's history.[11] In other words culture is dynamic, and it is the changing nature of culture that Hackman and Johnson caution against classifying cultures.[12] Similarly, Paul G. Hiebert defines culture as 'the more or less integrated systems of ideas, feelings, and values and their associated patterns of behaviour and products shared by a group of people who organize and regulate what they think, feel and do.'[13] Kwame Bediako echoes Hiebert, and defines culture as 'the ways of thinking and behaviour shared by a substantial social grouping of persons which give them identity in relation to other social groupings'.[14] Similarly, A. S. Glasser's definition of culture states that:

Culture embraces the totality of the response of any people to the environment. It includes all deliberately defined religion, mores, and social organization. It is the integrated, organized, and distinctive way of life that distinguishes one people from another people. Its components are the technological, the sociological, and the ideological – not tools, weapons, and techniques by which people sustain their corporate life and exercise their will over other peoples.[15]

In comparison to Ela, Hiebert and Bediako, Glasser's inclusion of 'all deliberately defined religion' and the distinction of what entails cultural components best describes the IoC. Some rituals, ceremonies and festivals associated with the IoC and observing religious rites are often described as culture.

Cultural traditions look to the past for their mandate, authority and authenticity as cultural traits are regarded as society's norms handed down the generations.[16] To introduce some new aspect is therefore often too much of a challenge. Kwame Gyekye points out that when a cultural value has gone through several generations, it turns into a tradition. Hence, the expression 'cultural tradition' and 'it would be more correct to say that culture constitutes the content of tradition, that tradition consists of, - is the bearer of, - those cultural products that have persisted over generations of people.[17] Some chieftaincy practices are mostly guided by culture and cultural traditions assumed to conflict with the Christian faith. The next section narrates chiefly political structures, rituals and responsibilities among the Akan and Mamprusi and examines contentious issues between Christianity and the IoC.

3.2. The Akan Chiefly Political Structures, Rituals and Responsibilities

One of the reasons that the chieftaincy institution is deeply woven into the fabric of the people can be traced to its link to the family system. Rattray, an early interpreter of the Akan indigenous knowledge explained that: 'The various family groups in course of time came under the head of a particular extended family: to him all important matters and appeals were made.'[18] These initial developments that Rattray noted eventually led to the establishment of royal lineages and political structures which in some cases were ratified by consulting the ancestors through the traditional priest.

3.2.1 Royal lineages and political structures

The origin of royal families started with the head of a settlement. According to Nana Dankwa, the head with most leadership qualities and referred to as the *Odikro* (owner of the village), was always selected from members of the founding family or first settlers of the land.[19]

The *Odikro* is the first step towards the level of hierarchy in the IoC. Brobbey outlines the statutory categorisation of chieftaincy hierarchy as follows: a) Paramount Chiefs, b) Divisional Chiefs, c) Sub-Divisional Chiefs, d) Adikrofo and other chiefs recognized by the National House of chiefs.[20] The Akan describe the paramount chief as the *Omanhene,* which means chief of his traditional area. Next is the divisional chief described by the Akans as *Obrempong,* which means 'very powerful' and has chiefs ranked below him. Chiefs below the divisional chiefs are known as sub-divisional or wing chiefs such as the *Adontenhene* or *Dzaasehene.* The Adikrofo acts as a caretaker to oversee the lands and properties for the traditional area on behalf of his superior chiefs. Chiefs below the Adikrofo can also be created that are recognised by the National House of Chiefs under Act 759, s 58(e).[21] The unique nature of the Ashanti chieftaincy system makes the Asantehene head of all levels of chiefs in the Ashanti kingdom. During installation the Odikro swears allegiance to the Obrempong, the Obrempong swears to the Omanhene, the Omanhene swears to the Asantehene, with the Asantehene swearing to the people and kingmakers. Akan chiefs are considered the custodians of the land and customs of the people and royal lineage are by right in a limited sense, traceable in matrilineal system to the progenitor or originator of the royal family.[22]

3.2.2 The Akan rules of succession

The Akan political offices known as *adehye nnwa,* (royal stools) are vested in lineages of certain clans such as the Aduana, Asona, Asinie, Asokore, Agona, Beretuo, Ekuona, and Oyoko in the Asante communities. Members of a clan had the same *akyiwadee,* (taboos or avoidances) and recruitment to the royal family is through the mother on the basis of having the same *mogya* (blood).[23] The assumption is that mothers transmit royal blood and fathers are considered to transmit *sunsum* (soul) and therefore do not share their blood with children as mothers do.[24] Women are regarded as experts on family genealogies and that is why the *Ohemma* (Queen mother) has a key role in the selection of a stool occupant. Candidates are asked to validate their claim to the stool by giving a detailed account of his matrilineal descent to the original occupant of the first stool.[25]

In the selection procedures, a reigning Chief can appoint a successor with the advice and consent of the queen mother and council elders. When a successor is not appointed before a vacancy is created for the stool, the queen mother and council of elders elects the new stool-holder. It is both hereditary and election-based because there could be several candidates eligible for the vacant post.

Those who argue that chieftaincy has exclusionist tendencies and is undemocratic are wrong in that nomination, election and installation of a candidate is done on the basis of electoral college.[26] The social conditions of the Akan political communities generally favour peaceful selection of stool-holders (chiefs).

A traditional educational programme known as *Apatam* is organized for selected royals and teaches key values of Asante customs and acceptable norms such as public speaking, self-control, relationships with other chiefs and the history of the state. Candidates are kept for 40 days, 21 days or 14 days for this educational programme depending on the status of the chief-elect in the royal political structure.[27] The council of elders then sets aside two days for his enstoolment in the *nkonuafieso*, (stool-room) and followed by his public installation for the consent of the people as the stool-holder.[28]

At a private ceremony of enstoolment for the new chief, the new chief takes a stool name, usually one of the deceased occupants and, being supported by some principal subordinates, is slowly lowered three times with incantations and prayers. He is then lightly seated on the stool of his namesake. In lightly touching the stool with the buttocks of the new chief, he is indirectly informed that he is distinct from the stool which represented the nation and believed to be immortal.[29]

3.2.3 The Akan royal stools

A stool is one of the commonest items that can be found in every house in Ghana. It is a wooden seat that has a base, the middle portion and top. Apart from its role as a wooden seat, the word *stool* is used as a term for the office of a chief or king among the Akans.[30] Brobbey states that the stool is a symbol of authority of a chief and conveys spiritual messages in its use in chieftaincy affairs.[31] It is a symbol that binds the people, chief and community together. It is said to confer divine leadership on the reigning chief and symbolises ancestral influence on the living. That is why a ritual of blackening the stool is done to preserve its memory and for instructive information of its significance to future generations. The stool symbolises the soul of the community that 'has life which is never extinct, until such time that certain events occur or certain conditions are satisfied'.[32] This explains the determination behind the Ashantis protecting the *Golden Stool* from being captured during wars with other tribes and more importantly with the Europeans as stated in chapter two.

There are different kinds of stools for Akan chiefs in accordance to their status. The most important is the *Golden Stool* which is believed to be made of gold. Sarpong disagrees that it is made of all gold but describes it as a wooden stool covered with pure gold leaf, because if it was made with entire gold, it could not be carried by one person[33] during festivals as seen in figure 3.2. The Golden Stool is laid on its own stool or skin, kept with the strictest security and precaution. It is considered sacred that no one sits on it and must not touch the earth or ground. Okomfo Anokye (the Priest Anokye), considered as the greatest and most respected priest of Ashanti, facilitated the arrival of the *Golden stool.*[34]

Next to the Golden Stool is the ancestral blackened stool. Founders of villages, elders of clans, generals of wars, queen mothers and chiefs' stools are often blackened and kept after their death for remembrance.

Carrying the Golden Stool

Ashanti King state sitting with the
Sika Dwa Kofi (Golden Stool)

ɔsram Dwa (The Moon Stool)

ɔsebo Dwa (The Leopard Stool)

Ahemmaa Dwa The Queen Mother Stool)

Agyenyame Dwa (Except God Stool)

ɛsono Dwa (The Elephant Stool)

Kɔtɔkɔ Dwa (The Porcupine Stool)

Figure 3.2 Kinds of Akan royal stools[35]

Among the many stools that the chief uses, his immediate successor takes the one he often sat on to have it consecrated by being blackened and kept in the stools room. Some think that the stool used for this ceremony is the one he sits on to eat, or the one he sits on to bathe or even the one used to bathe the corpse before being laid in state for burial. Whichever one is used it is believed that the soul of the departed chief remains on the blackened stool.[36] Sarpong sums up the reasons for blackening the stools as being so that they may not appear too nasty, whilst properly representing the dead as black signifies sorrow for the departed chief, producing a feeling of reverence in people who appear before them and making them last longer.[37]

3.2.4 The Akan festivals, rites and ceremonies

Festivals are special feast-days devoted to honouring the ancestors.[38] Festivals are one of the best ways of showing the rich culture of the people and are important historically, religiously, economically, politically, socially and culturally.[39] The religious aspects of these festivals allow priests to work alongside coordinating rituals. The presence of chaplains at these festivals might seem to compromise some Christian values but also be an opportunity for Christian witness. The two most important for the Ashantis in which the chief plays important roles are the *Odwera* and *Adae* festivals.

The *Odwera*, meaning 'purify or cleanse' is the Akan annual yam festival of purification held for one to two weeks during September or October. The festival is used to remember the dead, offer thanksgiving for harvest and settle any prevailing disputes to enable peaceful coexistence in the community. Festivals also serve 'as important means of social control'[40] for the community. In an analysis of Busia's extensive account[41] of how the *Odwera* ceremony is carried out as he observed it at Wenchi, Safo-Kantanka suggests the following: first of all, the festival celebrates the feast of first fruits that involves yam-eating by the gods, sacrifices to the ancestors at the stool room, yam-eating by the ancestors at the royal mausoleum and yam-eating by the stools. Secondly, there is a symbolic procession around the town. Busia explains it is an expression of the watch that the ancestors kept over the town throughout the year. Finally, there is the cleansing ceremony which involves particular offering to the ancestors and the soul-washing purification rite.[42]

The *Adae* festival of Akans is used to cleanse ancestral stools and shrines of state deities; making repairs of regalia or additions of them and for offering food and drinks to the ancestral spirits, state deities and subjects.[43] This festival is celebrated every 21 days, which falls on a Wednesday or Sunday. When it is celebrated on a Wednesday, it is called *Wukudae* and the one held on a Sunday is called *Akwasidae, Addae Kese.* The rite takes place in the *stool-house* that contains the stools of deceased chiefs and prominent people of the land. The chief assumes the role of a chief-priest and servant. Assisted by few elders, he leads the delegation to the stool-house and offers drink and meat to the ancestors and prays "To-day is Adae, come and receive this and eat, let this town prosper, let the bearers of children bear children, may all the people get riches, life to me; long life to the nation".[44] A public celebration is held after this private rite in the stool-house where the chief sits in state to receive homage from his subordinates and the general public.

In recent times, the festivals are more than just performing religious rites, having historical education with feasting and dancing. Muller notes that the celebration of *Asanteman Adae Kese* in Kumasi between March and May 2004 coincided with the fifth reign and birthday of Asantehene Osei Tutu II. The theme for the festival was '*Asanteman Adae Kese:* promoting traditional leadership for accelerated development', which in Muller's view sought to promote the role of modern "traditional rulers as development workers, to support current development projects and to educate the Asante youth on Asante traditional culture."[45] Contributions to the fund are made by various individuals and organisations in cash and kind during these festivals.[46]

There are other rites and ceremonies that are constantly associated with the chieftaincy institution. Some are observed annually, seasonally or when the need arises. However, there is the need to give a brief account of burial and funeral rites of a deceased chief. When an Akan chief dies, he is said to have gone to the village, because the people do not consider death as the end of life but only in transition to another world. Traditional rites and rituals are observed following the passing of a chief which includes black-ening the royal stool and burial ceremonies. Chiefs who know about this tradition keep a stool in their bedroom that is used later after their death, or one is bought and taken to a forest called *Werempe* and guarded for seven days before the blackening process.[47] On the day of the ceremony at the stool-house, the new chief pours libation with palm wine on each stool and invokes blessings for the occasion. Broken eggs mixed with soot collected from the kitchen and spider web are used to smear the stool until it becomes as black as coal.[48]

The pre-burial ritual starts with firing of musketry to announce the death of the chief and to drive away evil spirits followed by public mourning, dancing and the laying-in-state ceremony.[49] The *fɔntɔnfrɔm* (drum ensemble) is used to invoke ancestral spirits and ask their blessings for successful burial and for the soul of the departed to enter the realm of the *nsamanfoɔ* (ancestors). The *Adinkra* symbols of courage and hope are used to depict that a great warrior always has a royal sword of rest and hope is needed to complete the journey to the world of royal ancestral spirits. The Akans believe that not all rulers automatically become ancestral spirits. Those who are asocial end up as vagrant spirits and others never reach the ancestral world. Even in such cases, the local priest will have to perform special rituals so that the wandering souls will cease disturbing the living and make it to the ancestral world. Widowhood rites are also performed for the late chief's wives and some rites for the children. Several musicians that include the *Manhyia Kete Nnwokorɔ* (Palace cultural singers) and dancing groups such as the *adowa* would be there to perform. An experienced indigenous priest dressed in white cloth, who often gave spiritual advice to the deceased royal, will perform the *akɔm* ritual dance.[50]

According to Muller, some rituals are private, secret and sacred which is why some respondents could not share everything concerning what needs to be recorded. Funeral rituals that also show the status of the family are sometimes celebrated with lavishness and high expenditure that leaves financial burden on the deceased family afterwards. On the other hand, some argue that funerals have economic benefits as the ceremonies sustain several businesses, provide employment opportunities for artisans, media and entertainers, textiles, food and hotel industries. In general, high spending on rituals of royals is accepted because they are considered earthly representatives of the ancestral spirits.[51]

3.3 The Mamprusi Chiefly Political Structures, Rituals and Responsibilities

The Mamprusi Kingdom is known for exhibiting rich cultural values on chieftaincy over many centuries. The Mamprusi king's title *Nayiri,* meaning king's house or chief's house, is unique and accorded the place of being at the very centre of governance, where *Nayiri* is the source of *naam* (chieftaincy), the mystical aspect of chiefly power.

The rules and cultures of chieftaincy from *Nayiri* (Mamprugu king) have influenced most tribes in northern Ghana. According to Schlottner, Mamprusis took over the control of political administration of the people they conquered and constituted themselves to the ruling elite (*Nadema*), while assigning few of the vanquished to the position of elders (*Na kpaambaya*) and the rest as commoners (*Tarima*).[52]

3.3.1 Royal lineages and political structure

The Nayiri of Mamprugu (King of Mamprusi), has the same status of an overlord, who has authority to install and promote chiefs to paramount status within their traditional areas.[53] Apart from the Nayiri of Mamprugu, other overlords within the northern region who have similar chieftaincy cultures are the *Ya Na* of Dagomba, the *Yagbonwura* of Gonja and the Bimbila-Na of Nanumba. Where necessary, references to the other kingdoms and the Dagombas in particular will be made due to the similarity of cultures. These kingdoms have a centralised political system where kings or chiefs exercise jurisdiction over well demarcated 'boundaries within which operates well-developed administrative, legislative and judicial institutions for governance of the territories.'[54] According to Drucker-Brown, the Nayiri of Mamprugu represents the mystical connection between living chiefs and deceased kings in serving the people as a whole, while other chiefs serve smaller local communities and less powerful ancestral spirits. The Mamprusi say the *Nayiri* is, 'owner of the world, all rocks and trees and all living things.'[55]

The Mamprugu Kingdom comprises the province of Nalerigu and five other divisions or paramouncies of Kpasenkpe, Janga, Wungu, Yunyoo and Kparigu. As overlord of the Mamprugu, the current Nayiri known as Naa-Boahagu Mahami Abdulai-Sheriga administers the province of Nalerigu with the assistance of elders and princes who qualify to become *Nayiri*. Tonah, who is a lecturer at the department of sociology, at the University of Ghana, states that although the Nayiri appoint various paramount chiefs and allocate the office of *naam* (chief) at the installation ceremony, they administer their territories autonomously. The term *naam*, 'is not only associated with political power but has also religious functions involving the veneration of the ancestors and the rituals of sacrifice'[56] and in most cases through the assistance of the fetish priest.

The main administrative organ of the Mamprusi is the chief's court. It is the place where public installation ceremonies are held, as well as judicial cases to settle disputes, disrespect to chiefly authority, witchcraft, taboo breaking, sorcery and the denigration of the ancestors. Persons found guilty are made to pay animals or cash and the *Nayiri in the precolonial* era had power over life and death of his subjects. Moreover, the chief's additional functions in spiritual matters are visible in the many sacrifices and the veneration of ancestors that tradition expects him to observe at all levels. These spiritual functions are regarded as a source of power, prestige, respect and provide a general foundation for the legitimation of rulers.[57] It is for this reason that Christian chaplaincy should engage with chieftaincy so as to provide alternatives in matters relating to spirituality.

The Mamprusi practise a patrilineal family system just like other tribes in northern Ghana. A patrilineal family system is where related family members are believed to be connected by descent from a common male ancestor. Where greater social significance is attached to male descent, the people practise a patrilineal system of succession and inheritance.[58] This applies to the elite royal lineages where sons inherit the chiefly positions of the fathers. The chief's children are born princes and princesses and, in some areas, the privilege is extended to grandchildren and great grandchildren who can trace their descent to a male ruler in the past.

3.3.2 The Mamprusi rules of succession

The Mamprusi political offices are known as *Naam Gbana,* (Royal Skins) which will be considered in detail in the next section of this chapter. These royal skins were vested in lineages of certain clans of the community. Recruitment to the royal family is through the father on the basis of having the same ancestral descent. At any level of chieftaincy, all sons and in some areas grandsons of past chiefs are considered candidates to be the next chief when the position is vacant. In some cases, the gate[59] system is used to allow rotation of succession to the royal skin. According to Mamprusi tradition, the first son is installed as regent following the death of the chief. Thereafter, the race for the vacant position begins as candidates publicly declare their intention to be the next chief. The candidates then have to wear a white turban around their head as a public display of their participation in the contest and as an indication that the village or province has no leader.[60]

During the entire period of the competition, it is usually the practice of candidates to withdraw from public life, avoiding eating and drinking in public for fear that their opponents might poison them.[61] The contest for chieftaincy in Mamprugu is as much of a spiritual and psychological battle than anything else; that is why candidates would consult soothsayers, diviners, mallams and spiritualists to foretell their chances of winning and also protect them from the evil plans of their opponents. The Mamprusis believe that a candidate can use spiritual powers to eliminate their opponents from the competition by making them physically deformed, ill, or even killing the strongest rivals.[62] The pursuit for spiritual powers does not end during the contest but it is rather the beginning in my view. It is believed that the successful candidate does not only have the support of the ancestors but has on his own acquired spiritual powers to help him rule. Just like the Mamprusis, Dagombas have similar ceremonies[63] in the selection and installation of a new chief.

3.3.3 The Mamprusi royal skins

The *Naam Gbana* (Royal Skins) of Mamprusi kingdom are the symbol of authority for the office of chieftaincy. These are simply animal skins that chiefs sit on and the commonly used ones are cows, lions or leopards. Some use more than one skin at a time, like placing a lion skin on cow skin.[64] The use of animal skin as a symbol of authority for any group of people should not be anything to worry about. However, the significance, rituals, and ceremonies associated with animal skins considered as royal skins due to belief systems are worth going through some theological reflections by

Pentecostals and Christianity in general. For the Christian chaplain, this is an opportunity to facilitate some kind of understanding on how Christians can relate to royal skins of their communities.

Brobbey states that the procedure is not the same within the three regions of northern Ghana where royal skins are used for enskinment. There are some considerable differences from one traditional area to the other.[65] Among the Mamprusi, the chief's status determines the kind of animal skin that should be used. According to Drucker-Brown, when the Nayiri installs a new chief, he gives the Nayiri a white sheep that is sacrificed to the royal ancestors on the morning of the chief's departure where the Nayiri then blesses the chief and gives him the skin of the sacrificed sheep. This sheepskin becomes the first of the skins that the new chief will sit on in his court, later on adding other animal skins that he himself sacrifices.[66] During the installation rite of the Nayiri, he sits on a snow-white sheepskin laid on a grass mat on the ground before one of the ancestor shrines. The Nayiri would have other animal skins added to sit on afterwards, such as a lion skin which is 'regarded as the embodiment of deceased kings'.[67]

3.3.4 The Mamprusi festivals, rites and ceremonies

The Mamprusis have two main festivals that are also observed by the Dagombas and Nanumbas in the northern region. These are the *Bugum Toobu* and *Damma Kyuu* festivals held annually. The *Bugum Toobu* (Fire Festival) is one of the earliest festivals used to begin the new year. Oral tradition states that at some point in time, one of the king's sons went missing. The community searched for him with torches of lights at night until they found him lying under a tree. The king named the tree as an evil tree for being responsible for hiding his son. The king then announced that this day would be celebrated annually to remember the event by lighting the first torch. Others consider the event is held to remember a plentiful harvest of crops after previous years of famine, praying to the gods and hoping never to experience another famine. The influence of

Islam has added another twist to the event, as Muslims consider it to commemorate the landing of Noah's ark after the flood, saying that torches were lit to know if the ark landed on dry ground.[68]

However, the manner in which it is celebrated across other tribal groups like the Dagombas in particular does not support the Moslem claim in my view. According to MacGaffey, the fire festival is a celebration where sacrifices are made to the gods and ancestors. The people do not only hold flaming torches at night but also cutlasses, swords, guns, bows and arrows. The atmosphere is tense and disturbed. Anyone witnessing it for the first time has the impression that something bad will happen. Some men use the occasion to test their magical powers by asking to be shot at or cut with machetes. If they are not hurt, it means their powers are working.[69] MacGaffey's description supports the oral historical account of a search party looking for a missing son of the king, ready to fight to rescue the king's son from his captors.

The *Damma Kyuu* is also one of the earliest festivals of the Mamprusi held to celebrate chieftaincy culture and commemorates the origins of kingship.[70] The event brings chiefs and people together at the *Nayiri's* palace for this celebration that lasts three days in a span of one week. Oral tradition and rituals associated with the celebration predates the arrival of Islam. However, some claim the festival commemorates the birth of the founder of Islam, prophet Muhammad, and have included animal sacrifices on the first and second days of the festival.[71] The dates of celebration are normally on the 11th, 17th and 18th of the Damma calendar month. People gather at the festival ground or chief's palace on these dates to see their chiefs dressed in their regalia for the celebration that includes cultural displays, dance, and feasting. The festival is used to pay homage to the king as well as a display of historical and cultural heritage for public education. It also promotes economic and social benefits through tourism and family reunions.

Mamprusi chieftaincy observes several rituals, rites and ceremonies during the funerals and enskinment of chiefs. Drucker-Brown provides relevant insight through her research on Mamprusi chieftaincy[72] and describes the death rites of the king 'that reveals the unique and terrible powers attached to it.'[73] The Dagombas, who have similar cultural practices as Mamprusis, consider the death of a king to bring calamity to nature and nation.[74] When the *Nayiri* dies, an elder at the king's palace *Sapkanaba* leads a ritual to verify the death, before a public announcement which is done wordlessly, but with the *Timpani* (talking drums).[75] Special rites are observed, before the forbidden stone object known as *Naa Moari* (King River)[76] is removed from the palace and hidden somewhere until the day a new king is to be enskinned. Another rite is performed after the burial where the king's elder son sacrifices a white ram to his father's spirit. The palace elders then give the dry skin of the ram to the deceased king's elder son as the regent *Gbanaraana* (skin-owner) and he wears the sheepskin over his gown throughout the funeral. The regent, *Paanaba* (female king) and elders have roughly six months after the burial to plan the final funeral rites.

At the final funeral, Drucker-Brown describes the rite of entry[77] that is performed to end the reign of the former king and also paves the way to select a new king. The regent is the last to perform this rite. The regent rides on horseback, followed by the female king carried aloft leads a procession of mourners around the palace thrice before entering.[78] We must acknowledge that God and his will is accepted in this important ceremony. The role of the *Nayiri's* grandchildren who perform mock kingship during the funeral cannot be ignored as it gives the youth an opportunity to partici-pate in the process to learn culture, tradition and religious practices.[79]

The rites and rituals for enskinment for the next king follow imme-diately after the final funeral rites of the former king. Royals who attend and participate in the final funeral rites do not leave the capital until a successor is announced. A much more detailed account of these rites and rituals are narrated in Drucker-Brown's writings.[80] What is significant about the enskinment of the next Nayiri is the role of the earth-priest who is a commoner with a chieftaincy title *Sagadugunaba* (chief of the Porridge-Pot). He secretly arrives at the capital at night to do the investiture and leaves at dawn the following morning. The king-elect provides a cow and sheep which are sacrificed to the ancestors and cooked in the palace that night.[81] The king-elect observes some rituals between midnight and dawn and his transformation takes place as he sits on the forbidden object, King-River. 'Anyone who sits on that object, for however brief a span, becomes king, and if he has children they become princes.'[82]

Drucker-Brown describes the next stage of the enskinment as the king is dressed[83] and led for further rituals at the elders' shrines. He is presented before two senior elders' shrines. He chooses to visit one in a house, where he receives further protection, and the other secluded. Next, he is presented as humble, riding slowly backwards on a donkey which shows reluctance and protected by a pressing crowd to the shrine. At the shrine he is seated on a snow-white sheepskin laid on a grass mat on the ground with extreme care to not let his feet or body touch the earth.[84] The priest pours libation to the ancestors, asks blessings for the new king and shares a drink mixed with millet flour with the king which marks the end of the installation.[85]

The final rites and ceremonies continue with the return of princes and royals to pledge their allegiance and support[86] before the outdooring of the king. The ceremony yet again acknowledges the will of God in the choice of a successor, a promise to accept the result and abandon litigation or war for continuity and peaceful co-existence. The king is then led to a secluded place for a period where he escapes to his lodging.[87] At the king's lodging, the courtship stew is cooked overnight which contains species of some animals to host the royals present before their departure.[88] The public gathers for the first seating of the new king.

Mamprusi Ba'ek=tugu (Soothsayer)   The Mamprusi King lights the first torch
for the night of Bugum Kyuu (Fire festival)

Figure 3.3 Chiefs sitting on royal skins[89]

The king chooses three names that depict an expression of his reign. One of these names is chosen and added into kings' lists. He then addresses the princes, calling for peace and blessings on the kingdom. His speech is brief and proverbial: 'No prince should go to his home disheartened. In time, every dog gets a chance to chew the bone'.[90]

3.4 Christianity and the Institution of Chieftaincy: Contentions, Criticism and Why?

Though many African Christians do not hesitate to accept the Christian faith into their traditional worldview, that introduction of Christianity has been characterized by conflict with African religious culture.[91] This is true in the Ghanaian context, where some chieftaincy cultural practices are often linked to ATR. The conflict has mainly involved Africans to whom, in their view, Christianity is alien, has nothing to do with the religiosity of Africans but seeks to replace ATR.[92] In their understanding, the Christ of Christianity cannot be given prominence and supremacy over the revered African deities of ATR.[93] Peel has commented that in comparison to other West African cultures, such as the Yorubas, the Asante and other Akan groups were relatively hostile to Christianity and the rate of the uptake of this world religion in the Akan forest belt was notoriously slow.[94] In Ghana, Pentecostals have been the ones worst affected due to the aggressive form of Christianity and their tendency to demonize African culture.[95] The proposal for chaplaincy as a missional model for the IoC in this study seeks to address these perceived tendencies through sustained Christian witness.

3.4.1 Chiefs as spiritual leaders and custodians of religious shrines and gods of the kingdom

From the Asantehene's presentation of the functions of a modern chief, we can see that spiritual leadership and being custodian of religious shrines and gods of the kingdom is important to the IoC.

But what is this role? Whilst chiefs see this role as a cultural heritage, Pentecostals assume that it links chiefs to ATR beliefs and practices, creating tensions.[96] According to Meyer, the proponents of Ghanaian Pentecostalism regard local gods and spirits as agents of Satan and should be eradicated.[97] Amanor states that the confrontation and antagonism that exist among Pentecostals and promoters of African culture 'has mainly been due to the formers' demonization of the African cultural heritage and the latter's veneration of that heritage.'[98]

However, Amanor further argues and I agree that there is no need for this conflict between Christianity and the IoC.[99] Rather, Christian leaders should look for ministry opportunities that exist between both institutions to facilitate engagement. Nketia suggests that the contemporary relevance of shrine cultures should cause the church as part of its social responsibilities to deal with human problems that draw people to shrines.[100] Dankwa, Safo-Kantanka and Opuni-Frimpong support the call for engagement, dialogue and understanding between Christianity and the IoC in dealing with religious beliefs and cultural practices.[101] Amanor cites Anderson and Hollenweger that the holistic African worldview which does not separate the 'physical' from the 'spiritual' is restored in Pentecostalism and provides the opportunity for friendship rather than an enemy to African culture.[102] Dankwa, an insider of the IoC comments that the role of chiefs as spiritual leaders does not necessarily make them divine or given divine authority as some perceive. What is supposed to make the chief sacred during installation, limits the chief's powers by the oath he swears to the elders and his people.[103] In this respect, spiritual leadership function is similar to the role of a Christian minister who is considered a shepherd of God's flock,[104] it says something about divine presence in the minister's spiritual responsibility to members of a congregation. In this case, a chief is an exalted person who is considered first among equals and has no divine rights.[105] The presence of Christian chaplains to the IoC would help explore the friendship between Christianity and African culture which plays a major role in chieftaincy that Amanor and other writers have expressed and is echoed by respondents in this study.

3.4.2 The cult of ancestors and ancestral veneration/worship

The role of the chief's association to ancestors and ancestral veneration or worship is another area that raises conflicts and tensions between Pentecostals and the IoC. Pentecostals see the process of enstoolment or enskinment of a chief are linked to the cult of ancestors. The secrecy in crowning a chief which involves blood sacrifices raises questions as to whether it is mere ancestral veneration or worship.[106] However, a description of the installation ceremony of a chief[107] acknowledges that God is not left out but is considered the ultimate focus of sourcing divine powers. Hence, there is the need to make a distinction between ancestral veneration and worship to God through the sacrifices in these ceremonies.[108]

Even so, Pentecostals consider blood sacrifices during these ceremonies as idol worship. For them, Christ is the ultimate sacrifice and there is no more need for any form of blood sacrifice.[109] Nevertheless, Pentecostals stating their case of rejecting any form of blood sacrifices should not mean abandoning the IoC. I agree with Safo-Kantanka that 'as long as the church sits back and blindly condemns everything in the Ghanaian culture as fetish, our members will be living at two levels – a divided identity.'[110] Gehman cites Mbiti who holds such a view that:

> The old nonsense of looking at African background as devilish, and fit only to be swept away … should be gone by now. African religious background is not a rotten heap of superstitions, taboos, and magic; it has a great deal of value to it. On this valuable heritage, Christianity should adapt itself…[111]

Asantehene Nana Prempeh I took steps towards adaptation when he converted to Christianity. His conversion to Christianity through the ministry of chaplaincy had a great influence on the royal family and some culture and customs of Asanteman. The manager of the Manhyia Palace museum attributed the abolition of human sacrifice that occurred during the death of Asantehene, as part of the funeral rites, to the conversion of Asantehene Prempeh I to Christianity. After his return from exile in the Seychelles in 1924,[112] the King advocated that there was no need to take human life at the death of any king and that his faith as a baptized Anglican would not allow it. Instead, they should use animal sacrifice in place of human beings for those ceremonies, which has been so until today.[113] It is significant to note the role of an Anglican chaplain in the spiritual journey of Edward Prempeh as a Christian. In this case, it is possible that the proposal of chaplaincy as a missional model would enable Pentecostals to ensure intentional engagement with the IoC so it could adapt itself within the valuable heritage of chieftaincy culture in the light of gospel witness.

3.4.3 Chiefly rituals, festivals and loyalty to the kingdom

Chieftaincy culture involves the practices of rituals, observance of festivals and ensuring subjects' loyalty to the kingdom. Pentecostals assume that the rituals practiced during chieftaincy installation and festival celebrations involve blood sacrifices to invoke spiritual powers from deities. The purpose of the *odwire* and *adae* rites is in part to purify the community and maintain the power of the ancestral stools by reanointing them.[114] The power of the ancestral stools known as the 'Black Stools' made during the 19th century was derived in part from human sacrifice.[115] For Pentecostals, the idea of human sacrifice is an abomination and against biblical instructions on the value of human life[116] created in God's image. Though it has been argued that in recent times that human sacrifices have been terminated[117] and replaced with animal sacrifices, the use of secrecy[118] in African chieftaincy culture tends to undermine this claim.

In a positive contribution, the termination of human sacrifices in chieftaincy rituals and festival celebrations is in part attributed to the influence of Christianity[119] and modern civilization. That is to say, Christianity has already made an impact in challenging the cultural practices of the IoC to some extent. As such, Pentecostals should rather build on this by engagement not abandonment. If animal blood sacrifice which has replaced human sacrifice is not acceptable, what should Pentecostals offer as an acceptable alternative to maintain chieftaincy cultural norms? It is possible that an acceptable biblical alternative can be given if Pentecostals have an intentional missional model of chaplaincy to engage with the IoC. The effect of undermining some aspects of chieftaincy culture in the past has often resulted in undesired consequences. Historically, politicians and other interested parties that one may term as 'outside forces' that have tried to influence the cultural tradition of the process involved in the nomination and installation of chiefs, have often led to chaos, instability, property destruction and loss of lives. MacGaffey commenting on the Dagbon crisis in the nomination and enskinment of a new *Ya Naa* (Dagbon king), states that the utter failure of politics and institutions have led to a moderate opinion on the need to return to tradition.[120] Even so, these traditions, guided by 'flexible customs' adapt to change and 'have survived the introduction of Islam, the intrusion of the British and the volatility of Ghanaian politics.[121] The 'flexible customs' in traditions offer Pentecostals an opportunity to make meaningful suggestions towards changes in cultural practices of the IoC through chaplaincy.

The previous chapter acknowledged how achieved documents revealed the strain in relations between Christian leaders, missionaries and some chiefs. These were issues relating to Christians and native customs, fetish days, festivals and the persecution of Christian converts who refuse to perform certain duties because of their faith.[122] K. A. Busia, Prime Minister of the Republic of Ghana from October 1969 to January 1972, made a close study in the early 1950s of the interaction of Akan converts with their indigenous cultural practices. He observed that the Akan converts kept distance from their cultural practices. The Akan converts were not encouraged to recognize their own indigenous leadership structures. Busia wanted a more integrative approach to the interaction between Christianity and African culture that is why he called for the ennoblement of the Akan culture.[123] Missionary presence did not function differently from their colonial authority in Akan society. Church leadership and the missionary headquarters became centres of authority for church members instead of traditional leaders and the palace.[124] Christians rejected activities which had little religious significance like communal labour or road construction just because it came from the traditional leaders. Addo-Fening narrates how chiefs opposed the conversion of state functionaries and cited the Okyehene as:

> Must I let my horn-blowers, my drummers, my pipers, my hammock carriers etc. become Christians? If I do, then I can no longer carry out...ceremonies, nor can I receive foreign embassies worthily. Whoever has an obligation to serve me...will never be allowed to become a Christian.[125]

This affected Christian mission in certain parts of the country. The traditional leadership became afraid of their own people because Christians could count on the support of church leadership and colonial influence against them. It is possible that the presence of chaplaincy ministry could have avoided some of the tensions.

3.5 Current Relationship Between the Institution of Chieftaincy and Christianity

The situation that characterised 19th century and early 20th century Christians engaging the IoC has changed. Chiefs are full members of various denominations and are among leadership as lay preachers in some congregations. According to Asante, the underlying factors for the change of relationship between Christianity and the IoC may be considered as change in the Christian theological thinking as an aspect of the nationalist movement, the affirmation of African cultural values and practices and the accommodation or toleration of Christianity by the IoC.[126] The question of whether a Christian can be a chief or not centres around the religious role of the chief and the sacred nature of chieftaincy. It is this religious basis of the chief's obligation to perform certain rites that brings Christianity into conflict with it. According to Sarpong, 'nobody doubts the right of a Christian to become a chief per se or indeed the advantage, even to Christianity of a Christian becoming a Chief'[127] but the controversy is the chief's role in rituals, ceremonies which make prominent mention of the ancestors considered by some as idolatry and against the first commandment of God.[128] Asante also comments that many of the religious rites associated with chieftaincy which constituted a bone of contention with Christianity in the past are losing their religious characteristic and becoming more civil.[129]

Moreover, there are recent calls on both institutions to strengthen the understanding that is developing and bridge the gap that existed in the past. For instance, the Paramount Chief of Ada and President of the Greater Accra Regional House of Chiefs in an address to the congregation of the Trinity Presbyterian Church of Ghana, called for a closer collaboration between Christianity and Chieftaincy. He admonished Christians not to persist in seeing chieftaincy as heathen but that both institutions have divine mandate from God and should work towards unity and peace to serve humankind.[130] The General Secretary of the Christian Council of Ghana also admonished pastors to preach the Gospel of Jesus to Chiefs. He noted that the church in Ghana and Africa as a whole has failed to extend its mission work to traditional rulers. He also commented that 'majority of the people in the chieftaincy institutions are seeking for support of pastors and Christians in general to provide them with spiritual and leadership support'.[131] The

Vicar General of the Catholic Diocese of Ho in the Volta region of Ghana, urged Christian churches to allow their members to be made chiefs. He added that Christians becoming chiefs will have the opportunity to purify and Christianise kingship and that 'to allow such a precious opportunity to slip by will be a miserable failure, with regard to the urgent need for the evangelization of cultures.'[132]

In this case, two reasons that call for active engagement include: firstly, the chiefs' role outlined above provide missional opportunities proposed in chapter five for Christian leaders to engage with the IoC. Secondly, the change in attitude that seeks cooperation between the leadership of the two institutions in recent times as noted above should interest the church community and church leaders to be proactive in considering chaplaincy as a missional model to engage with traditional rulers.

3.6 Theological Reflections

This section explored chiefly rituals, responsibilities and criticisms from missionaries and Christian leaders just as sustained contact of Christianity increased. The narration reveals how chieftaincy is shrouded with rituals and cultural practices linked to ATR that Christians criticise. Historically, the gospel proclamation encountered similar issues that were dealt with accordingly. Christian converts were not expected to abandon cultural loyalties consistent with the gospel.[133] The IoC as a political structure, providing leadership and governance is among the leadership and authorities that Christians are encouraged to pray for, as they are accountable to God.[134] Referring to the event of the 'Day of Pentecost' in Acts 2:1-12 as a clear sign of the global significance of Christianity,[135] Christian leaders needed to have an open and more tolerant approach to issues related to the IoC.

The key to resolving this challenge was for Christian leaders to understand the cultural and social structures of the people, analyse them, and produce relevant strategies to facilitate the mission of the church. Understanding culture does not imply compromise. Rather, it offers Christian leaders an opportunity to evaluate their theology and produce a more practical form of church life that positively represents Christ within the cultural context of the people. Instead, what prevailed in many parts of the nation showed that new Christian converts kept a distance from their culture. This method of keeping believers away from their culture was not peculiar to Ghana. Isichei stated that missionaries like their counterparts elsewhere in the late 19th century, 'tended to found Christian villages, in the belief that converts needed to live apart from traditional society if they were to develop a pure and fervent spiritual life.'[136] However, we cannot continue to blame missionaries who have done their best and have since handed over to nationals.[137] Hence, there is the need to treat cultural practices with respect and dignity in order to avoid a situation where the church would continue to look like an alien institution before the people.[138]

For instance, the significance of *Odwira* festival among the Akans noted above would be areas that could be used to facilitate any need for contextualisation for the Christian missiologist. The words and themes used to describe the importance of the festival such as purify, cleanse, remembering the dead, thanksgiving for harvest, settling disputes, reconciliation and peace are commonly used in Christianity. Following these analyses, Afriyie and Safo-Kantanka point out that there are a number of parallels in this festival found also in the Old Testament which suggests some redemptive analogies.[139] There is the consecration of the priests before they serve the Lord and a description of the process.[140] Next, the day of atonement is celebrated annually and the feast of first fruits which the people were instructed to bring to the priest.[141] Isaiah's prophetic role to Israel and the nations of the world outlined in chapter 1-39 and Daniel's service in kings' courts expresses God's mission to the world.

Safo-Kantanka agrees with Bishop Sarpong that Ghanaians tend to lean on Parrinder's Triangle Theory of religious thought where God is at the apex of the triangle. This highest position that God occupies, has made him unknown. It is very well understood in the Akan religious thought that God cannot be represented in any form of art. According to Bishop Sarpong, 'images of God are almost non-existent, and rarely are temples built for him.'[142] That is why God is denied public worship and sacrifices, which are rather ignorantly given to ancestors and deities perceived as known and closer to the people. Safo-Kantanka again referred to the author of Hebrews' argument on the Old Testament sacrifices being a shadow of what God was going to do in Christ and suggests that the traditional sacrificial system of Odwira, Adae and other ceremonies were also a shadow of things to come in Christ. I may not be able to agree with all his analogies due to the fact that I have not done any biblical exegesis on his suggestions given on these ceremonies, as it was not the focus of this work. Nevertheless, redemptive analogies can be a useful cultural contextual bridge that may be used with an awareness of the weaknesses. These redemptive analogies from the Old and New Testaments should provide the bases for which the chaplains might assume the roles of 'Prophets and Priests' proposed in the missional model in the next chapter. Priests in the pastoral role provide spiritual care and prophets as agents of change challenges the status quo to facilitate cultural transformation.

Furthermore, there are challenges that need to be addressed. According to Louis Luzbetak, worldview is one of the cultural domains that reveals a people's mentality and provides answers to questions such as: Who belongs to the invisible world and what are the invisible forces in the world? What about life after death?[143] Answers to these questions in ATR make royal objects and symbols such as 'stools' and the 'King River', believed to contain the spirits of deceased kings which are fearfully protected with rituals and are to be worshiped. This contradicts Bible teaching that all acts of worship should be given to Almighty God alone.[144] In addition, the numerous animal sacrifices offered to these objects of worship, taboos observed, mysticism and the display of spiritual powers during these celebrations limits chaplaincy involvement. Christians believe that Jesus Christ was the final sacrifice that puts an end to all sacrifices and any sacrifice to replace that of Christ is an abomination to the Lord.[145] Pentecostal chaplaincy faces the challenge of creating an impression of endorsing ATR practices when seen around the ceremonies and festivals. For years, Pentecostals have 'demonised' chieftaincy and asked members to abstain from practices associated with it. A change of perception is needed to facilitate missional engagement in this case. I agree with Safo-Kantanka that there should be a distinction between that which is purely fetish from ceremonial service.[146] In this case, the proposal to adopt 'hybridity' will help facilitate this difference, allowing traditional leaders to handle roles exclusively carried by them alongside Christian services offered to the IoC.[147] This distinction will help theologians contextualise what is appropriate for Christian participation and the eventual transformation of such practices which chaplaincy to chieftaincy as a missional model can play an important role. In spite of the challenges, the data reveal that there is the need for Christian witness with the IoC which reinforces the hypothesis that the proposal of chaplaincy as a missional model would enable Pentecostal denominational involvement with chieftaincy.

3.7 Summary

From this study of chiefly rituals, responsibilities and examined contentious issues between Christianity and the IoC, it was evident that the attitudes and actions of some Christian leaders to address conflicts between members and the traditional authorities did not help to build any good relation between the two institutions, as government structures were often relied upon to the advantage of Christians over chiefs. Civilization and modern enlightenment in education have to some extent facilitated the diffusion of the tension that existed as both institutions acknowledge the benefits that would be derived in collaboration and partnership. Furthermore, the changing role of the chief in recent times from spiritual and military responsibilities to focusing on education, economic development, social integration and moral leadership of the community, offer the church ministry opportunities to facilitate this change and not to shun away from it. That is why I am proposing the introduction of Christian Chaplaincy as a missional model to the IoC from Pentecostals in particular. The next chapter examines the ecclesial, contemporary cultural and institutional contexts of chaplaincy ministry.

---

1. Brobbey, *The Law*, p. 2.
2. See Figure 3.1.
3. The Constitution of the Republic of Ghana, http://www.ghana.gov.gh/images/documents/constitution_ghana.pdf [accessed 4 November 2017].
4. Dankwa, *Chieftaincy*, p. 1., Donald I Ray & E. Adriaan B. van Rouveroy van Nieuwal, 'The New Relevance of Traditional Authorities in Africa', *The Journal of Legal Pluralism and Unofficial Law*, (1996), 28:37-38, 1 38, DOI: 10.1080/07329113.1996.10756473 [accessed 17 January 2017], Alhassan Sulemana Anamzoya, 'Neither fish nor fowl': an analysis of status ambiguity of Houses of Chiefs in Ghana', *The Journal of Legal Pluralism and Unofficial Law*, 46.2, (2014), 218-234 DOI: 10.1080/07329113.2014.902652 [accessed 12 February 2017], Janine Ubink, 'Traditional Authority Revisited: Popular Perceptions of Chiefs and Chieftaincy in Peri-Urban Kumasi, Ghana, *The Journal of Legal Pluralism and Unofficial Law*, 39:55, (2007), 123-161, DOI: 10.1080/07329113.2007.10756610 [accessed 12 February 2017].
5. Dankwa, *Chieftaincy*, p. 2.
6. Asantehene Otumfuo Osei Tutu II, 'The Role of Modern Traditional Chiefs in Development in Africa', an address delivered at the 2nd Bonn Conference on International Development Policy, World Conference Centre, Bonn, Germany, 27th-28th August 2009, <http://manhyiaonline.org> [accessed 2 November 2014].
7. Kleist, 'Modern Chiefs:', p. 634.
8. Brobbey, *The Law*, pp. 33-34.
9. Dankwa, *Christianity*, p. 46.
10. According to the West Africa Report the IoC composed of some 32000 in 1991. Canada: Immigration and Refugee Board of Canada, 'Ghana: Information on the number of paramount chiefs and wing chiefs including the names and the authority they wield', 1 May 1993, <https://www.refworld.org/docid/3ae6acdd5c.html> [accessed 27 November 2017].

11. Jean-Marc Ela and John Pairmain Brown, *My faith as an African*, (Eugene, OR: Wipf and Stock Publishers, 2009), p. xv.
12. M. Z. Hackman and C. E. Johnson, *Leadership: A communication perspective*, (Long Grove, IL: Waveland Press, 2000).
13. Paul G. Hiebert, *Anthropological Insights for Missionaries*, (Grand Rapids, Michigan: Baker Book House, 1985) p. 30.
14. Kwame Bediako, 'Gospel and Culture: Some Insights for Our Time from the Experience of the Earliest Church', *Journal of African Thought*, 2.2. (1999), pp. 8-17.
15. A. S. Glasser, *Kingdom and Mission*, (Pasadena, CA: Fuller Theological School of Mission, 1989), p. 309.
16. Nketia, 'Christianity and African Culture', p. 15.
17. Kwame Gyekye, *Tradition and Modernity – Philosophical reflections on the African Experience*, (New York: Oxford University Press, 1997) p. 219.
18. R. S. Rattray, *Asante Law and Constitution*, (London: Oxford University Press, 1929), p. 63.
19. Dankwa, *Chieftaincy*, p. 11.
20. Brobbey, *The Law*, p. 49.
21. Brobbey, *The Law*, pp. 50, 51.
22. Brobbey, *The Law*, pp. 103, 104.
23. Arhin, *Traditional*, pp. 28-30.
24. Opuni-Frimpong, *Indigenous*, pp. 123, 124.
25. Arhin, *Traditional*, pp. 30, 31.
26. Dankwa, *Chieftaincy*, pp. 14-18.
27. Opuni-Frimpong, *Indigenous*, p. 119; Arhin, *Traditional*, pp. 36, 37; Dankwa, *Chieftaincy*, p. 50.
28. Arhin, *Traditional*, pp. 35, 36.
29. Brobbey, *The Law*, p. 152; Arhin, *Traditional*, p.36.
30. Peter Sarpong, *The Sacred stools of the Akan*, (Accra: Ghana Publishing Corporation, 1971), pp. 7, 8.
31. Brobbey, *The Law*, p. 91.
32. Brobbey, *The Law*, p. 91.
33. Sarpong, *Sacred* p. 17.
34. Sarpong, *Sacred*, p. 30. 'The day was Friday. Anokye had summoned all the chiefs of the Union to a great gathering at Kumasi. At that gathering he brought from the sky, with darkness and thunder, and in a thick cloud of white dust, a wooden stool, adorned with gold, which floated to earth and landed gently on Osei- Tutu's knee'.
35. Sarpong, *Sacred*, pp. 17 - 59; <https://uk.images.search.yahoo.com/yhs/search;_Hand-carved-Ashanti-Unity-Stool-Ghana> [accessed 26 September 2016].
36. Sarpong, *Sacred*, p.36, Brobbey, *The Law*, pp. 91, 151, Opuni-Frimpong, *Indigenous*, pp. 148-53.
37. Sarpong, *Sacred*, p. 38.
38. Safo-Kantanka, *Christian?* p.16.
39. Festivals in Ghana, <http://www.ghanagrio.com/festivals/> [accessed 29 October 2016].
40. Nukunya, *Tradition*, pp. 64, 65.

41. In the account Busia states that: 'In the old days, it was a feast of the dead; it was closely connected with first-fruits, it was a cleansing of the nation from defilement, and a purification of the shrines of the ancestral spirits and national gods.' Safo-Kantanka, *Christian?* p. 17.
42. Safo-Kantanka, *Christian?* pp. 17-21.
43. Arhin, *Traditional*, p. 68.
44. Safo-Kantanka, *Christian?* p. 16.
45. Muller, *Religion*, p. 183.
46. Some of these contributions are realised during the Akan festivals. Businessmen who pay homage to the Asantehene during these festivals give gifts in cash or kind. Muller, *Religion*, p. 184.
47. Opuni-Frimpong, *Indigenous*, p. 149.
48. Sarpong, *Sacred*, p. 42.
49. Muller, *Religion*, pp. 155-56.
50. A description of this dance is found in: Muller, *Religion*, p. 166.
51. Muller, Religion, pp. 168-71.
52. Michael Schlottner, 'We Stay, Others Come and Go': Identity among the Mamprusi in Northern Ghana', in Carola Lentz and Paul Nugent, (eds.), *Ethnicity in Ghana. The Limits of Intervention*, (London: Macmillan Press, 2000), pp. 49-67.
53. Brobbey, *The Law*, p. 16.
54. Nukunya, *Tradition*, p. 67.
55. Drucker-Brown, 'Mamprusi installation' and 'Horse, dog', *The Journal*, p. 486 and p. 72.
56. Steve Tonah, 'Defying the Nayiri: Traditional Authority, People's Power and the Politics of Chieftaincy Succession in Mamprugu – Northern Ghana', *Legon Journal of Sociology*, 1 (1) (2004), 42-58.
57. Tonah, 'Defying,' p. 45.
58. Arhin, *Traditional*, p. 3, 4.
59. The gate system is used to let respective gates present a preferred candidate to contest the other gates for the vacant royal skin. In the case of the Nayiri, one should be a reigning chief of one of the qualifying gates in order to be eligible to contest.
60. Tonah, 'Defying', p. 47.
61. Drucker-Brown, 'Ritual', *African Studies*, (1975).
62. Tonah, 'Defying', p. 47.
63. These ceremonies include: i) the selection of a new Na through divination; ii) the presentation of gifts to the elders of the Na's household; iii) the investiture and admonition of the new Na; iv) the flight and capture of the new Na; v) the Na's public affirmation of his duties with the Koran and distribution of gifts. Arhin, Traditional, p. 49.
64. Brobbey, *The Law*, pp. 90, 156.
65. Brobbey, *The Law*, p. 156.
66. Drucker-Brown, 'Mamprusi', p. 498.
67. Drucker-Brown, 'The Court and the Cola Nut', p. 137.
68. Heidi William, Trey & KJ's, 'The Hauns in Africa', <http://haunsinafrica.com/2014/11/10/bugum-fire-festival/> [accessed 29 January 2017].

69. Wyatt MacGaffey, 'Death of a king, death of a kingdom? Social pluralism and succession to high office in Dagbon, northern Ghana', *Journal of Modern African Studies, 44, 1* (Cambridge: Cambridge University Press, 2006), pp. 79-99.
70. Drucker-Brown, 'Horse', p. 86.
71. Arts Ghana, 'Damba as a festival and dance form', *Admin*, 11 July 2014, <http://artsghana.org/damba-as-a-festival-and-dance-form/> [accessed 30 January 2017].
72. Drucker-Brown, 'Mamprusi', 'Horse', 'The Court', and 'The grandchildren's',
73. Drucker-Brown, 'Horse', p. 76.
74. MacGaffey, 'Death?', pp. 79-99.
75. Drucker-Brown, 'The grandchildren's', p. 183.
76. Drucker-Brown, 'Horse', p. 77.
77. One of the true sons of the deceased king starts the rite, followed by all royals who hope to become the new king. In an orderly way, the royals arrive one after the other on horseback with armed warriors. He gallops to the palace gate brandishing his sword and shouts at the palace guard 'What is happening here' and the guard replies 'it is God's will'. The royal ends the exchange which is repeated thrice in the manner of an oath shouting: 'if it were not God's will, I will avenge his death.'
78. Drucker-Brown, 'Horse', pp. 78-79.
79. Drucker-Brown, 'The grandchildren's', pp. 188-89.
80. Drucker-Brown, 'Horse', p. 79.
81. The heavily medicated cooked meal is supervised by a barber-cum-circumciser and assisted by the senior widow of the immediate past king and the senior wife *Ma Paani* of the king-elect. A powerful symbol of continuity of naam chieftainship, ensuring unity and peaceful transfer of leadership in my view.
82. Drucker-Brown, 'Horse', p. 80.
83. The king is roped in a white gown and covered by a red hooded *bulmusu* which veils his face. This part is secretly done and possibly with rituals but not commented upon. Drucker-Brown, 'Horse', pp. 80-81.
84. 'the care taken to prevent contact between the king's body and the earth is a public demonstration of how powerful his physical person has become.' Drucker-Brown, 'Horse', p. 81.
85. At the public installation, the king is surrounded by townspeople rather than royals and lineage kin. When he is offered the water to drink, the people stretch out their right hand in a gesture to show their support. People say, it is as though they were holding the calabash for the king to drink.
86. Drucker-Brown, 'Horse', pp. 81-82.
87. At the secluded place, the king receives strengthening medicines, further protection and education in kingship.
88. The king initiates the distribution, using both right and left hands to share. Accepting the meal is an act to demonstrate one's willingness of obedience and loyalty to the king.
89. Google Images, 'Northern Ghana Chiefs', <https://www.google.co.uk/search?q=northern+ghana+chiefs&client> [accessed 20 December 2016].
90. Drucker-Brown, 'Horse', pp. 82-84.
91. John S. Mbiti, *Introduction to African Religion*, 2nd ed. (Oxford: Heinemann Educational Publishers, 1991), pp. 180, 196.

92. K. Bediako, *Jesus in Africa: The Christian Gospel in African History and Experience*, (Carlisle: Paternoster Publishing, 2000) p. 50.
93. Y. Turaki, *Christianity and African Gods: A Method in Theology*, (Potchefstroomese: S. A. Christian Higher Education Press, 1999), p. 36.
94. John David Yeadon Peel, 'History, culture and comparative method: a West African puzzle', in Ladislav Holy, (ed.), *Comparative Anthropology*, (Oxford: Basil Blackwell, 1987), pp. 88-118.
95. Birgit Meyer, 'Translating the Devil: Religion and Modernity among the Ewe of Southeastern Ghana', *Ghana Studies Review*, (2001), p. 5.
96. Gilbert, 'The Christian Executioner', p. 315.
97. Meyer, 'Make a complete break with the past', pp. 316-49.
98. Amanor, 'Pentecostal and Charismatic churches in Ghana', p. 126.
99. Amanor, 'Pentecostal and Charismatic churches in Ghana', p. 126.
100. Nketia, 'Christianity and Culture', p. 14.
101. Dankwa, *Chieftaincy*, p. 68, Safo-Kantanka, *Christian*, p. 67 and Opuni-Frimpong, *Indigenous*, p. 233.
102. A. H. Anderson and W. J. Hollenweger (eds.), *Pentecostals after a Century: Global Perspectives and a Movement in Transition*, (JPTSup, 15; Sheffield: Sheffield Academic Press, 1999), p. 190.
103. Dankwa, *Chieftaincy*, pp. 70 – 71.
104. Acts 20:28; 1 Pet. 5:1-3.
105. Dankwa, *Chieftaincy*, p. 70.
106. Safo-Kantanka, *Christian*, p. 12.
107. See Chapter 3.2.2.
108. Safo-Kantanka, *Christian*, pp. 37-41; Dankwa, *Chieftaincy*, pp. 68-70, Opuni-Frimpong, *Indigenous*, 119-66
109. Heb. 10:14-18.
110. Safo-Kantanka, *Christian*, p. 40.
111. Richard J. Gehman, *African Traditional Religion in Biblical Perspective*, (Nairobi: East African Educational Publishers Limited, 2012), p. 249.
112. *A Guide to Manhyia Palace Museum*, (Kumasi: Otumfuo Opoku Ware Jubilee Foundation, 2003), p. 1.
113. Brobbey Justice, Interviewed at Manhyia Palace Museum, (Kumasi: 14 February 2014).
114. Afriyie, 'Christ our Perfect Sacrifice', pp. 26, 31; Dankwa, Chieftaincy, p. 73.
115. Feeley-Harnik, 'Issues in Divine Kingship', p. 302.
116. Gen. 9:5; Exod. 20:13; Lev. 20:1-5, 24:17; Hos. 13:2.
117. Gilbert, 'The Christian Executioner', p. 352.
118. Feeley-Harnik, 'Issues in Divine Kingship', p. 296.
119. Dankwa, *Chieftaincy*, pp. 67-81; Safo-Kantanka, *Christianity*, pp. 16-36; Opuni-Frimpong, *Indigenous*, pp. 149-53.
120. MacGaffey, 'Death of a king', pp. 93-94.
121. Davis, 'Then the White Man came', pp. 644-46.
122. W. G. Waterworth to Arthur J. Philbrick, (Coomassie: West Africa, 11th September 1914).
123. K. A. Busia, *The Position of the Chief in Modern Political System of Ashanti*, (Oxford: Oxford University Press for International African Institute, 1951), p.135.

124. Opuni-Frimpong, *Indigenous*, p. 60.

125. Addo-Fening, 'From Traditionalist to Christian Evangelist...', p. 6.

126. Emmanuel Asante, 'The Relationship between the Chieftaincy institution and Christianity in Ghana', in Irene K. Odotei and Albert K. Awedoba, (eds.), *Chieftaincy in Ghana: Culture, Governance and Development*, (Accra: Ghana, Sub-Saharan Publishers, 2009), p. 235.

127. Peter Kwasi Sarpong, *Libation*, (Accra: Anansesem Publication, 1996), p. vii.

128. Sarpong, *Libation*, p. vii.

129. Asante, 'Relationship', p. 243.

130. Dzetse Nene Abram Kabu Akuaku III, 'Clergy and Traditional Rulers need to work together', Ghana News Agency, 12th April 2013, <http://www.ghanaweb.com> [accessed 15 January 2014].

131. Kwabena Opuni-Frimpong, 'Let's take the Gospel to the Palace', *Christian Council of Ghana*, (Accra: GNA, 21st January 2014), <http://www.ghanaweb.com> [accessed 10 February 2014].

132. Reverend Monsignor Anthony Kornu, 'Christians can be Chiefs', *Catholic Diocese of Ho*, (Accra: GNA, 23rd June 2013), <http://www.ghanaweb.com> [accessed 17 March 2014].

133. Graham, Walton and Ward, *Theological Reflection: Methods*, p. 218.

134. Rom. 13:1, 5-6.

135. Graham, Walton and Ward, *Theological Reflections Methods*, p. 220.

136. Elizabeth Isichei, *A History of Christianity in Africa: From Antiquity to the Present*, (London: Society for Promoting Christian Knowledge, 1995), p. 195.

137. Nketia, 'Christianity and African Culture', p. 18.

138. Opuni-Frimpong, *Indigenous*, p. 63.

139. Afriyie, 'Christ our Perfect Sacrifice', pp. 31-33; Safo-Kantanka, *Christian*, pp. 22-31.

140. Exod. 28:1-29:9.

141. Lev. 16 and 23:9-14.

142. Safo-Kantanka, *Christian*, p. 26.

143. Louis J Luzbetak, S.V.D. *The Church and Cultures: New Perspectives in Missiological Anthropology*, (Maryknoll, NY: Orbis Books, 1988).

144. E. K. Marfo, *The Christian Faith & Traditional Rituals*, (Kumasi: Ed-Jay Services Ltd, 2009), p. 40.

145. Marfo, *Christian*, pp. 45-47; Heb., 10:5-7.

146. Safo-Kantanka, *Christian*, pp. 37-40.

147. Shaw, 'Beyond Syncretism', pp. 6-15.

FOUR

Chaplaincy Ministry

4.0 Introduction

All this is from God, who reconciled us to himself through Christ and gave us the ministry of reconciliation: that God was reconciling the world to himself in Christ, not counting people's sins against them. And he has committed to us the message of reconciliation. We are therefore Christ's ambassadors, as though God were making his appeal through us. We implore you on Christ's behalf: Be reconciled to God.[1]

The church as the body of Christ is designed in such a way that believers are saved to serve. The call to serve is emphasized in the above text where the Scripture admonishes Christians to acknowledge the divine assignment entrusted to serve humanity as God's representatives on earth. This service comes in different forms, one of which is the chaplaincy ministry. A ministry that addresses the place of religion and its representation in public spaces in the context of a pluralistic society. In spite of the debate of religious authority and the Church's social status in public institutions, chaplaincy practice and roles have been growing in number and diversity in recent times.[2]

This chapter therefore considers chaplaincy ministry in relation to the various contexts within which it is situated. These contextual perspectives are the ecclesial context, the relationship between the Church and the prevailing culture, and the institutional context. As Slater notes, the decision to embrace a faith community and its practices is a matter of choice among many alternatives in a place that offer the promise of personal and spiritual fulfilment.[3] The IoC is one of the public spaces that offer alternative choices with regards to faith practice. There is therefore the need to discuss the wider contextual influences that shape chaplaincy ministry.

4.1 Chaplaincy and the Ecclesial Context

The type of chaplaincy ministry that is mainly the subject of this book is placed in the public structure of the IoC. It therefore represents the institutional churches and the IoC. This means that chaplains are not only in dialogue with the prevailing culture of the IoC but also, the churches they represent. Churches have their own local culture, understood as their way of life, customs, shared meanings, values and beliefs at a particular time.[4] This is reflected in the various denominational traditions of the Church. I argue in the next chapter that churches should be responsible in appointing chaplains to the IoC as part of their missional policy. This will facilitate good working relationships between chaplains and local churches in the area. In countries where chaplaincy have long been established and widely used in Christian ministry at various institutions, reveal a disconnection in the working relationship between chaplains and the church.[5] The research showed that many chaplains did not feel the Church cherished, supported or acknowledged the significance of their work in the same way it did for congregational ministry.[6]

The findings in the 2014 Church of England research for instance, revealed lack of accurate data of chaplaincy at local and national levels of church life. There was no reliable quantitative data about the type and number of chaplaincy roles that exist, the number of people involved in chaplaincy ministry and how they were resourced. Most chaplains were employed by organizations other than the Church of England. It indicates an investment from secular institutions that demand accountability from chaplaincy practices that suit employers' mission rather than the Church. The figures showed that 93 per cent of full-time ordained chaplains were employed by someone other than the Church of England.[7] Swift comments on this perceived disconnection between the theology and concerns of the Church and chaplains who work independently within the social structures of society as 'the silent exile of the chaplains from the central preoccupation of the Church.'[8] Slater suggests that one fundamental reason for this disconnection can be attributed to the recent growth in innovative chaplaincy-type roles that has far outstripped any theological reflection on practice.[9] The consequences of disconnection affects the mission of the Church. As a result, there can be a lack of a clear theological rationale for chaplaincy that can be represented to and heard by the Church. These findings noted above may serve as lessons and a guide to the church in Ghana. As of now, a lot of theological and other resources have been devoted to other places of Christian ministries rather than IoC. In view of this, I suggest that the Church should resource chaplaincy ministry to the IoC. The training, deployment and sustenance of personnel either voluntarily or in full-time paid chaplaincy ministry to the IoC should be the Church responsibility. This reflects participants' view in this study that called for chaplaincy involvement in the IoC.[10]

The spiritual and numerical growth of the church in Ghana requires its ability to develop capacity to serve the whole community in the country. There is the need to ensure a growing and sustainable Christian witness in every local community where there is both greatest need and greatest opportunity. The vision of chaplaincy ministry enables the Church to be represented in the very midst of society, rather than at its margins.[11] If the Church through chaplaincy ministry is set within the midst of IoC as a community – the nation – in a sense, genuinely engaging with the national community about its concerns and ambitions, then there is a real chance of achieving the vision of the Christ for every day in the wider society. Christianity has both an inward and outward dimension. It is about having a personal relationship with God and how to live as a member of the body of Christ in a wider society. It is possible that the varied roles of chaplaincy ministry will enable the Christian traditional leader to fulfil the latter within the structures of the IoC as a community in the wider society. If the Church in Ghana truly has a vision of mission that is broader and more profound than a focus on growth in numbers, then there is the need to see chaplaincy ministry to the IoC as the frontier of the mission of the Church in this century.

4.2 Chaplaincy, the Church and the Contemporary Cultural Context

In countries where chaplaincy ministry is well established, its growth in chaplaincy roles at a time that church attendance is in decline is described by authors such as Callum G. Brown and poses the question of what this means for the relationship of the church and chaplaincy with their social and cultural context.[12] Ballard is of the view that the growth of these chaplaincy-type roles represents one of the ways in which the Church is adapting to the dispersed, diverse and fluid nature of contemporary life.[13] In today's lifestyle, one live in a place, work in another and have a variety of work, social and leisure networks. This is arguably the case for most people who are constantly on a move between different roles and places either real or virtual spheres of activity. People have become increasingly mobile and with a decline to geographical central gatherings, chaplaincy ministry can be seen as one response to this context. In effect, it is an attempt to re-enculturate the gospel in contemporary society to express the relevance of Christianity in every context in which we live our lives. Slater suggests that chaplaincy can be considered as an ecclesial adaptation to the cultural context.[14] This is important, because as the empirical study has shown, chaplaincy ministry to the IoC as a particular cultural context, has missional significance.

The continually recurring task of the Church is to discern how to fulfil its mission in and to the world. Considering the fact that it is imperative to engage with the whole of society, the Church should resist the temptation to turn inwards under financial and cultural pressure. In this context, if traditional leaders will not come to the church building then church ministries have got to go where the traditional leaders are. In this case, chaplaincy ministry ability to relate to different cultures and contexts proves to be a resource that could enable Pentecostals' thinking and practice at this particular cultural context of the IoC. The kind of theological approach appropriate to take towards engagement with chieftaincy cultures lies at the sharp edge of practical theology where the focus is on praxis. Our theology is expressed every day through our practice. People know what we believe as they see what we do as Christians. As one participant remarked, you always pray for leaders and people in authority in your churches but it is good if the chief hears you praying to God in his palace.[15] A good theological reflection on chaplaincy practice with the IoC that brings lived experience is possible through having dialogue in order to bring to awareness the meanings and significance of the practice. This process would enable what is good to be affirmed and the discernment of what might need to be changed or developed. An example could be taken from my own experience. I attended the *Akwasidae* festival held in Kumasi at the *Manhyia* Palace grounds as part of my research participant observation. Once the celebration was over and I returned home, I called one of the senior ministers and told him of my visit to *Manhyia* Palace. To my surprise, his immediate reaction was a word of caution for me to be careful in visiting the place because my head could be cut for rituals. This caution was based on the public perception of human sacrifices held in the past at some chiefs' palaces that continued to make some people feel unsafe to visit such areas which is not the case today. The discrepancy between the importance of church ministry that people wanted to believe and exercised at the confines of the chiefs' courts and the reality of the practice would be a fruitful focus for practical theological reflection. In order for there to be a chance of that process taking place, it is possible that chaplaincy ministry to the IoC would enable the awareness of the theological nature of our practice.

This is particularly true in relation to the theological approach that is taken towards the prevailing cultural context. The kind of approach taken will reflect certain assumptions about the nature of mission and the relationship between the Church and the IoC as a society. If Pentecostals adopt the approach that the Church is dispersed within the society rather than the gathered as the assembly of the faithful, they will follow the particular calling of the Church to discern where God may be at work and seek to participate in God's redemptive purposes. There is the need for genuine dialogue between the Church and its social and cultural context. The contemporary society context requires the church to engage from the position of listening and conversation that are characteristic of chaplaincy in its engagement with people's lived experience. Walters is of the view that the chaplain stands in the world as a representative of the Church, looking around many people who have no encounter with it.[16] They are there witnessing the transformative love of Christ through the work of the Holy Spirit bringing about the Kingdom of God. Similarly, Todd suggests that given that chaplaincy embraces a practical and dialogical method of engagement with society which the Church urgently needs to adopt, its style of engagement may serve as a sign of the future shape of the Church.[17] In this case, I argued in the next chapter that chaplaincy ministry is fundamental to the vision of mission rooted in God's initiative, calling believers to serve the *Missio Dei* in the world.

4.3 Chaplaincy and the Institutional Context

Ministry in an institution requires a special understanding and awareness of the particular institution. Chaplains serve in the context of complicated issues and potentially compromising situations. When chaplains enter the institutional culture without having ever been a part of that culture, they are faced with the challenge of building trust and credibility with the institution and its members. For this reason, there is the need to put in place proactive steps to minimize chaplains' vulnerability and protect them and the institutions they represent and serve. Chieftaincy as an institution, is a public place with multi-faith personalities which the chaplain needs to take into consideration for ministry. The rules and expectations may not be quite clear, as there may be few ambiguities. Challenging or disregarding those expectations could result in fines or criminal charges. A consistent presence and interest in chieftaincy governance, coupled with intentional observation and study of the culture and distinctive traits of chieftaincy would assist the chaplain in understanding the basics of the IoC.

The chaplain should therefore endeavour to be led by the Holy Spirit and the ethics for ministry laid out by the church. Where there is doubt, the chaplain would do well to utilize good skills such as clarification and self-examination through dialogue to process difficult situations, evaluate interventions and assess effectiveness. In order to accomplish some understanding of the institutional culture will require building relationships with members within the institution of chieftaincy.[18] As spiritual people providing spiritual ministry, God requires the right response from chaplains as his people. They are accountable to God for their attitudes, motives and actions. The Scriptures state: *He has shown you, O mortal, what is good. And what does the Lord require of you? To act just-*

ly and to love mercy and to walk humbly with your God.[19] In this text, God requires chaplains to love mercy by having a compassionate heart that demonstrates godly action.

After a presentation of the research outcome at some annual regional council meetings of the Assemblies of God Ghana,[20] one of the ministers from the north west shared his ministry experience at the palace of his station. He stated that his initial visits went unnoticed by the elders of the palace until they noticed he was a consistent participant in events at the palace. This led to the chief asking him to pray in one of the gatherings which led to other ministry opportunities thereafter at the palace. Today, he is one of the respected religious leaders at the palace and the chief would always give him his offering to be sent to church on his behalf. Another minister from the north east narrated how he and some elders of the church's ministry to one of the Dagomba chiefs near Yendi earned his respect and praise. He stated that the chief acknowledged that all their prayers offered at his palace have been answered as the place now enjoys some peace after a long conflict. A minister from Ashanti north also shared how he has the opportunity of consistent ministry at a palace due to the chief's wife Christian faith. Similar accounts of this nature can be found in several places across the country. The common feature of these examples is that ministers embarked in a continued ministry and valued the institutional culture of chieftaincy with their presence that gained trust and enhanced a better relationship between ministers and the IoC.

4.4 Summary

This chapter has presented the ecclesial, contemporary cultural and institutional contexts of chaplaincy ministry in relation to its praxis. The exploration of these contexts demands an ecclesial response if the church is to engage with the IoC and actively participate in conversations in the public square. There are signs that the church is responding to this challenge as shown in this study. Although this exploration may be suggestive of the significance of chaplaincy, such assertions need to be grounded in research into practice. The next chapter therefore presents the case for chaplaincy to chieftaincy. This provides the basis for developing the empirical evidence of why and how the missional model of chaplaincy would enable Christian witness and ministry with the IoC.

---

1. 2 Cor. 5:18-20 *NIV*, (All Scriptural references are from the New International Version of the Bible unless stated otherwise).
2. Slater, *Chaplaincy*, p. 2.
3. Salter, *Chaplaincy*, p. 3.
4. Hiebert, *Anthropological Insights*, p. 30
5. A. Todd, V. Slater & S. Dunlop, *The Church of England's involvement in Chaplaincy*, (The Cardiff Centre for Chaplaincy Studies & The Oxford Centre for Ecclesiology and Practical Theology, 2014)
6. Slater, *Chaplaincy*, p. 6
7. Todd, Slater & Dunlop, *The Church*, pp. 14, 20
8. C. Swift, *Hospital Chaplaincy in the Twenty-First Century, 2nd ed.* (Farnham: Ashgate, 2014)
9. Slater, *Chaplaincy*, p. 7
10. See Chapters 7 and 8.
11. Caperon, Todd, and Walters, *The Christian...*, p.136
12. Callum G. Brown, *The death of Christian Britain, 2nd ed.* (London: Routledge, 2009)
13. P. Ballard, 'Locating Chaplaincy: A Theological Note', *Crucible: The Christian Journal of Social Ethics, July-September* 2009, pp. 18-24.
14. Slater, *Chaplaincy*, p. 9.
15. NRTL2, Interview, (Nalerigu, 2nd February 2014).
16. James Walters, 'Twenty-first Century Chaplaincy: Finding the Church in the Post-Secular', in J. Caperon, A. Todd and J. Walters, (eds.), *A Christian Theology of Chaplaincy*, (London: Jessica Kingsley Publishers, 2018), p. 51
17. A. Todd, 'Chaplaincy Leading Church in(to) the Public Square', *Crucible: The Christian Journal of Social Ethics*, October-December 2011, pp. 7-15.
18. Paget and McCormack, Chaplain, pp. 96-97, 123
19. Micah 6:8
20. These meetings were held at the 5th Annual Regional Councils of the North West held at the Northern Campus of Assemblies of God Theological Seminary, Kumbungu, North East held at Toma AG Saboba, Ashanti West held at Grace Chapel AG Kumasi, Ashanti North held at Calvary Charismatic Centre AG Kumasi and Ashanti East held at Living Waters Chapel AG Kumasi from 13th January to 7th February 2020.

FIVE

Chaplaincy to Chieftaincy

5.0 Introduction

A key objective of this thesis is to identify the role of chaplaincy to enable Pentecostals' involvement with the IoC. Having previously considered the historical encounter between Christianity and chieftaincy, I now turn my attention to chaplaincy as a missional model for Christian leaders ministering within the social context of chieftaincy.

The primary focus of this thesis is to assess the extent to which Pentecostal denominations can be involved with the IoC in Ghana. As such, chaplaincy as a missional model must be considered within this context. An overview of chaplains from denominations other than Pentecostals and the role of ATR priest to chieftaincy is necessary but is confined here to assist in the understanding of how chieftaincy heavily relies on religious leaders or priests for counsel and insight in dealing with spirituality. ATR priests do this in their quest to provide good leadership that honours God and assist chiefs to fulfil their responsibilities in the community. Therefore, with that in mind, this chapter seeks to provide a response to Christian chiefs' dependence on traditional priests by reasserting the importance of Christian chaplaincy as a distinct alternative to traditional priests to help reflect the teachings of Christ consistent with biblical narratives in the IoC. I argue that the ministry of chaplaincy has extended to diverse institutions in recent times in the UK but not in Ghana, and within this context should now include the IoC.

5.1 Existing Chaplains from Denominations Other Than Pentecostals

The Roman Catholics, Anglicans, Methodists, Presbyterians and Baptists exerted their presence in some parts of the country before the arrival of Pentecostal churches. It will therefore be appropriate to explore whether these churches have designated chaplains for the IoC as pioneers of Christian evangelization of the nation, so as to learn from their experience. However, this does not appear to be the case, as very little is known of formal engagements of the use of chaplaincy in these denominations with the IoC. The lack of formal engagement of chaplaincy within chieftaincy even with other denominations makes the purpose of this dissertation more pertinent.

The previous chapter reported on the conversion of the Ashanti King Prempeh I whilst in exile to Seychelles as a prisoner for twenty-four years from 1900 – 1924). It is reported that Prempeh chose to become Anglican after learning that the King of England was an Anglican and suggested that all kings should have the same religion as the King of England.[1] The ministry of chaplaincy played a vital role in the Christian formation of King Prempeh. His desire to be a Christian influenced his close family who were with him as political prisoners to convert to Christianity. King Prempeh is credited for much of the conversion of the Ashanti royal family to Christianity and for the Anglican church in Kumasi being considered their official church.[2] However, the chaplaincy service that King Prempeh experienced while a political prisoner, was not offered at his palace when he returned from exile. Opuni-Frimpong noted that prayer books had names of royals for regular intercessions by the church but failed to teach converts how to remain a traditional leader (Chief) and a Christian.[3]

The failure to address Christian involvement in traditional leadership was not limited to this alone but extended to public services. Commenting on the debate 'should Christians be involved in Government leadership?', O'Donovan acknowledged the positive influence of biblical examples like Joseph, Moses, Esther and Daniel in government services but admitted that the bad experience of many Christians in government calls for believers to be very sure of God's leadership in seeking political roles.[4] He encouraged Christians to obey God's command to pray for government leaders since that can bring about changes in policies and hearts from evil to good, rather than seeking political office for themselves unless they are certain of God's leadership.[5] I disagree with O'Donovan in that, if God can change policies and hearts through prayers as suggested above, then it will be proper to encourage Christians to seek roles within government leadership, since those we are praying for are more likely to respond to God's dealings as Christians than unbelievers. Such caution might have influenced Church leaders to distance themselves from traditional leaders, failing to do much to minister to them, although these traditional leaders maintained constant presence in church functions in the communities when invited. Traditional leaders, who were Christians before being installed as chiefs, lost the right to full membership in some churches. The lack of formal chaplaincy roles within chieftaincy is echoed in Opuni-Frimpong's recent call for the church to appoint Christian chaplains to Akan palaces, where he admits that the Presbyterian Church of Ghana and the Methodist Church Ghana, have provided chaplaincy services to schools, hospitals, industries, prisons, police and military but not to chiefs. He calls on the church to consider the palace as a mission field and appoint chaplains to serve there. He argued that palace chaplains will assist Christians selected and installed as chiefs to maintain their Christian principles as well as their traditional values.[6]

One of the early strategies that the Presbyterian church adopted, aiming to have pastoral oversight on traditional leadership, was the establishment of a Christian community with traditional leadership structures at Abokobi, situated in the Greater Accra Region, off the Accra-Aburi road. It all started in 1854 when two Basel Missionaries namely Johannes Zimmermann and William Steinhausser acquired a piece of land and settled there with their thirty converts to start a church and community.[7] The missionaries appointed a well-behaved indigenous Christian to handle local issues under their supervision with the title 'Headman' as they concentrated on church growth and evangelism.[8] Brobbey considers the Abokobi community as part of the 'second protagonists' people who believe that some practices in chieftaincy constitute idolatry and are sacrilegious for Christians to be involved.[9] A candidate for chieftaincy in Abokobi must be a proper Presbyterian and also meet the criteria set for church leaders according to the Scriptures in 1 Timothy 3:1-7 and Titus 1:7-9.[10] The elected candidate is installed as *Abokobi Mantse* (Abokobi Chief) in a purely Christian ceremony, officiated by Presbyterian clergy and conducted inside the Zimmermann Presbyterian Church devoid of any traditional rituals.[11] Since he was nominated, elected, and installed in accordance with the customs of the people of Abokobi as a chief, his name is registered in the Register of Chiefs at the National House of Chiefs.[12] Those who advocate that Christians can be chiefs often refer to the Abokobi community as a case study. If that should be the case, then we are looking for communities that are entirely Christian and need no evangelization. Chaplaincy to chieftaincy as argued in this thesis is to have Christian witness amongst chiefs that still need the gospel as well as standing alongside Christian chiefs who need the support of church leaders to enable their faith to influence their reign as chiefs. Nevertheless, the Abokobi community establishes the fact that given the chance, chieftaincy has a place in Christianity and they are not incompatible. The Christian minister is available to offer spiritual guidance and direction to the chief who often relies on the traditional religion priest as shown in the next section of this chapter.

It is important to note that mainline churches have formal chaplaincy ministries in the security services (armed forces, police and prisons), health and educational institutions. This is evident among the Roman Catholics and Anglicans who have erected church buildings within the communities of some of these institutions and provided trained clergy for ministry.[13] However, formal ministry of chaplaincy with chiefs is very minimal as compared to other institutions. Mainline churches might not have formal chaplains, but their relationship with the IoC is far greater than Pentecostals. Many chiefs would identify themselves as members of mainline churches and the ministers of these churches are seen more often in palaces, ceremonies, festivals and events that chiefs organize than ministers from Pentecostals.

5.2 The Role of an African Traditional Religion Priest to Chieftaincy

African traditional religion is practised in such a way that it is not separated from the rest of life, but rather permeates the social life of the traditional African with a traditional world view of all its values and beliefs.[14] The arrival of Christianity and its missional emphasis should have minimized the presence of African Traditional religion if not eradicated it entirely. However, the linked revival of African cultures with religion in recent times may not have been so if Evangelical Christians had thought through traditional religious heritage, evaluating the beliefs in the light of the Scriptures so as to know what is moral, just, good and upright before the Lord.[15] The proposal of chaplaincy to chieftaincy will help facilitate thinking through traditional religious heritage that considers the chief as the central figure in Ghanaian cultures.

In the previous chapter I defined the function of a chief, which includes some important roles requiring the assistance of a priest. The ones to be considered in this section are the chief's role as the custodian of cultures, ceremonies and festivals of the community; and that of successor to the ancestors[16] in his reign. In some cases, the service of a priest starts in spiritual ceremonies leading to the birth of the chief's child as a prince, and more specifically during his installation and death. The chief's inability to fulfil some functions without the service of a priest offers the office of priesthood an opportunity to influence chieftaincy. Priests in ATR serve in shrines of various divinities. The priest as a religious figure offers prayers, serves as a mediator and leads in the rites that require sacrifices in ceremonies, festivals and customs. He also acts as the spiritual counsellor to the chief in matters pertaining to spirituality which is fundamental to his reign in the area of ancestral worship or veneration.

Festivals are occasions for ritual cleansing of ancestral stools and shrines of state deities. The state priests lead the ceremonies by offering food, meat (sheep) and drinks (local palm wine) and imported schnapps to ancestral spirits.[17] These religious ceremonies are considered essential for the prosperity of the whole community. For the Tallensis in northern Ghana, the priests are believed to have powers to perform magico-religious rites for ensuring rainfall in times of drought, whilst the 'chiefs' also offer sacrifices to the spirits and perform magical acts before hunting and fishing expeditions to ensure successful hunting and fishing in the rivers.[18] In other cultures such as the Akans, there are some sacrifices when the chief becomes an *Ohene Komfo* (chief priest) and offers sacrifices himself during the *Akwasidae* and *Addae Kese* festivals.[19] The chief being able to perform some priestly duties is significant in two ways for the Christian faith. Firstly, the Scriptures acknowledges believers to be a royal priesthood[20] who are capable of performing certain priestly services without necessarily being official priests or ministers. Secondly, the chief who in most part of his life is often served, as culture demands, becomes a servant on these occasions and reverently offers drink and meat to the ancestors whilst praying for prosperity, fruitfulness and long life for himself and the people.[21] Service to God and fellow human beings are important values in the Christian faith. The chief seeing himself as a servant and praying for the welfare of the people, are values that the Christian chaplain can relate within his service to chieftaincy.

The priest is involved in the religious rites following the death of a chief as well as leading to the selection and installation of a new chief. The death of a chief or any other person raises questions as to what and who caused it. To find answers to the cause of death, a priest or medicine man is called to consult the ancestral spirits.[22] The priest cannot be ignored because of the religious aspect of ancestral veneration tied up with idol worship, which makes the chief play a subordinate role to the priest. Even though the chief is the political and administrative head of the community and derives his authority by being the link between the living and ancestors, he still lacks the ability to know what the ancestors want. The fetish priest who claims to know what the ancestors want through divination, virtually makes the chief a worshiper of his idol and wills power over him. The solution to being freed from this domination is the introduction of Christian chaplaincy as a missional model to chieftaincy.

5.3 The Theory, Practice and Theology of Chaplaincy

In theory, chaplaincy ministry has its roots in history where religious personnel often accompanied armies into battle as priests.[23] It is noted that 'Chaplains sailed with Sir Francis Drake in the sixteenth century and fought with George Washington during the Revolution War.'[24] What justified chaplaincy ministry then and now, was the provision of spiritual care outside the confines of religious structures. This is significant due to the role that kings and chiefs play in leading their armies to battle in that era. Chiefs in Ghana proved their authority through military conquests to extend territories and defend their people from invaders. Chiefs needed the services of priests to consult the gods before going to war and for special spiritual protection to escape any attempt on their lives during battles.[25] Muslim clerics capitalised on this spiritual need for chiefs, and for many years since the arrival of Islam in Ghana, have given the *Malam* an important spiritual role in most palaces.

Chaplains are members of religious faiths who chose to minister to people outside the designated public worship places of their religion.[26] To a large extent, institutions engage chaplains to serve their clients and employees. In this case, it is of great significance that chaplains do not get so "institutionalized" and lose their faith-based distinctiveness.[27] Chaplaincy is defined as 'a practice of care involving the intentional recognition and articulation of the sacred by nominated individuals authorized in this task for secular situations.'[28] The ministry of chaplaincy allows chaplains to 'provide the opportunity for everyone to practice, or not practice, religion as an individual choice and style.'[29] Slater comments on the different perceptions of chaplaincy with little or no conceptual clarity in its genre of ministry.[30] In her view, chaplaincy looks different in different contexts, and is understood and perceived differently depending on one's theological, ecclesial and vocational standpoint. For Slater, 'such divergent perceptions of what it means to be a chaplain simultaneously epitomize the difficulty of saying anything at all about it and the necessity to do so.'[31] I agree. Nevertheless, it is important to acknowledge this diversity, whilst ministering in a pluralistic society. The proposal of chaplaincy as a missional model for Pentecostal engagement with chieftaincy in this study adds to the divergent perceptions of what it means to be a chaplain.

The practice of chaplaincy which began with the military and served the armies of the world, later on extended to the health-care services from the early twentieth century. This is because hospitals were first created as an extension of care services for members of their own religious groups and later on extended the service to members of other faith traditions.[32] The ministry of chaplaincy has developed from military and health-care services to many social settings in the West in particular. Slater confirms that some kind of chaplaincy activity can be found in any social context such as: nursing and care homes, police, military, prisons, courts, emergency services, sports clubs, retail centres, airports, waterways, the homeless, and the lists could go on.[33] The development of chaplaincy ministry is as the result of people needing spiritual care even when they are not in church or their faith equivalent and especially when in crisis situations.[34]

In an article on situating chaplaincy in the United Kingdom, Pattison attributes the rise of chaplaincy to the decline of the traditional church in the West. He referred to Linda Woodhead's statement that organised religion today has become toxic in public perception and attendance at services and church membership continue to decline.[35] In contrast, chaplaincy has recently expanded, diversified and flourished due to its ability to adapt to different situations acceptable to the groups where they minister.[36] The level at which these extended roles of chaplaincy ministries are witnessed in the West cannot be said to be so in the Ghanaian context where few institutions are privileged to have such services. Nevertheless, it provides the basis for the argument that given the opportunity, chaplaincy ministry can thrive in any social context. That is why it would be appropriate if the church in Ghana considered chaplaincy to chieftaincy as a missional model.

When one considers the ministry tasks and competencies for the chaplain, it is appropriate that such ministry be offered to the IoC. The chaplain as a Minister is able to perform religious rites, rituals and ceremonies that people expect from a clergy without the physical structure of the religion represented. The unique role of chaplaincy requires that the chaplain provide religious ministry that relates to faith traditions, but also provide spiritual care to those who profess no religion.[37] I disagree with the provision of spiritual care to those who profess no religion if that service is devoid of the values of Christian principles. That is why a missional approach is needed by the presence of a Christian chaplain. If the definition of spirituality given by Paget and McCormack is to be accepted, and its provision would 'help people find meaning and purpose in their existence and all they hold sacred',[38] then the provision of spiritual care should not be obligatory to the Christian chaplain. Why should Christian chaplains be made to facilitate the understanding of an individual's beliefs and values that gives meaning to a person's life without God when the Christian faith emphasizes that true life is found in God.[39] However, if spiritual care involves assessing the need of an individual, offering counsel, emotional support, physical assistance and being there for the person as a servant leader, then it would be an ideal way of ministering to people of other faiths or no faith at all by Christian chaplains. Moreover, one does not have to make reference to God or set aside religious values for, 'it is possible to pursue what are believed to be religious purposes without referring to that explicitly'.[40]

One of the thirteen fundamental truths listed as non-negotiable Tenets of Faith which all AoG churches in Ghana adhere to is 'the ministry'. It emphasises the belief in the Lord to provide divinely called and scripturally ordained ministers to lead the church in worship of God, evangelization of the world, building a body of believers in the image of his Son, and meeting human needs with ministries of love and compassion.[41] One of the Scriptures given to support the minister's role of meeting human needs with ministries of love and compassion states that - *Therefore, as we have opportunity, let us do good to all people, especially to those who belong to the family of believers.*[42] Chaplaincy to chieftaincy should be one of the ministries that ministers can use to meet the spiritual needs, as well as showing love and compassion to those in traditional leadership. There is no justification whatsoever to neglect traditional leaders of the community where the church exists and show them love and compassion because of their belief, let alone when some of them join the Christian faith and now belong to the family of believers as the above scripture admonishes.

In their argument for the biblical (theological) basis of chaplaincy, Paget and McCormack used Matthew 25 to set out their case which I agree with. When Jesus spoke about ministering to the 'least of these',[43] he referred to the value of all persons, not just those who share our ethnicity, culture and religion. Jesus pointed out in this text that if the 'righteous' are to 'inherit the kingdom' of God, then they must minister to all people especially the 'least of these'. According to Paget and McCormack those that Jesus considered the least are still with us today and chaplains must minister to the disenfranchised of the society – the 'least of these'.[44] If that is the case, traditional leaders can be classified as being among the 'least of these'. Whereas there is tension between chaplaincy as ministry to all founded on a doctrine of common grace and one which preaches the exclusive claims of Christ for salvation, Pentecostals tend to lean on the latter with which I agree. Nevertheless, in a pluralistic society where religion or belief is a human right, theological response calls for dialogue in multi-faith teams and spaces.[45] The IoC is a multi-faith space, that is why an open approach based on the incarnational role of chaplaincy presence is included in the missional model of this study.

Paget and McCormack also pointed out that the text in Matthew 25 states some things that resonate with chaplaincy which are; 'Go' to those in need of ministry and 'Good Works' must accompany faith.[46] In this case, chaplains usually take the initiative to look for people that need spiritual care. For instance, the condemned inmate sentenced to life imprisonment or being prepared for execution according to the law in favour of serving justice for the heinous crime committed might not call but chaplaincy ministry will reach out to that individual. In the same way, some traditional leaders might look unrepentant to Christian values and heading towards spiritual destruction but that should not deny them the opportunity of receiving the ministry of Christian chaplaincy who will take the initiative to be there as Christian witness despite their unbelief. For Paget and McCormack, the 'good works' of giving people food, water, shelter and clothes that Jesus used in the text does not limit spiritual care to practical needs. But as it is pointed out in James 2:14-17, good works will enable others to see that the Christian faith is genuine.[47] Similarly, 'good works' as social ministry is service of love inspired by the example of Christ expressed in mission.[48]

Jesus' call on the disciples to 'keep watch' with him in the Garden of Gethsemane in Matthew 26:36-45 is another concept modelled for chaplaincy who stay with people during their darkest moments, according to Paget and McCormack. When people realise that they are not alone and abandoned in times of suffering, emotional, physical or spiritual pain, that may enable them to believe that God has not abandoned them either. The Christian chief will need the ministry of chaplaincy during festivals and ceremonies which are the hallmark of celebrating the cultures of the people where sometimes sacrifices to idols and invoking of ancestral spirits are made. It is a spiritual battle that should not be left to the converted Christian chief to handle alone when he is in the midst of other unsaved traditional leaders who will demand that these rituals be followed according to tradition. In addition, recognizing the 'unknown God' in diversity as noted in Acts 17:16-34 shows that one can be sensitive to the pluralistic cultural setting of listeners in ministry. In this case, chaplains recognize the 'unknown God' in diversity as well as respecting differences in cultures, religion and provide opportunities for people to make choices.[49] Christian chaplaincy to chieftaincy will definitely encounter other religions such as ATR and Islam where compassion and love is needed to hold high the testimony that Jesus is the real and genuine saviour that must be sought by all who seek God and eternal life.

Threlfall-Holmes and Ryan admit to this conflict of interest in chaplaincy and suggested that there should be different models of chaplaincy in two categories – theological and secular. The theological models allows the chaplains to see their vocation as missionaries, pastors, incarnational or sacramental, historical-parish and the prophetic or challenging whilst the secular models provides pastoral-care, spiritual-care, diversity, tradition/heritage, and meta-model: specialist service providers.[50] Chaplains also need to be critical, creative and reflexive thinkers due to the occasional crisis cases that they encounter in performing their duties.[51] That is why it is paramount that they are strong in faith so as to draw from the wealth of their experience to help others in need. Chaplaincy to chieftaincy is a unique social setting where religious practices are explicit; that is why the proposal of a missional model is appropriate.

5.4 The Missional Model of Chaplaincy

The term 'missional' is considered a fairly recent origin developed out of the 'gospel and culture' debate from the second half of the twentieth century. It is a concept built on theological ideas relating with the mission of God and serves as a reminder that Christians are to focus on mission.[52] The term, which has acquired many different uses, is employed here to indicate that Christians should be living missionally, in a way that bears witness to God's purposes in Christ that certainly contributes to church planting and growth but is basic to all Christian values. It is God's on-going work of restoration that includes social, political and physical salvation as well as personal redemption and forgiveness.[53] The term missional invites us to consider a new way of being the church that is shaped by mystery, memory and mission.[54] In mystery - God has chosen the church to represent him on earth;[55] in memory – the church through the Holy Spirit manifests the life, death and resurrection of Jesus Christ as the people of God; and in mission – is the result of mystery and memory where God calls the church for the sake of the world.[56] If this concept is applied, it means chaplains should see their role with the IoC as working with God to bring salvation, physical redemption and forgiveness as well as restoring the social and political structures of the people, which in my view is the holistic approach to *Missio Dei* (God's Mission). The shifts in missionary thinking of God's Mission, is well documented in Bosch's summary of world missionary conferences held since the Edinburgh conference in 1910. By the time the conference was held at Accra, Ghana, in 1958 the opening statement was 'the Christian world mission is Christ's, not ours.'[57] Newbigin published the consensus after the Ghana Assembly, stating that 'the church is the mission... the home base is everywhere,'[58] which means placing mission at the centre of every local church whose mission field is their community. In this case, the church in Ghana should consider the IoC as part of their mission field. Bosch comments that God's reign on earth is revealed as the church participates 'in the ongoing struggle between that reign and the powers of darkness and evil.'[59] The perception of some participants' view on chieftaincy as a dark institution in chapter seven, further supports the need for the church to intentionally engage with the IoC.

Hence, the missional model should encompass the theological models of chaplaincy being missionaries, pastors, incarnational or sacramental, historical-parish, prophetic or challenging to serve God's mission with the IoC. Threlfall-Holmes and Ryan state that the missionary model enables the chaplain to proclaim the gospel and reach those traditionally unreached by the church, whilst the pastor model provides a specific focus on the caring aspect of the ministry.[60] Similarly, the historical-parish model allows the chaplain to provide spiritual services to those unable to attend a local church, whilst the agent of challenge or 'prophet' and the incarnational or sacramental models enable the chaplain to challenge or confront behaviour and also demonstrate God's love on the simple fact of the chaplain's presence.[61] Although the theological models do pose a challenge in some institutions, adopting them would enable Pentecostals' provide spiritual care to Christian chiefs and Christian witness to the IoC. Pentecostals should be responsible in sending chaplains to the IoC as part of their missional policy and not vice versa. This model supports the case for chaplaincy as 'Representative of a Religious Tradition'.[62] By so doing, chaplains would not lose focus of their missional mandate of sustaining their theological integrity and ministerial identity[63] as it is with secular models of chaplaincy where chaplains operate within institutional policies.[64] It is possible that the provision of chaplaincy as a missional model would enhance cultural transformation.

The term 'cultural transformation' is used here to mean the dynamic process of changing chieftaincy cultural norms, policies and behaviours through gospel knowledge, acceptance and values. Transforming culture is quite a challenge but not impossible. It begins with the personal transformation of the leader. The power of the gospel to transform people must affect their behaviours[65] and cultures. The gospel calls on all cultures to change structures and practices that are evil.[66] In effecting such changes, one needs to find what is working and what is not and identify specific areas that need change. In his attempt to facilitate cultural transformation, Theophilus Opoku understood well that religious conversion to Christianity 'involve[s] challenging people to a serious dialogue, and that this required a deep understanding of traditional beliefs and practices.'[67] I agree. Unfortunately, this study reveals that Pentecostals have since not taken the initiative to engage with the IoC to facilitate dialogue. Their concerns on syncretism can be addressed through engagement and not abandonment.

According to Hiebert, syncretism is a mixture of other religions and Christian ideas in converts. For instance, 'Santa Claus' as a hero character in the Christmas story of the birth of Christ shown to converts of Hindi background from India. He argued that the wholesale rejection of old cultural ways and customs created problems and left vacuums that needed to be filled. As a result, pagan customs are practiced in secret, along with public celebration of Christian teachings to form Christopaganism – a syncretistic mix of Christian and non-Christian beliefs.[68] Hiebert's solution to syncretism is to theologically critique the people's worldview – the core of a culture. I agree. In addition, the argument for hybridity is one possible way to address concerns of syncretism. The role of a historical-parish, prophet or agent of change in the proposed missional model of chaplaincy provides the opportunity to instruct and also learn chieftaincy culture for theological reflection to facilitate cultural transformation.

The proposal for the Pentecostal church to have chaplaincy as a missional model to chieftaincy is intended to place emphasis on the fact that God's mission also includes the restoration of political and social structures of the redeemed. The fact that the political and social roles of chieftaincy are linked to ATR does not mean that Christians should abandon the entire institution. It should rather be an opportunity for the church in her mission to engage in genuine conversation to facilitate authentic witness. Slater echoes this and states that chaplains seek to understand social contexts from within and still maintain their identity as representatives of faith communities with the capacity for prophetic witness alongside pastoral care and service.[69] The recent changes developing in the IoC due to the conversion to Christianity of some prominent chiefs and kings indicates that political and social restoration is possible.

5.5 Summary

This chapter has sought to argue for the role of chaplaincy ministry to the IoC. It revealed the absence of formal chaplaincy ministry with chieftaincy among mainline churches who are pioneers of Christian evangelization in Ghana, although they have demonstrated some visible presence and impacted chieftaincy over the years. Further, it narrated the role of the traditional priest to enable a chief to fulfil responsibilities as a political and social leader of the community. It noted that the chief's dependence on priests for spirituality in relation to ATR are challenges which confront total commitment to a converted Christian chief. An essential response in dealing with these issues is the introduction of Christian chaplaincy, where the role of minister would provide spiritual care for the chief. Therefore, I looked at the theory, practice and theology of chaplaincy to support my argument and proposed chaplaincy as a missional model to engage with the IoC.

The next chapter will look respectfully at the development and growth of Pentecostal denominations that reveal a lack of chaplaincy to chieftaincy.

---

1. A. Adu Boahen, 'Agyeman Prempeh in the Seychelles, 1900-1924', in A. Adu Boahen, Emmanuel Acheampong, Nancy Lawler, T. C. McCaskie & Ivor Wilks, (eds.), *The History of Ashanti Kings and the whole country itself' and other Writings by Otumfuo, Nana Agyeman Prempeh I*, (Oxford: Oxford University Press, 2014), pp. 21, 27, 28.
2. Boahen, 'Agyeman Prempeh', pp. 28, 29.
3. Opuni-Frimpong, *Indigenous*, p. 250.
4. Wilbur O'Donovan, *Biblical Christianity in Modern Africa*, (Carlisle, UK: Paternoster Press, 2000), pp. 182–85.
5. O'Donovan, *Christianity*, p. 186.
6. Opuni-Frimpong, *Indigenous*, p. 250.
7. Brobbey, *The Law*, p. 172.
8. E. A. Aryeetey. 'A Paper on the Abokobi Chieftaincy Institution' to Commemorate the 10th Anniversary Celebrations of the Installation of Nii Samuel Adjetey Mohenu as Chief of Abokobi (Presbyterian Women's Centre, Abokobi, 4th August 2007), p. 1.
9. Brobbey, *The Law*, p. 169.
10. Brobbey, *The Law*, p. 170.
11. Aryeetey, 'Abokobi', p. 3.
12. Brobbey, *The Law*, p. 171.
13. The St. George Church – Police Depot was recently elevated to a Parish in April 2016. A Very Rev. Fr. was also installed as Chaplain with the full faculties of a Parish Priest. <http://accracatholic.org/st-george-church> [accessed 24 July 2016].
14. Gehman, *African*, p. 18.
15. Gehman, *African*, p. 18.
16. Safo-Kantanka, *Christian*, p. ii.
17. Kwame Arhin, *Traditional Rule in Ghana: Past and Present*, (Accra: Sedco Publishing Limited, 1985), p. 68.
18. Arhin, *Traditional*, p. 12.
19. Safo-Kantanka, *Christian*, p. 16.
20. 1 Pet. 2:9.
21. Safo-Kantanka, *Christian*, p.16.
22. Gehman, *African*, p. 63.
23. Paget and McCormack, *Chaplain*, p. 2.

24. Paget and McCormack, *Chaplain*, p. 2.
25. A description of the Asante war of liberation against Denkyira held from 1700 – 1701 indicates that Okomfo Anokye (Prophet Anokye) performed some spiritual powers to enable the Asantes to gain victory over their enemies. Boahen, Acheampong, et al., (eds.), *History*, pp. 107-09.
26. Paget and McCormack, *Chaplain*, p. iv.
27. Threlfall-Holmes and Newitt, *Chaplain*, p. 136.
28. Swift, Cobb and Todd, *Chaplaincy studies*, p. 2.
29. Paget and McCormack, *Chaplain*, p. 4.
30. Slater, *Chaplaincy*, p. 86.
31. Slater, *Chaplaincy*, pp. 87-88; Stephen Pattison, 'Situating Chaplaincy in the United Kingdom: The Acceptable Face of 'Religion'?', in C. Swift, M. Cobb and A. Todd (eds.), *A Handbook of Chaplaincy Studies*, (Farnham, Surrey: Ashgate Publishing Limited, 2015), pp.13-30.
32. Paget and McCormack, *Chaplain*, p. 3.
33. Slater, *Chaplaincy*, p. xii.
34. Paget and McCormack, *Chaplain*, p. 4.
35. Linda Woodhead, 'Introduction', In L. Woodhead and R. Catto (eds), *Religion and Change in Modern Britain*, (Abingdon: Routledge, 2012a), pp. 1-33.
36. Pattison, 'Situating Chaplaincy in the United Kingdom:', p. 15.
37. Paget and McCormack define religion 'as the practice of a particular system of faith and beliefs within a cultural setting. Spirituality may be defined more broadly as the search for understanding and connection to beliefs and values that give meaning to a person's life.' Paget and McCormack, *Chaplain*, p. 17.
38. 'For many, this 'sacred' could be God, but it could also be the transcendent, family, nature, or community' Paget and McCormack, *Chaplain*, p. 17.
39. John 17:3; 1 John 5:20.
40. Fraser Watts, 'The interface of Psychology and Spirituality in Care', in C. Swift, M. Cobb and A. Todd, (eds.), *Chaplaincy Studies*, (Farnham, Surrey: Ashgate Publishing Limited, 2015), p. 143.
41. The General Council of the Assemblies of God, Ghana, 'Assemblies of God Statement of Fundamental Truths', <http://www.agghana.org/gchq/fundamental-truths.html> [accessed 11 August 2016].
42. Gal. 6:10.
43. Matt. 25:40.
44. Paget and McCormack, *Chaplain*, p. 5.
45. A. Todd, 'A Theology of the World', in Caperon, Todd and Walters, (eds.), *Chaplaincy*, pp. 21-42.
46. Paget and McCormack, *Chaplain*, pp. 6, 7.
47. Paget and McCormack, *Chaplain*, pp. 7, 8.
48. Daniel Eshun, 'A Study of Social Ministry of some Charismatic Churches in Ghana' *Thesis, (MPhil)*, (Accra: University of Ghana, 2013), pdf p. 136, <http://ugspace.ug.edu.gh> [accessed 17 November 2017].
49. Paget and McCormack, *Chaplain*, pp. 10, 11.
50. Miranda Threlfall-Holmes, 'Exploring Models in Chaplaincy', in Miranda Threlfall-Holmes and Mark Newitt, (eds.), *Being a Chaplain*, (London: SCPK, 2011), pp. 116-26; Ben Ryan, 'Theology and models of chaplaincy', in J.,

Caperon, A., Todd and J., Walters, (eds.), *A Christian Theology of Chaplaincy*, (London: JKP, 2018), pp. 79-100.

51. Mark Newitt, 'The Role and Skills of a Chaplain', in Threlfall-Holmes and Newitt, (eds.), *Chaplain*, pp. 109-12.

52. Ed Stetzer, 'A Brief History of 'Missional': Moving from Concept and Conversation to Leaving it out', *The Exchange: Missiology*, Feb. 23, 2016, <http://www.christianitytoday.com> [accessed 11 August 2016].

53. Martin Reppenhagen and Darrel L. Guder, 'The Continuing Transformation of Mission: David J. Bosch's Living Legacy 1991-2011', in David J. Bosch, (ed.), *Transforming Mission: Paradigm Shifts in Theology of Mission*, 20th Anniversary ed. (Maryknoll, NY: Orbis Books, 2016), pp. 4-11 and 533-55.

54. Alan J. Roxburgh, and M. Scott Boren, (ed.), *Introducing the Missional Church: What It Is, Why It Matters, How to Become One*, (Grand Rapids, Michigan: Baker Books, 2009), pp. 31, 32 and 45.

55. Eph. 1:15-23.

56. Luke 12:32; 1 Pet. 2:9-10; Roxburgh and Boren, (eds.), *Missional Church*, pp. 41-45.

57. David J. Bosch, (ed.), *Transforming Mission: Paradigm Shifts in Theology of Mission*, (Maryknoll, NY: Orbis Books, 2016), pp. 378-81.

58. Lesslie Newbigin, *One Body, One Gospel, One World: The Christian Mission Today*, (London: International Missionary Council, 1958), pp 25-38.

59. Bosch, *Transforming Mission*: p. 400.

60. Threlfall-Holmes, 'Exploring Models', *Chaplain*, pp. 118-120; Ryan, 'Theology and Models', *Chaplaincy*, pp. 86-88.

61. Threlfall-Holmes, 'Exploring Models', *Chaplain*, pp. 120-122; Ryan, 'Theology and Models', *Chaplaincy*, pp. 88-91.

62. Peter Kevin, and Wilf McSherry, 'The Study of Chaplaincy: Methods and Materials', in Swift, Cobb and Todd, (eds.), *Chaplaincy Studies*, pp. 47-62.

63. Slater, *Chaplaincy Ministry*, pp. 124-26.

64. Threlfall-Holmes, 'Exploring Models', *Chaplain*, pp. 122-25; Ryan, 'Theology and Models', *Chaplaincy*, pp. 93-97; Kevin, and McSherry, 'The Study of Chaplaincy', pp. 47-62.

65. Rom. 12:2; 2 Cor. 3:18.

66. Hiebert, *Anthropological insights for Missionaries*, pp. 54-56.

67. Michelle Gilbert and Paul Jenkins, 'The King, His Soul and the Pastor: Three Views of a Conflict in Akropong 1906-7', *Journal of Religion in Africa*, Vol. 38 (2008), p. 372.

68. Hiebert, *Anthropological Insights*, pp. 13, 184-186, 212.

69. Slater, *Chaplaincy*, p. 93.

SIX

The Development and Growth of Pentecostal Denominations That Reveal Lack of Chaplaincy to Chieftaincy

6.0 Introduction

This chapter considers the development of the Pentecostal church and its involvement in any type of chaplaincy with chieftaincy. The focus is on missional activities and denominational growth of Pentecostal churches such as AoGG, Apostolic Church, CAC, and the CoP and their engagement with chieftaincy. It revealed that Pentecostals' engagement with chieftaincy have been very minimal. Finally, it assesses the establishment of Christian chiefs' associations and their call for Christian involvement in chieftaincy.

6.1 Introduction of Major Pentecostal Denominations

6.1.1 The Assemblies of God, Ghana

This account captures a brief summary of my previous research on the history of AoGG.[1] The AoGG, was born out of the missionary efforts of AoG, USA through the ministry of a number of selfless missionaries since 1931. Margaret Peoples was born in Ireland and migrated to Philadelphia, USA in 1917 at the age of twenty-one after which she responded to the call to missions before marrying Lloyd Shirer.[2] The Shirers, who were the first missionaries to the Mosiland (Upper Volta), now Burkina Faso, came to the then Gold Coast (now Ghana) through the northern borders at this time 'to spy out the land which (they felt) the LORD GOD hath given'.[3] Convinced of what God would have them do in Ghana, the Shirers requested more workers from their Mission Board in the USA. In less than one year, two young people, Hickok and Buchwalter, answered the challenge.[4] Many more responded to this call over subsequent years and work began briskly from northern to southern Ghana.

The early years were years of consolidating the work. Their first station was at Yendi – the traditional capital of the Dagbon kingdom and later at Tamale – the administrative capital of the then northern territories in Ghana. It is important to note that when they arrived in Yendi, the *Ya Naa* (King of Dagbon) warmly received them and allowed them to begin their work of evangelizing the people. The fact that the Dagbon overlord received them meant that they could go anywhere in his kingdom to evangelize without anyone attempting to physically threaten their lives.

They began with language learning, translating choruses, and Sunday school lessons into Dagbani.[5] The Shirers had an advantage over their fellow missionaries in learning Dagbani as a result of ministering in Burkina Faso amongst the Mosi Kingdom, where they had learned how to speak Mori. The Mori language has the same linguistic roots as that of Dagbani. The fact that the Shirers could speak Mori made them the mouthpiece of the missionary team. It also served as a booster to the natives to hear white people speaking the language of their ancestral background. Rev. Shirer immediately earned the title *Monaba* which means Mosi 'chief'. He preached and communicated daily in Mori, which the natives of his new mission field understood until he learned Dagbani.[6] This gesture of conferring the title 'chief' to a missionary in my view was an opportunity for the church to consider asking searching questions towards contextualizing the IoC in light of gospel presentation.

The Shirers sowed the seed of the Gospel at Yendi in 1931 when they stood before the *Ya Naa* and announced their intention to evangelize the place. The Shirers started work at Yendi formally in 1932, whilst the Garlocks opened the Tamale station in the same year. Within the first few years of missionary work, many who converted to Christianity included Chiefs. Lehmann recorded and posted a picture of the Tamale Chief with his elders who came to church every Sunday in 1934.[7]

Within three decades from the time of entry into Ghana in 1931-1961, AoGG had opened a church in almost all major towns in the country. This was possible due to the spiritual power displayed by Pentecostal churches who believed in the scriptural authority of the Holy Spirit for effective church plants. The worldview of Ghanaian people involved with spiritual powers meant that it was far more contextual than the other Western missionaries' approach and could have easily been applied to chieftaincy as well. At the centennial celebration of AoG, USA held at Springfield Missouri from 5th – 10th August 2014 which the researcher was privileged to attend, the pioneering missionary to Ghana – Margaret Peoples Shirer - was named among the ten early AoG female missionaries whose respect for indigenous customs earned her open doors;[8] but this did not include chieftaincy customs in my view, as the church failed to theologically contextualize cultural values of chieftaincy even long after nationals took over leadership of the denomination until today.

The church celebrated its 75th anniversary in August 2006 with the theme: 'Declare His Goodness - Psalm 105:1'. As of 2013, AoGG has over 2400 churches, 1850 ministers and close to 515,000 members.[9] The members include statesmen such as the Chief Justice of the country, Mrs Georgina Theodora Wood, the immediate past President of the National House of Chiefs *Naa* (Chief) Professor John Nabila Sebiyam and immediate past President of the Republic of Ghana - John Dramani Mahama. The current leadership has, since 2015, embarked on establishing 3000 churches for the next five years as they take the gospel to the doorsteps of the people.[10] This laudable programme should in my view include intentional missional policies for the IoC which seems not to be the case.

AoGG is fast approaching its centennial anniversary, but available records show less intentional missional engagements with chieftaincy. AoGG, just like other Pentecostal denominations, mostly offer intercessory prayers for traditional leaders in obedience to the instruction *'pray for kings and all those in authority* (I Timothy 2:2)'[11] as well as occasional visits to chiefs' palaces. On one such visit to the palace, they presented a gift to the Ashanti King with the inscription *'I help Kings to govern...* Prov. 8:15 GNB'[12] as shown in figure 6.1

Figure 6.1: Portrait of the king with scripture inscription on it.

In my view, this image shows the church admits God helps kings to govern. On the other hand, we fail to engage with chieftaincy because their practices are mostly associated with ATR. Frimpong-Manso acknowledged that the actions of the Ya Naa's invitation for the first AoG, USA missionaries to evangelize his people was very instrumental in the history of AoGG. According to him, this action of the Ya Naa can be likened to God using King Nebuchadnezzar and Cyrus as his servants in Jeremiah 25:7-9 and Isaiah 45:1-3.[13] What is interesting is that his historical account of the denomination, which can be considered the most recent academic work, had little to say on the church influence on chieftaincy when he conceded the relevance of chiefs in the political, social and cultural settings of the people in Ghana.[14] He also failed in his conclusion and recommendations to challenge the church to missionally engage with chieftaincy. As a respondent in the interviews, he admits that there has not been much Pentecostal influence on chiefs because of the denomination's anti-chieftaincy and cultural views of previous years. He adds:

> We must redefine Christians' roles, see the biblical perspective of chieftaincy and educate them, and we should not throw out the baby together with the bath water. We must write a theology of chieftaincy in the light of the gospel and in the light of culture that will solve some of our theological concerns.[15]

The phrase 'do not throw out the baby together with the bathwater away' in ASRCL1 quote is a proverb that cautions against losing valuable aspects of what is generally considered not important. In this case, chaplaincy to chieftaincy would help preserve 'the baby' (within chieftaincy) from being thrown away together with bath water. The need for Pentecostals to address theological concerns on chieftaincy was reiterated by all respondents, which is further discussed in chapter seven.

6.1.2 The Apostolic Church

The Pentecostal revival in the early 1900s saw the rise of indigenous Christians along the coast of the then Gold Coast of West Africa. Some of these Christians who were seeking spiritual awakening in their lives and desired to know more about spiritual truths led them to contact missions abroad. An indigenous Christian group known as the Faith Tabernacle Brethren at Asamankese and led by Anim contacted the Apostolic Church in Bradford, United Kingdom to send a delegation for consultations. Pastor George Perfect, who was an Apostolic Church Missionary to Nigeria, was asked to visit this Christian group at Asamankese. After some deliberations with the leadership of the Faith Tabernacle, they 'accepted to become members of The Apostolic Church and whole-heartedly embraced the Tenets of the Church.'[16]

In March 1937, Pastor McKeown arrived in the country as the resident missionary of the Apostolic Church from Bradford. He fell sick of fever and was admitted for eleven days at a hospital in Accra where he recovered. However, some elders of the host church were unhappy about the medical treatment that Pastor McKeown had received. Richard Foli states the reason being that members of the Faith Tabernacle Church who had become the nucleus of the Apostolic Church were popularly known as *kyirbentoa* (no medicine) people.[17] They still held to their belief prior to becoming part of the Apostolic Church that believers were to trust God for divine healing and should not opt for any form of medical treatment when sick. The leadership of the church today refers to this view as the 'fanatic way' concerning the doctrine of divine healing.[18] The disagreement on the issue of divine healing led to a split in the church and by 1939 the group that left the Apostolic Church took the name Christ Apostolic Church. Despite the set-back resulting from the split, the Apostolic Church United Kingdom continued to send missionaries to support the work in the country. By 1952, the Apostolic Church had no less than fifty-three ordained African ministers, 512 local churches with a total membership of about 10,000.[19]

The church, through the visionary leadership of Apostle Abebrese and other senior ministers, has become more vibrant, progressive and dynamic in recent years. The denomination has 1500 local churches in Ghana and other branches in West Africa, United Kingdom and North America because it is passionate about seeing God's glory manifested in the world.[20] The writer has not come across any written intentional missional engagement of the church with chieftaincy from this group. They fall within the category of other Pentecostals who view most practices of chieftaincy as heathen and discourage member participation.[21] This view is changing now as the research reveals in this paper, hence the need for Pentecostal Christian chaplaincy to chieftaincy.

6.1.3 Christ Apostolic Church

The CAC traces its roots to Peter Anim's Prayer Group started in 1917 and later on became the Faith Tabernacle church in 1922. They pride themselves on being indigenous Ghanaian Pentecostals who experienced an outpouring of the Holy Spirit after five weeks of revival meetings held at Asamenkese (besides previous intermittent ones). However, the dissensions in the Apostolic church over divine healing (as stated above) led to a break away and the establishment of CAC.

Ten years later, the CAC also suffered a series of dissensions resulting in the formation of churches such as: New Day Church in 1949, Christ Revival Church in 1959, United Pentecostal Church in 1969, Christ Apostolic Reformed Church in 1979, the Harvesters Church in 1983, the Asanteman Christ Apostolic Church in 1989, and the Christ Anointed Church in 1991.[22] Nevertheless, the CAC's contribution to the Pentecostal denomination of Christianity cannot be overlooked and has branches in West Africa, Europe, Australia and the Americas.[23] The researcher is of the view that the fact that the church struggled with some of their doctrines at the initial stages, as demonstrated in that of divine healing, might have also influenced their attitude towards chieftaincy, which was often branded heathen and sacrilegious[24] similar to other Pentecostal denominations from their early years. They are among the group that Brobbey calls protagonists who view chieftaincy practices as constituting idolatry, and who argue no genuine Christian should be involved in them.[25] As a result, there is little or no documented intentional missional engagement with chieftaincy to refer to, although the church claims to have had a good traditional theologian in the person of their founder – Apostle Anim.[26] In my view, a good traditional theologian should have also engaged with the cultural practices of the people in which chieftaincy plays a major role. The call for the church to have an intentional missional engagement with chieftaincy would facilitate the interpretation of some aspects of Ghanaian cultural and traditional values in light of Christian theology.

6.1.4 The Church of Pentecost

The CoP credits its establishment to the dedicated service and leadership of an Irish Missionary known as James McKeown (1900-1989), sent by the Apostolic Church Bradford, UK to the then Gold Coast (now Ghana) in 1937.[27] The church split in 1939 due to doctrinal differences that led to the formation of the CAC although the other group stayed with the Apostolic Church Bradford. It grew rapidly only to split again in 1953 due to a constitutional crisis in the church. Foli comments that this constitutional amendment 'sought to introduce obnoxious and racialist tendencies into the Body of Christ'[28] to which McKeown and Cecil Cousen objected out of the 54 Council members present who affirmed the changes. The Apostolic Church Bradford dismissed McKeown who was on furlough at this time in England and Cousens as ministers. The church in Ghana backed McKeown and Cousen upon hearing the developments in England and called on McKeown to return to

Ghana as their spiritual leader without the support of the Apostolic Church Bradford. The church adopted the current name – the CoP in 1962[29] and has since grown to become the largest Pentecostal denomination in the country.

The CoP in its earlier years did little to engage with the IoC as generally noted of other Pentecostal churches in Ghana. Christians' conversions during the early 20th century were often identified as authentic when the members were willing to renounce traditional world-views and practices which included chieftaincy as one of the corrupt cultural practices of the people. Smith comments that an elected Christian who opted to become a chief forfeited full membership of the church, but might, and invariably did, remain an adherent.[30] What Smith noted in his work with the Presbyterians about elected Christians to chieftaincy is also the position of Pentecostals in general. Nevertheless, the CoP just like other Pentecostal churches is currently adopting some doctrinal changes that would allow cultural integration without compromising Christian values. According to Quayesi-Amakye, the CoP now trains members on how to become chiefs and still maintain their Christian identity. The CoP leadership have noted that a Christianised chieftaincy increases the church's witnessing space in its cultural environment. The leadership commitment to engage with chieftaincy was further demonstrated when the national chairman – Apostle Dr Opoku Onyinah ordained a chief, Nana Antwi Agyei Brempong II, Atwimahene (Chief of Atwima) as an elder of the church during 'All Ministers and Officers' retreat held in Kumasi in 2012.[31] This is a significant development and change in theological view of Christianity and chieftaincy from the early years.

Due to the significant numbers of Christian chiefs in CoP, the leadership called for their first 'Conference for Christian Royals' in 2014.[32] The minister for chieftaincy and traditional affairs who addressed the conference on the theme 'Impacting generations: The Church's Mission to the Palace' acknowledged contributions made by both church and Palace (Traditional Rule) to peace and development of the society.[33] Whilst in Ghana for data collection, I visited the national office of CoP to enquire about this conference; the general secretary could not give me any details, admitting that this step was still new to them giving the impression that the chairman – Apostle Onyinah - was leading the church into this missional engagement with chieftaincy. It is therefore no coincidence and a step in the right direction that this research is conducted at a time when some Pentecostal church leaders have started initiating plans to intentionally engage with traditional rulers.

6.2 Christian Chiefs' Associations and Their Call for Christian Involvement in Chieftaincy

After exploring Pentecostal denominational growth that shows minimal involvement in chieftaincy, this section acknowledges the formation of Christian chiefs' associations and their call for Christians to engage with traditional rulers. One of such groups is the Northern Ghana Christian Chiefs Association (NGCCA) facilitated by Northern Empowerment Association (NEA). The NGCCA is ecumenical, as membership is open to all Christian chiefs in northern Ghana.

The founder of NGCCA saw the need to provide an environment where Christian chiefs could meet to share experiences and learn how their faith could help them govern as Christian chiefs. This led to organising the first conference held at Carpenter in 2011.[34] According to Brenda Mensah, 120 chiefs from 13 tribes attended the three-day event of the conference where it was decided that it should be an annual event.[35] At this maiden event, the convener of the conference, David Mensah - Mo/Deg *Gyasehene*, spoke from the text: *But you are a chosen people, a royal priesthood, a holy nation, a people belonging to God, that you may declare the praises of him who called you out of darkness into his wonderful light* (1 Peter 2:9). According to Mensah, one of the special moments of the conference that had so many representatives of tribal chiefs was when the Mamprusi and Kusasi chiefs requested to pray together during the group prayer sessions. The Mamprusi and Kusasi tribes were still in conflict, which resulted in some deaths and curfew imposition to restrict movements. However, Christian chiefs who came from these conflict zones seized the opportunity to pray for God's intervention to restore peace among their people. Mensah remarked:

> It is hard to put on paper the depth of this meeting. Seeing these leaders bowed together before the Lord was a powerful picture of what it means to know Christ and to be part of his family.[36]

The fourth conference coincided with my trip to Ghana for data collection in 2014. I attended the conference and interviewed some of the participants. The conference agenda included daily devotions, Bible study, discussion and ratification of the association constitution, evening celebration service of praise, testimony and prayer. The final day included a communion service. The highlight of the conference for me as I observed, was witnessing how these chiefs expressed their passion and desire to serve God and being part of every activity held. The 2014 conference registered 250 in attendance, out of which 190 were chiefs as captured in figure 4.2.

The GRID and NEA continue to facilitate annual conferences for Christian chiefs and in 2017 participants learned about leadership, community development and peace building in Christian perspectives. What this association lacks is the provision of chaplaincy services for chiefs at their respective communities. This is a ministry opportunity for the church to engage the chiefs with chaplaincy. Some of the chiefs gave their thoughts about the importance of the Association and its annual conferences in their role as community leaders where one of the chiefs' remarked:

> This association has helped me stop pagan practices in my chiefdom. People in my community have seen a drastic change in

their lives. I am very glad... Being a Christian chief is good because there is liberty in Christ. I am free of entanglements.[37]

GRID Newsletter May 2014 p. 2

Christian Chiefs' Conference 2014
by Doug Webster

The 2014 Chiefs Conference was was generously funded by the partners from Stronger Together. Doug and Virginia Webster were in Ghana for the conference, where Doug was a keynote speaker. Doug writes:

One hundred degrees in the shade but a hundred percent worth the experience.

One hundred and ninety chiefs came for the four-day conference with their entourage for a total of 250 people to be fed three good meals a day from Wednesday through Sunday. In conversation with a couple of the chiefs I asked how many this conclave represented. They figured at least a thousand per chief.

What we know for certain is that The Lord was in our midst in a powerful way.

In three languages – Mo, Twi, and English – we studied biblical models of leadership, drawing mainly on the Old Testament narratives of Cain and Abel, Abraham and Lot, Jacob and Joseph, Samuel and Saul, along with the David story. The chiefs were attentive throughout the four days, and if they weren't they were poked by another chief.

We came together on Sunday for a four-hour worship service and I preached on the God Who Kneels from John 13. As always, David did a fantastic job translating, preaching, and leading the entire group.

In the afternoons the chiefs worked on a constitution to underscore their Christian identify and solidarity. Chief Adam and Dr. Adam played a key role in developing this document.

Virginia and I count it a rare privilege to participate in this work and to see the wonderful progress that The Lord has accomplished through David and Brenda Mensah and the entire NEA-GRID team. Thank you for your prayers.

Figure 6.2: Some of the chiefs at the 2014 conference.[38]

The above testimony demonstrates the power of the gospel to transform lives and emphasises the need for Christian chaplaincy presence in palaces.

Apart from the above account, similar stories can be recorded across the nation with calls for Christians and traditional leaders to work together. Dzetse Nene Abram Kabu Akuaku III, Paramount Chief of Ada and President of the Greater Accra Regional House of Chiefs called for closer collaboration between Christians and chieftaincy so as to foster unity and peace for development.[39] Another chief, Nana Kwarfo Opare, Mawerehene of Aburi Atwiesim in the Akuapem South District of the Eastern Region constructed a church building and appealed to his colleague chiefs to help spread Christianity by putting up more church buildings.[40] Togbe Kotoku XI, Paramount Chief of Kpenoe, who is also an Evangelist, told the Ghana News Agency that he faced no challenge in his twelve years as a chief. He added that 'It is basically a leadership role and not so much of rituals.'[41]

This section narrates the steps that Christian chiefs have taken to form associations to learn and share experiences that would enable them perform their roles. Such initiatives need support from the church and provide the opportunity for chaplaincy ministry in the IoC.

6.3 Theological Reflections

The historical overview of Pentecostal denominations in this chapter broadly reveal lack of sustain Christian witness in the IoC. Whereas respondents wanted a situation where the church is actively involved in issues relating to chieftaincy, the reality is that such involvements are in obscurity. As some respondents made reference to Daniel, the Old Testament narration of Daniel's ministry at kings' palaces re-echoes the need for Christian witness with the IoC. Though Israel's exile led to Daniel's capture and transportation to Babylon, his life and ministry as well as other righteous Israelites shows how God's name was exalted through their services to the heathen kings. Daniel excelled in service to the kings and their kingdom despite several tests and trials he faced.[42] Though Daniel was a statesman at the king's service, his prophetic, ability to interpret dreams and more importantly in his righteous life and presence in the mist of ungodliness, witnessed to the heathen the manifold wisdom and power of God.[43] He was God's light and witness in an evil and unbelieving environment. That is the calling Christ has given to the church, that Christians are salt and light to the earth.[44] Like the 'Daniel model', - where Daniel is seen as God's servant ministering in kings' courts; the missional model of chaplaincy allows the minister to bring the gospel to the unchurched as a missionary, care for the people through sharing God's love as a pastor, sees his presence at a palace to symbolize God's incarnational presence, uses his presence to engage in conversation leading to formal and informal confessions as a historical-parish and as a prophet or agent of change, challenges 'the status quo and speaking prophetically into unjust or ungodly structures'[45] in ministering to the IoC.

A theological response is needed to reset the course of Pentecostals' anti-chieftaincy and cultural views, to pursue a missional policy with the IoC. There are loose structures in place that are useful, because ministers occasionally visit chiefs' palaces, and some churches have members of the IoC attend services. Pentecostals have missional policies on evangelism through conventions, campuses and student groups, performing arts, electronic and print media.[46] Why not also intentionally have missional policies for the IoC? There is the need to have policies from the leadership of Pentecostal denominations directing intentional mission to the IoC. One of the methods realized in 'Theology of the Vernacular: Contextual Theologies' came from the Second Vatican Council (1962-65) – where it emerged that the Council endorsed contextual and global theologies in the evangelization of cultures.[47] Among others, its concern was to shape 'Christian mission to meet the needs of its host cultures.[48] Such a high-profile endorsement was needed to direct mission from within the Roman Catholic church. Similarly, a theological response can be achieved through establishing theological colleges of Pentecostal traditions to theologically reflect on each specific cultural and geographical context of the IoC. Here, chaplains serving at the IoC would be resourceful with knowledge gained through continued ministry with chiefs in understanding chieftaincy culture.

In my recent trip to Ghana from the 10th January – 15th February 2020 to present the outcomes of this research findings at five regional councils of AoGG in the Northern and Ashanti regions, the overwhelming response received from ministers and church delegates revealed the need for intentional engagement with the IoC. One of the highlights of the trip was a visit to the Greater Accra West Regional Council of AoGG. The regional superintendent reported that through the missions outreach of Revival Restoration Centre Assemblies of God at Roman Ridge, three churches were planted in Obontser, Nasawadze and Asempayin. 'The chief of Obontser was converted from Islam to Christianity, he then followed up with the donation of a piece of land to the church.'[49] The question is what next after a chief's conversion? Such conversions happened in the past and still do as reported. However, there is the need to go beyond isolated occasional conversions to building a sustained Christian witness within the confines of the chief's court. Participants' call for chaplaincy to chieftaincy in this study suggests that it is possible that the missional model of chaplaincy proposed would enable Pentecostal missional engagement with the IoC.

6.4 Summary

One of the places that Christian leaders can effectively influence chieftaincy is within the confines of traditional leadership exercised in the palaces. This should be done not through the imposition of legal codes but through lifestyles that reveal authentic Christian living. Unfortunately, this has not been the case as Pentecostal denominations have sought to distance themselves from any involvement with chieftaincy in the past until recently that some are making efforts to engage with traditional leadership.

The chapter revealed lack of intentional missional engagement with chieftaincy in the development and growth of Pentecostal denominations. It also acknowledged the recent steps taken by Christian chiefs to form associations that would help promote their Christian faith in fulfilling their responsibilities as traditional rulers. It is within this context, that there is the need for Christian leaders to adopt missional strategies and policies to engage with traditional leadership. Having examined the lack of Pentecostal denominational engagement with chieftaincy historically, the next chapter will analyse the data as it pertains to participants' perceptions of the IoC.

------

1. Gabriel Namsori Yidana, Pentecostalism in Northern Ghana: Origins, Growth & Potentials', *MTh Thesis*, (Mattersey Hall: University of Wales, Bangor, 2006).
2. Rosemarie Daher Kowalski, 'What Made Them Think They Could? Ten Early Assemblies of God Female Missionaries', *Assemblies of God Heritage: Celebrating 100 Years of the Assemblies of God*, Vol. 34, (Springfield, MO: GPH, 2014), pp. 67-73.
3. H. S. Lehmann, 'The Ghana Story', *Assemblies of God Ghana 1931-1981*, (Accra: AoG Printing Press, 1981), p. 10; Kalu, *African Pentecostalism*, (2008).
4. Lehmann, 'Story', p. 10.
5. Peter D. Yamusa, *A History of Assemblies of God, Ghana*, (Kumbungu: n.d.).
6. Lehmann, 'Story', p. 11.
7. Lehmann, 'Story', p. 2.
8. Kowalski, 'What? pp. 67-73.
9. Frimpong-Manso, 'Origins', p. 120.
10. AoGG, Vision 3000, <http://www.agghana.org/v3000/vision-3000.html> (accessed 1 February 2017).
11. 1 Tim. 2:1-4.
12. I was told it was part of the gifts given to Nana Opoku Ware II by AoGG members on one of their occasional visits. Manhyia Palace Museum, (Kumasi: 12 February 2014).
13. Frimpong-Manso, 'Origins', p. 40.
14. Frimpong-Manso, 'Origins', pp. 46-52.
15. ASRCL1, Interview, (Accra: 26th January, 2014).

16. The Apostolic Church Ghana, <http://www.theapostolicchurch.org.gh> [accessed 12 September 2014].

17. Richard Foli, *Christianity in Ghana: A Comparative Church Growth Study*, (Accra: SPL, 2012), p. 39.

18. The Apostolic Church Ghana, <http://www.theapostolicchurch.org.gh> [accessed 12 September 2014].

19. Foli, *Christianity*, p. 40.

20. The Apostolic Church Ghana, <http://www.theapostolicchurch.org.gh> [accessed 12 September 2014].

21. Brobbey, *The Law*, pp. 167, 169.

22. Foli, *Christianity*, pp. 41-42.

23. Christ Apostolic Church International, <http://cacihq.org> [accessed 26 October 2015].

24. Brobbey, *The Law*, p. 167.

25. Brobbey, *The Law*, p. 169.

26. Christ Apostolic Church International, <http://cacihq.org/history/2/> [accessed 15 February 2017].

27. The CoP, Ghana, <http://www.thecophq.org> [accessed 3 November 2016].

28. Foli, *Christianity*, pp. 43-44.

29. The CoP, Ghana, <http://www.thecophq.org> [accessed 3 November 2016].

30. Noel Smith, *The Presbyterian Church of Ghana – 1935-1960*, (Accra: Ghana University Press, 1966), p. 273.

31. Quayesi-Amakye, *Christology*, pp. 220–21.

32. See Appendix 3.

33. See Appendix 4.

34. NRTL1, Interview, (Tamale, 5th February 2014). GRID & NEA <https://grid-nea.org/about> [accessed 12 April 2017].

35. Brenda Mensah, '2011 Christian Chiefs Conference', *GRID & NEA Sustainable Development in Ghana*, May 2011, p. 3, <https://grid-nea.org/wp-content/uploads/2011/05/GRID-Newsletter-May-2011.pdf> [accessed 12 April 2014].

36. Mensah, '2011 Christian Chiefs Conference', p. 3.

37. GRID & NEA, *GRID Update: News from Northern Ghana*, Spring 2017, <https://grid-nea.org/wp-content/uploads/2017/03/GRID-Newsletter-Mar-2017-vFin.pdf> p. 3 [accessed 12 April 2017].

38. Doug Webster, 'Christian Chiefs Conference 2014', *GRID & NEA Sustainable Development in Ghana*, (GRID Newsletter May, 2014), p. 2 <https://grid-nea.org/wp-content/uploads/2014/05/GRID-Newsletter-May-2014.pdf> [accessed 12 April 2017].

39. Ghana News Agency, 'Religion', 12th April 2013, <http://www.ghanaweb.com/GhanaHomePage/religion> [accessed, 7 November 2014].

40. Ghana News Agency, 'Religion', 2nd January 2013, <http://www.ghanaweb.com/GhanaHomePage/religion> [accessed, 3 January 2013].

41. Ghana News Agency, 'Religion', <http://www.ghanaweb.com/GhanaHomePage/religion> [accessed, 3 October 2015].

42. Dan. 1:18-20, 2:12-16, 5:11-17 and 6:3-23.

43. Dan. 1:18-21, 2:16-48, 4:8-27, 5:13-29, 7, 8 and 10.

44. Matt. 5:13-14.

45. Threlfall-Holmes, 'Exploring models of Chaplaincy', pp. 118-122.

46. Peter White and Cornelius J. P. Niemandt, 'Ghanaian Pentecostal Churches' Mission Approaches', *Journal of Pentecostal Theology*, 24, (2015), pp. 241-69.
47. Graham, Walton and Ward, *Theological Reflection Methods*, pp. 229-31.
48. Graham, Walton and Ward, *Theological Reflection Methods*, p. 230.
49. Ernest Birikorang, 'Annual Report by the Regional Superintendent', *Assemblies of God Ghana: Greater Accra West Region*, (Accra: AoGG, February 2020), p. 21.

SEVEN

Perceptions of the Institution of Chieftaincy

7.0 Introduction

The first part of this thesis presented the historical account of chieftaincy in Ghana revealing how the institution is central to the culture, political, social and religious life of the people. Muller acknowledged the complexity of indigenous religion and chieftaincy and reported on how early missionaries compiled a large body of oral traditions in written form as a means to learn what it meant to convert the Asante to Christianity.[1] The church's failure to follow through some of this early missionary engagement has led to the current situation where Pentecostals in particular have had little engagement with chieftaincy as the study has shown in previous chapters.

The aim of this and the next chapter is to analyse the empirical data designed to examine participants' response to interviews conducted. How data analysis was carried out is captured in chapter 1.3.3.

7.1 Data Analysis and Results

As shown in column four of Table 7.1 (Appendix 1), using thematic network analysis,[2] three global themes emerged from the interview transcripts: 1. Perceptions of the IoC, 2. Role of chaplaincy in transforming the IoC and 3. Getting involved in chaplaincy. Thematic analysis is used to discover important themes in the text at different levels and thematic networks facilitate structuring these themes.[3] Thematic networks organize the extraction of identified codes from the data to form basic themes; the basic themes are then grouped together to form more thoughtful principles known as organizing themes; it then leads to express the principal phrase in the data as global themes.[4] This chapter will focus on using the organising themes and their related basic themes through the codes derived from the data to discuss and explain one of the global themes: perceptions of the IoC. The next chapter will capture the other two global themes.

7.2. Global Theme: Perceptions of the Institution of Chieftaincy

As shown in column three of Table 7.1 (Appendix 1), four organising themes emerged from the interview transcripts: 1. Chieftaincy as a dark institution, 2. Lack of education, 3. Divine protection required to succeed and 4. Heads of the community that explain the global theme: Perceptions of chieftaincy institution. These four organising themes and their related seven basic themes derived from codes out of the data are discussed below. This section offers the Pentecostal chaplain the opportunity of pursuing an informed understanding of chieftaincy culture for missional engagement with the IoC.

7.2.1. Organizing theme: Chieftaincy as a dark institution

The respondents' views on chieftaincy centred on their understanding of what the institution looks like. Christian leaders who were chiefs mostly used words and phrases such as 'corruption', 'satanic influence', 'taboos', 'rituals', 'sacrifices', 'idol worship' and 'shun chieftaincy'. All participants talked about the importance of chieftaincy for the community. However, they noted that in practice, it was not just simply about fulfilling a leadership role, but its religious obligations linked to ATR mostly conflict with other faiths. Some illuminating quotations from respondents include the following:

> Pentecostals look at the chieftaincy institution linked to African Traditional Religion which is against biblical principles. They will prefer not to meddle with chieftaincy linked to idol worship.[5]

> Pentecostals oppose most of the practices of African Traditional Religion and chieftaincy as evil and so they stay far, far apart from each other.[6]

In responding to a question on how they think early Pentecostal missionaries perceived chieftaincy, all respondents had views that contained some similarities with the concept that ATR was indeed linked to chieftaincy, although perceived views varied in the understanding of chieftaincy from Christian leaders and traditional leaders:

> I haven't really studied this; I must be honest, but just from what I have read and observed, I have the impression that most early missionaries would set the chief aside..., for anything spiritual... I am not saying that they ignored the chief ... I think most of them went to the chief and followed the customs when coming into the new area to get the approval of them being there but as to the chieftaincy, I would say that they mostly look upon it as not relevant or maybe... being negative.[7]

> They respected and honoured chiefs, sought their permission to preach and build churches. Once the chief did not show any signs of being converted, he was abandoned and branded devilish.[8]

Though Christian leaders' perception of the IoC included the use of words such as 'negative' and 'devilish', what followed was the need to identify and adapt missional policies and strategies that would enable Christians to engage with chieftaincy. This confirms missiologists' calls to contextualise biblical values with cultural practices of any targeted people group for gospel conversion.

The negative perception on chieftaincy identified as a basic theme shows how people's thought about the Christian God has been influenced, and what his acceptance meant for their culture, as noted below.

> You see, one problem with our missionary line is that they didn't study about our culture; they took everything as fetish, our way of life, our way of greeting, our mode of worship and that was myopic and they wrote off all that we had... The people saw the Christian God as a foreign God ... and that was a mistake.[9]

> They thought everything was wrong, it was evil, it was not correct and they really spoke against it and that has really had a negative effect on our culture all the way over 150 years now.[10]

A few of the respondents indicated the extent to which this negative perception has affected the cultural values of the people and for that reason, have lost the opportunity for cultural transformation:

> Missionaries branded traditions and customs as bad. This affected the way Christians engaged their own culture and traditions. A people without a culture is lost. Now as a Bible translator, I have noticed how we lost out in transforming our culture on biblical principles.[11]

The leaders noted with concern that though ATR was linked to chieftaincy, in practice, the majority of the taboos and rituals were designed to protect the sacredness of chieftaincy and reflect the culture of the people. Some of these taboos and rituals can be observed without religious obligations or making sacrifices to the gods, others may be entirely ignored without any consequences.

...cultural values not linked to religious sacrifices were not very much appreciated by our early Pentecostal missionaries and everything of the chieftaincy... was considered diabolic and we missed the way; we missed a great lot of it.[12]

People have wrong perceptions about rituals in the stool room. I did not even enter the stool room and chose a name from the history of one of the good kings.[13]

In responding to a question on whether their perceptions have influenced Christian involvement in chieftaincy, all the participants indicated that the influence was negative. This is because much is said about the dangers of Christians getting involved as noted in the table for data analysis in table 7.1 (Appendix 1). These dangers are primarily placed on rituals, taboos, sacrifices and satanic influence associated in festivals, and ceremonies involving chieftaincy. Due to these perceived dangers, Christians were advised to avoid chieftaincy.

... people have a very negative tendency about chieftaincy, everything is idolatry, everything is unchristian, so people were not concertized towards kingship, our kingdom is not here, chieftaincy is a worldly system...[14]

The church has brought a ban that Christians shouldn't get involved in chieftaincy institution. So, the church has a negative outlook about chieftaincy.[15]

With regards to dangers of Christian involvement and being asked to avoid chieftaincy, most of the respondents indicated the limited or lack of knowledge in determining the relevance and applicability of culture and traditions of the people in festivals and chieftaincy ceremonies which might have contributed to these decisions. Others also expressed concern about the lack of intentional cultural contextualization to aid decision-making in missional policies of the church.

> The church did not understand our culture and traditions, and has since not made any meaningful attempt to let Christians appreciate their cultural values as far as I know...[16]

> Early [Ghanaian] Christians did not understand the traditionalists, and once they didn't understand they had no place for it in their practice so they just thought that a lot of the things that we were doing were paganism or evil and for that matter they threw almost everything overboard and left us almost empty handed.[17]

> After reading Busia, Sarpong and other writers; I came to the conclusion that, after all, some of the things we do here in chieftaincy are not anti-Christ and are not anti-God, just that our cultures are embedded in that.[18]

This suggests that the minimal understanding of chieftaincy and ATR from Christian leaders and the lack of identification of intentions to contextualize chieftaincy culture to biblical values have caused this widened gap between chieftaincy and Christianity. Hence, there is the need for education which leads us to the next organising theme.

Despite this negative perception, it was discovered that participants wanted a situation where Christian involvement can influence chieftaincy. This is reflected in the following remarks by various respondents: One of such states,

Definitely, in order to have a positive influence. Nana Premper I's conversion to Christianity brought changes to evil practice of the kingdom. Elders should be Christians as well because of their advisory role to help the king.[19]

ASRTL1 as a traditional leader, commended the Roman Catholic and Anglican Churches for doing well with chieftaincy but urged Pentecostals to stop the condemnation of other religions and be tolerant, learning from each other. Another respondent ASRCL4 who has been part of the national leadership of AoGG states

> If I sit back and say as a Christian I cannot be chief because the world is already dark, then why am I the light? A light is meant to influence darkness and draw people from that darkness and let them have a view of the values of life. I would want to think that yes; a child of God should desire to be a chief.[20]

ASRCL4 further suggested that he would want to see Pentecostals rethink their theology about Christian's role in chieftaincy to enable proactive decisions acceptable through the gospel of Jesus Christ. A respondent states

> I always ask myself a personal question that if all Christians shun that institution, who will go there and reform it? If we leave it to people we know who are only part of traditional religion, then you won't see any transformation so I said, well I would go in, because as a Christian then we can impact...[21]

These narrations show that some respondents advocated for Christian participation in chieftaincy. Those from the northern region of the country had similar views.

> Definitely yes, chieftaincy is such an important institution even though corrupt as it is but these are the places that the Lord would

want us to influence and so I 100% think Christians should be involved in politics just as in chieftaincy.[22]

Another respondent comments:

That is why we need Christians to be chiefs because we have the mind of Christ and so if you have the mind of Christ and you become a chief, it means we can bring people near God and if God is on our side, who can be against us?[23]

On the other hand, some respondents showed disinterest in Christians becoming chiefs due to rituals, sacrifices and cultures linked to traditional religion. This supports the criticism of chieftaincy captured in chapter two. A minister who has held a national leadership role of AoGG commented:

Best for Christians to be chiefs but the system does not allow. It involves libation, blood sacrifice, black stool, festivals, idol worship so Christians can't be chiefs. That is more difficult for the Akans who have ancestral links with festivals. History shows all who tried to change things failed and ended up being compromised.[24]

ASRCL5 is of the view that convincing the traditional leaders would be difficult and the best is for Christians to stay away completely. He further comments that the opportunity for changes have been lost due to syncretism over the years as other Christian denominations other than Pentecostals have compromised with chieftaincy culture and worsened the attempt to enforce biblical principles. NRCL5 who also lectures at AoGG Bible College from the northern region echoes similar views stating that pressures from ATR lead to compromises in sacrifices, rituals and ceremonies. Nevertheless, he supports those who can withstand these pressures due to the impact they will make as Christian chiefs.[25]

The evidence presented suggests the need for chaplaincy to provide spiritual care and Christian witness with the IoC. That is why I agree with Onyinah that since culture strongly influences people in Ghana, it begs for Christian purification. Hence the need for Christians to become kings, chiefs and queens to allow the kingdom principles to work[26] as well as providing ministry opportunities for chaplaincy with the IoC.

7.2.2 Organizing theme: Lack of education

The traditional leaders and some Christian leaders indicated that certain Pentecostal perceptions of the IoC were due to their lack of education in the culture and traditions of chieftaincy. For them, this lack of education may be the reason for perceiving chieftaincy as a dark institution. They noted that there were opportunities right from the introduction of Christianity that leaders could have taken to facilitate learning from the host culture alongside fulfilling the church's mission of evangelizing the community. For instance, one of the common Ghanaian cultural traditions is hospitality, especially to strangers. The following quote from a respondent shows how chiefs tended to receive missionaries:

> They opened their arms to receive them because tradition says that when you receive a stranger well, he will take your good name wherever he goes. In some cases, as custom demands, they even provided some sheep or goat and some eggs so that the missionary would be entertained or take home to prepare their meal. So, what we realised was that, in fact when the missionaries came, the chiefs were not hostile.[27]

Although there was bound to be isolated instances where chiefs were hostile to some missionaries as shown in chapter two, most chiefs were and are hospitable to missionaries. What Christian leaders needed to do then and now, is to embrace this hospitable attitude of the chiefs to learn more of chieftaincy culture.

Chiefs respect and honour the office of any religious priesthood. They believe that priests are able to contact the spiritual world and thus become the intermediaries between the living and the ancestors. That is why traditional priests and Muslim Imams have special roles in certain courts of chiefs in Ghana. Some of the respondents noted that despite the fact that chiefs have the services of traditional priests and Imams, they still call on a Pastor for advice on certain difficult issues and prayers for the community.

> The Pastor is considered as one with knowledge and wisdom from God. That is why the chief calls him for advice. The question is that most of the Pastors do not make themselves available to the chiefs and because they are not going to the chiefs, sometimes when the chief has something to say, they find it difficult to call the pastors.[28]

> The ministers carry the mantle of God's anointing and as his mouthpiece, they cannot be ignored, we need their advice, prayers and support to rule our people.[29]

In responding to a question on whether a Christian should take up the responsibility of becoming a chief, some Christian leaders' responses showed ignorance or lack of education on how issues are handled in chieftaincy. They had an idea but were not sure what certain practices associated with chieftaincy mean. A quote from one participant states:

> That is a very controversial question... you know... we have an idea that apart from being leaders in your community there are certain rituals you have to go through and that is where at times we are not sure what that means, what that entails; so that is the dichotomy here but for the leadership roles I think wherever a Christian can be they can have an influence on the people. It is only the other roles, the taboos, the rituals, the libation aspect that at times [makes] you not sure how the Christian can go about those things.[30]

This is further revealed in the conflicting views amongst Christian and traditional leaders on one of the rituals held in the stool-room of the Akans during the rite of enstooling a new chief. Where one thinks that the chief-elect is made to drink a lot of alcohol and 'get boozed' another says he is blind-folded before entering the stool-room for the rituals of taking a formal name for his reign as shown below.

> If you become a chief, there are some processes you need to go through and those processes are usually what we think, what we believe... you know...they are demonic oriented....one of the processes is that one day they will make you become so boozed and you enter into the stool room...you are so boozed...so you go there naked and the stool that you point to will be your stool name.[31]

A traditional leader had a contrary view as follows:

> I have never heard it before that the new chief is made 'to booze'. What I have heard is that formerly they would blindfold your eyes and they would let you go to the stool-room and you take your hand to tap on one. The one that your hand touches, is the one they are going to name you after. This time is not like that, for me ... I prayed to get my own name...Nana Amankwaa Sarkodie ... without even entering the stool room.[32]

This suggests that the conflicting views of what happens in the stool-room as evidenced above calls for the need of education for proper understanding to enable taking decisions that are supported by facts not assumptions.

7.2.3 Organizing theme: Divine protection required to succeed

The participants' perception of the IoC centred on their understanding that chiefs required divine protection to be able to fulfil their responsibilities. They used words and phrases such as 'compromise', 'fear of distoolment', 'persecution', 'fear of death', 'fervent in prayers', 'God's protection', and 'God's strength'. Both Christian and traditional leaders noted that spiritual attacks and the temptation to compromise God's standards of righteousness on the part of Christian chiefs, are the reasons why they required God's power to succeed. Christian chiefs in particular described the threats and experience of spiritual attacks they constantly face. Generally, some of these threats and experiences of spiritual attacks are common for Christians living in heathen societies.

Nevertheless, 'spiritual attacks' can be more frequent and at a higher level in chieftaincy which is why across all the interviews, respondents emphasised the need for God's power to succeed. One of the Christian chiefs shared his experience of spiritual attacks:

> I remember there were quite some times I would find my brand-new trousers or cloth having holes like I have been shot with several bullets that would have gone through the cloth. I will show it to my wife ... and say spiritually they are shooting but they are shooting my cloth not catching me. They scared me with things like that... if you don't know the Lord well these things will scare you and you will just abandon chieftaincy, but I just thought well if they want to fight spiritually my faith in God would fight them... One night in particular I was going to have a bath; it was just like the Lord says "Watch!" and I looked carefully and there was a snake on the spot where I stood, ready and energized to strike but I killed it.[33]

The above account is not an isolated case as similar experiences including death threats were narrated from other chiefs. One chief remarked, when he was made chief, some predicted his death in three months' time for refusing to perform certain rituals and sacrifices for enskinment due to his faith as a Christian, but he survived the threat for 34 years.[34] Chiefs are more vulnerable to spiritual attacks because of the belief that they are considered the physical representatives of the ancestral world and are responsible to provide remedies of calamities that face the communities.[35] As such, chiefs are not only concerned about their own spiritual safety but that of the community as well. The need to meet what I will term 'social spiritual responsibility' drives many chiefs into seeking more spiritual powers. Fear of distoolment and death for not honouring this 'social spiritual responsibility' may lead some Christian chiefs to compromise God's standards for righteousness. The temptation to compromise God's standards was stressed across the interviews.

> When I became a chief, the first thing that my friends asked me was, "Would you pour libation? Would you supervise the slaughter of sheep? Would you partake of that sheep, the food?" and so on and so forth...[36]

> An elder told me, to become a chief, you don't just go there like that, like you are now; and he asked me have you visited or have you gone for any spiritual fortification? and I said yes. And he was pleased, very wonderful you have done that, so where did you go? but I said for me, I went to Christ. Then he began to draw back.... and went away.[37]

> If the Christian chief's faith is not strong, the elders could influence him negatively to do some things which are biblically wrong such as sacrifices to idols and ancestral worship.[38]

In responding to a follow up question on how they face all these threats of spiritual attack and temptation to compromise their faith as Christian chiefs, all participants noted the need for prayers in order to have God's strength and protection. Christian chiefs in particular stated how they have intensified their own personal prayers, trusting God for spiritual power and support. They also emphasised the need to have the church praying for them and chaplaincy ministry in the chief's court to affirm the church's support:

> The thoughts and experience of spiritual attacks so far as a chief makes me intensify my personal prayers with fasting sometimes. I know God alone can protect me and give me power...[39]

> I think from time to time the minister should be seen at the chief's palace as doing his work, I mean offering the needed spiritual support and advice to the chief.[40]

> ...at Manhyia, this year is full of activities for the Asante kingdom. Before the king opens this celebration, he will invite Bishop Sarpong to open the celebration with prayer... the king has known that as a leader he cannot do anything without the priest.[41]

The fact that Christian chiefs constantly face threats of spiritual attacks and are also vulnerable to compromise their faith should cause the church to pray always for the institution. Most especially for chiefs who acknowledge that their success in fulfilling their duties depends on God's power and protection. As some of the chiefs have acknowledged, it is not enough to pray in church for them as they are made to believe that Christians do, but 'there is also the need to pray with them in their courts.'[42]

7.2.4 Organizing theme: Chiefs are heads of the communities

The final organising theme derived from the analysis was that chiefs are seen as heads of the communities that they represent. Participants used words and phrases like 'leaders', 'influencers', 'role models', and 'chiefs are adored' to describe their views. The participants noted that the introduction of central governance in Ghana through democratic rule has changed the role of chieftaincy in recent times. The chief is now a development-oriented leader and plays a pastoral role to that effect for his community. It is the provision of this kind of leadership that all participants stated that

Christians should no longer shy away from chieftaincy but have the moral responsibility of being involved.

> A Christian can become a chief and give the people Christian leadership. For today we have some Christian chiefs who are giving the people leadership and they are giving them the right leadership.[43]

> The chief who is good is much concerned about the development of his people. It is for this reason that some Christians involve themselves in chieftaincy to try and help improve the lives of the people...traditional leaders also know that church brings development to the community.[44]

> Someone once said that I shouldn't have become a chief but rather a pastor. And I told her that the two roles are almost the same. A pastor is the head of a congregation and a chief is also a head of a community.[45]

Interestingly, it was not only ASRTL2 who compared the chiefs' role to that of ministers as community leaders, but others from both institutions had similar views. Hence, the basic theme identified under this section of the analysis: 'chiefs play a pastoral role'. They stated that just as pastors are called by God to do ministry, chiefs also rise to their role through divine appointment. 'God is the king and he appoints and de-stool chiefs, unless God chooses we can't.'[46] That is why during the process of finding a new chief, human deliberations are conducted alongside consulting the gods for divine guidance to choose the most qualified candidate amongst those contesting to fill the vacant role. This supports what has already been discussed in chapter two where among the Mamprusis for instance, royal families and contestants for chieftaincy accept the death of a chief and the enskinment of a new chief as God's will. Some quotes from participants include the following:

> If God appoints you to be a chief, you have to take it. Because if I
> may cite myself as an example, I think my being a *Taraana* is by
> divine intervention.... The church must accept that chieftaincy is
> also divine calling.[47]

> If we understand leadership, God did not just create the world and
> left it without leadership. So, wherever you find people there is
> leadership. God looks for leaders and chooses leaders in the
> community... So, chieftaincy I will say is God given and so we
> cannot look down on chieftaincy.[48]

All those interviewed acknowledged the importance of chiefs being
leaders of communities as privileged roles that makes them role
models, influencers and as such they are adored. As such, they
decide the course of the community. The general view was that
decisions on the course of the community are evidenced in development projects that affect the welfare of the people. One Christian
leader for instance, noted:

> One of the things that made *Otumfour* succeed was his ideology of
> the role of a modern chief. I heard him say several times when
> advising his subjects; he will tell them that; *Nananom, kane no na ye*
> *nananom ko ku, ene yenko ku, enti nne de3 nea ewos3 yetumi ye ne s3,*
> *yenboa yen nkrofo no na won abrabo no etumi ko soro.* Literally, you
> see...formally, chiefs were going for wars, and these days we don't
> go to war anymore. What we are called to do or yes what we are
> made to do is that we need to help our people develop and that is
> why we are made chiefs.[49]

7.3 Discussion

To my knowledge, this study is the first of its kind to examine the
perception of the IoC in Ghana from the perspectives of Pentecostal
Christian leaders and traditional leaders. Ubink's research focused
on the popular perception of chiefs and chieftaincy roles.[50] This

chapter described the understanding of participants' perception of the IoC as: Chieftaincy is considered a dark institution due to lack of education, chiefs require divine protection to succeed and they are leaders of communities.

7.3.1. Chieftaincy as a dark institution

The views expressed by the participants suggest that people have a narrow view of understanding cultural practices of chieftaincy which showed conflicting statements about chieftaincy portrayed as a dark institution. Most Christian leaders' main sources of information were what they heard from others and personal views as they observed these cultural practices from afar. This suggests knowledge that is sufficiently framed can sometimes be easily accepted as true or valid. At one level, this finding is in line with the wider literature which suggest that religions other than ATR and Christianity in particular, view chieftaincy as a dark institution.[51] However, this view frustrates Christian scholars who seek interaction between Ghanaian culture and the Christian faith to facilitate integration. One of such scholars was Busia concluding in his paper on 'The African World-View'; he asked a question, 'Can the African be Christian only by giving up his culture, or is there a way by which Christianity can be ennobled?'[52]

The African can be a Christian without giving up his culture whilst upholding the dignity in Christianity. God through his Holy Spirit is enabling the church to present the gospel to people in the cultural context. In a recent paper, Allan Anderson comments that Pentecostalism has contributed to contextualization through the planting of indigenous churches where the Holy Spirit is responsible for everything that takes place. 'The Spirit causes people to worship, sing, prophesy, speak in tongues, heal, exorcize demons, have visions and dreams, live holy lives—and generally the Spirit directs the life and worship of these churches.'[53]

It is against this background of the Spirit's leadings that Pentecostals object to sacrifices and rituals in chieftaincy linked to ATR.

In the previous chapter under Pentecostal theological concerns regarding rituals of chieftainship, it was evident that the disinterest and lack of involvement in chieftaincy were due to blood sacrifices and the invoking of ancestral spirits through fetish priests. Therefore, blood sacrifices to idols and the invoking of ancestral spirits they consider, must be abolished. It is possible therefore to argue that through engagement, the church can provide alternatives as well as draw redemptive analogies from some of the practices – echoed by other writers.[54] What they seek in offering blood sacrifices is found in the Scriptures and fulfilled in Jesus Christ.[55] Chaplaincy is therefore required for the chaplain to act as a recognized representative of the church for ministry opportunities argued for in the proposed missional model in chapter three. The chaplain's presence assures the Christian chief the provision of spiritual services relating to his faith and as a witness to the nonChristian chief. Though Christians generally accept the importance of chieftaincy, the issues relating to chiefly rituals are approached differently. For instance, whereas mainstream denominations see the pouring of libation as a form of prayer, Pentecostals see the call on ancestral spirits, spirits of the earth and water bodies and other objects of creation seen or unseen whilst pouring libation as idol worship[56] and must be abolished. I agree with the latter. It is possible that chaplaincy ministry roles as 'Prophets and Agents of change' to the IoC would assist in facilitating the need for chiefly cultural ennoblement for Christian chiefs.

7.3.2 The need for education

The need for education to understand cultures for effective interventions and strategies to aid cross-cultural missions has been widely acclaimed.[57] Some churches see their social relevance in their contribution to the development of education in Ghana.[58] Surprisingly, most of the Christian leaders in this study had a minimal knowledge of cultural practices associated with chieftaincy needed for contextualisation in missions. This is evidenced in their response that often-contained phrases like: 'I think that', 'I did not study', 'I feel like', 'I have heard' and also complained of lack of access to relevant primary research produced locally. Furthermore, the opportunity to educate traditional leaders on biblical values would lead to changes in their worldviews that have been the bases for beliefs and practices associated with chieftaincy.

Within the field of Missiology, Hiebert notes that: 'If behaviour change was the focus of the nineteenth century mission movement, and changed beliefs the focus of the twentieth century, transforming worldviews must be central to the mission task in the twenty-first century'.[59] According to Tengan,

> A people's worldview is always a culturally constructed world… It is also seen as the foundation for their ethical and moral norms. As a design for living, such a cosmological vision is thus held sacred by members of the society. A challenge to it would mean shaking the very foundations on which their social structure, ethical values and notions of personal identity are based.[60]

In the same vein, Luzbetak notes that worldview provides answers to basic questions on human identity, life, visible and the invisible world.[61] In support of the above scholars' statements on worldview and its role in post-modern missions, it is important that church leaders have some ways of understanding the cultures they engage for ministry. Chaplaincy ministry to the IoC would enable Christian leaders to learn and understand chieftaincy culture.

7.3.3 Chiefs need divine protection to succeed

The participants in this study saw chiefs as community leaders responsible for administration, leading in development projects; but also needed divine assistance to succeed. Acknowledging the role of leadership and spirituality in chieftaincy by the participants is worthy of note. Those who argue for Christian involvement in chieftaincy state that Christians are able to provide better leadership and are also privileged to have God's support in discharging their duties.[62] However, as the study has shown, these traditional leaders work within a complex spiritual environment where there is the tendency to display the spiritual competence and supremacy of one spirituality over another especially in public gatherings. That is why chiefs become overly concerned with seeking spiritual protection.

In such circumstances, Marfo suggests that when confronted with a choice between God and the gods, one should follow Joshua's example by rejecting idols and choosing the Lord who alone can offer the required protection and assistance in life.[63] God protects the Christian in his kingdom from the malevolent use of spirit possession, black magic, witchcraft and all such powers which are of the reign of Satan.[64] These findings have been reported in a similar study where traditional rulers are identified as community leaders and maintain sacredness as ritual figures to keep relations with ancestors on whom the living depend for help and protection.[65] The presence of a Christian chaplain offers some assurance to the Christian chief that he is not alone in dealing with spiritual issues within the IoC.

7.4 Theological Reflections

The perceptions of participants about the IoC were split into two categories – negative perception and lack of education. Regarding the first, it is important to note that the negative perception was not questioning the importance of chieftaincy, rather it centred around rituals and blood sacrifices linked to ATR. They all acknowledged that chiefs needed divine assistance as they provided leadership to the communities. The Scriptures reveal God's support for righteous rulers and his condemnation on evil rulers. Beyond the good and bad kings of Israel as a chosen nation, God referred to rulers like Cyrus as his servant.[66] The previous chapter acknowledged the contribution of chiefs as they received Christian leaders and protected the interest of Christianity to establish churches.[67] Such a response required that the church needed to theologically reflect on the role of chieftaincy after conversion. Following conversion, a sustained ministry with the IoC would be an opportunity for Christians to understand chieftaincy culture which traditional leaders felt Christians lacked.

Vincent Donovan's ministry with the Masai people of Tanzania led him to theologically reflect on their symbols and cultural values to produce the Masai creed – 'An African Creed' organized along traditional lines drawn from its African setting.[68] Likewise, theological reflection on rituals and blood sacrifices associated with chieftaincy would enable Pentecostals to engage with the IoC. John wrote about the continual advantage that the church has through Jesus Christ: *The light shines in the darkness, and the darkness has not overcome it (John 1:5).*[69] Certainly, the gospel light needs to shine in the perceived areas of darkness in chieftaincy. The Great Commission commands Christians to *go and make disciples of all nations (Matthew 28:19)*[70] – literally, whole nations or states such as Ashantis, Mamprusis and other Ghanaian cultural groups are being referred to here, not just individuals. If that is the case, a decision for Christ obviously will mean the transformation of individuals and whole cultures. The proposal of chaplaincy as a missional model for the IoC in this study seeks to enable Pentecostals to engage with chieftaincy.

7.5. Summary

The results from this chapter provide a unique study of how participants interviewed perceived chieftaincy. Whilst some of the participants saw chieftaincy as a dark institution, others were of the view that there is the need for education in order to enlighten people on culture and practices relating to chieftaincy. Given that participants in this study identified leadership and the need for divine help in fulfilling chieftaincy roles, this study supports the call for Christian involvement in chieftaincy. It is important that Christian leaders adopt policies that would address challenges facing believers with traditional cultures and provide the needed training that would equip members of their congregations for efficient missional activities. Furthermore, it is appropriate to acknowledge that not all Christians entering chieftaincy would be successful in that role but being there as witnesses to kingdom principles is necessary for the church's missional mandate.[71]

The next chapter continues on the empirical evidence from the questionnaires showing two more global themes identified from analysing the data.

---

1. Muller, *Religion,* p. 49.
2. See Chapter 1.3.3 data analysis.
3. Attride-Stirling, 'Thematic', p. 387.
4. Attride-Stirling, 'Thematic', p. 388.
5. NRCL9, Interview, (Bawku, 7th February, 2014).
6. NRCL8, Interview, (Tamale, 3rd February, 2014).
7. ASRCL8, Interview, (Lomé, 27th January, 2014).
8. NRCL8, Interview, (Tamale, 3rd February, 2014).
9. ASRCL2, Interview, (Kumasi, 13th February, 2014).
10. ASRCL1, Interview, (Accra, 26th January, 2014).
11. NRCL9, Interview, (Bawku, 7th February, 2014).
12. ASRCL4, Interview, (Kumasi, 12 February 2014).
13. ASRTL4, Interview, (Kumasi, 17 February 2014).
14. NRTL7, Interview, (Nalerigu, 2 February 2014).
15. NRCL8, Interview, (Tamale, 3 February 2014).
16. NRCL13, Interview, (Tamale, 29 January 2014).
17. NRTL2, Interview, (Nalerigu, 2 February 2014).
18. ASRTL2, Interview, (Kumasi, 13 February 2014).
19. ASRTL1, Interview, (Kumasi, 13 February 2014).
20. ASRCL4, Interview, (Kumasi, 12 February 2014).
21. ASRTL3, Interview, (Kumasi, 12 February 2014).
22. NRTL1, Interview, (Tamale, 5 February 2014).
23. NRCL8, Interview, (Tamale, 7 February 2014).
24. ASRCL5, Interview, (Kumasi, 13 February 2014).
25. NRCL5, Interview, (Tamale, 7 Feb 2014).
26. Quayesi-Amakye, *Christology,* p. 221.
27. NRCL13, Interview, (Tamale, 29 January 2014).
28. NRTL8, Interview, (Wulugu, 2 February 2014).
29. ASRTL7, Interview, (Kumasi, 17th February, 2014).
30. ASRCL2, Interview, (Kumasi, 13th February, 2014).
31. ASRCL3, Interview, (Kumasi, 13th February, 2014).

32. ASRTL4, Interview, (Kumasi, 17th February, 2014).
33. NRTL1, Interview, (Tamale, 29 January 2014).
34. NRTL9, Interview, (Tamale, 31 January 2014).
35. NRTL2, Interview, (Nalerigu, 2 February 2014).
36. ASRTL7, Interview, (Kumasi, 15 February 2014).
37. ASRTL2, Interview, (Kumasi, 13 February 2014).
38. NRCL22, Interview, (Nalerigu, 2 February 2014).
39. NRTL4, Interview, (Wulugu, 1 February 2014).
40. ASRTL8, Interview, (Accra, 26 February 2014).
41. ASRTL1, Interview, (Kumasi, 14 February 2014).
42. NRTL2, Interview, (Nalerigu, 2 February 2014).
43. NRCL3, Interview, (Tamale, 29 January 2014).
44. NRCL4, Interview, (Tamale, 31 January 2014).
45. ASRTL2, Interview, (Kumasi, 13 February 2014).
46. ASRCL1, Interview, (Accra, 26 January 2014).
47. NRTL2, Interview, (Nalerigu, 2 February 2014).
48. NRCL14, Interview, (Tamale, 30 January 2014).
49. ASRCL3, Interview, (Kumasi, 13 February 2014).
50. It was an 'extensive qualitative and quantitative field research conducted from 2002 to 2005 in nine peri-urban communities around Kumasi, Ghana.' Ubink, 'Traditional Authority Revisited:' pp. 123-61.
51. Arhin, *Traditional*, (Accra: SPL,1985), Safo-Kantanka, *Christian*, (Kumasi: PPL,1999), Dankwa, *Chieftaincy*, (Accra: KAF, 2004), Muller, *Religion*, (Zurich: LVG & C0., 2013).
52. Opuni-Frimpong, *Indigenous*, p. 50.
53. Allan H. Anderson, 'Contextualization in Pentecostalism: A Multicultural Perspective', *Academia*, https://www.academia.edu pdf, [accessed 28 February 2020].
54. Safo-Kantanka, *Christian*, (Kumasi: PPL, 1999); Opuni-Frimpong, *Indigenous*, (Accra: SLP, 2012); Nketia, 'Christianity and African Culture: Remodelling Tradition', Addo-Fening, 'From Traditionalist to Christian Evangelist and Teacher', and Afriyie, 'Christ Our Perfect Sacrifice', *JACT*, 2010, 2004, 2014.
55. Afriyie, 'Christ Our Perfect Sacrifice', p. 33.
56. Sarpong, *Sacred Stools*, p. 67.
57. A. B. Tengan ed., *Christianity and Cultural History in Northern Ghana*, (Oxford: P.I.E. Peter Lang, 2013); C. H. Kraft, *Christianity in Culture*, (Maryknoll, New York: Orbis Books, 2002); G. Van Rheenen, *Contextualization and Syncretism: Navigating Cultural Currents*, (Pasadena, CA: Evangelical Missiological Society, 2006); A. S. Moreau, *Contextualization in World Missions*, (Grand Rapids, MI: Kregel Publications, 2012); P. G. Hiebert, 'Transforming Worldviews', *Mission Focus: Annual Review*, Vol. 10, 2002, <www.anabaptistwiki.org> [accessed 20 February 2017]; R. Horton, 'African Conversion', *Africa*, 41 (2), (1971).
58. Eshun, 'Social Ministry', pp. 135-36.
59. Hiebert, 'Transforming', p. 11.
60. E. Tengan, *The Land as Being and Cosmos: The Institution of the Earth Cult among the Sisala of north-western Ghana*, (Frankfurt-am-Main, New York: Peter Lang, 1991), p. 2.
61. Luzbetak, *The Church and Culture:* p. 252.

62. Marfo, *Christian*, (Kumasi: Ed-Jay Services Ltd., 2009), Sarpong, *Sacred*, (Accra: GPC, 1971), Opuni-Frimpong, *Indigenous*, (Accra: SLP, 2012); Safo-Kantanka, *Christians*, (Kumasi: PPPL, 1999).
63. Marfo, *Christian*, p. 61.
64. Rheenen, *Communicating Christ*, p. 139.
65. E. Asante, 'The relationship between the chieftaincy institution and Christianity in Ghana', in Irene K. Adotei, and Albert K. Awedoba, (eds.), *Chieftaincy in Ghana: Culture, Governance and Development*, (Accra, Ghana: Sub-Saharan Publishers, 2006); Busia, *The Position*, (Oxford: OUP, 1951).
66. 2 Chr. 36; Ezra 1, 3-6 and Isa. 44:28-45:13.
67. See Chapter 6.1.1.
68. Graham, Walton & Ward, *Theological Reflection Methods*, pp. 231-33.
69. John 1:15.
70. Matt. 28:19.
71. Quayesi-Amakye, *Christology*, p. 221.

EIGHT

Call for Chaplaincy Involvement and Its Role in Transforming the Institution of Chieftaincy

8.0 Introduction

This chapter continues from the previous chapter, which showed the results of data analysis. There I identified three global themes from the analysis of the interview transcripts as indicated in Table 7.1 (Appendix 1) of that section. One global theme has already been discussed in chapter seven. The remaining two global themes: the role of chaplaincy in transforming the IoC and calls for chaplaincy involvement in chieftaincy are the focus of this chapter.

Led by the research objectives and questions as stated in chapter one, and the successive data gathered by the instruments discussed in the previous chapter, this chapter presents a continuation of the research analysis and discussion. The intent of this chapter is to point out the perceptions of those interviewed of chaplaincy involvement with the IoC as proposed and discussed in chapter five. This aims at providing a link between the data gathered and what is discussed in the previous chapters of this study.

This chapter is divided into three sections. Section one looks at participants' perceptions of the role of chaplaincy in transforming the IoC. Section two deals with the calls for chaplaincy involvement to fill the void of Pentecostal Christian witness and presence in chieftaincy, and lastly, section three discusses the findings in relation to other literature, followed by summary and interpretation of data. By so doing, this chapter fulfils the second objective of this study, namely to assess the possibilities of chieftaincy cultural transformation through chaplaincy involvement in Christian witness with the IoC to meet the spiritual and physical needs of the people. The chapter ends with a conclusion of the discussions.

8.1 Global Theme: Role of Chaplaincy in Transforming the Institution of Chieftaincy

Chapter five of this study looked at the seemingly indispensable role of the ATR priests to chiefs and proposed chaplaincy as a missional model to chieftaincy. The conclusion of chapter five revealed the purpose and potential for chaplaincy ministry in the palace to enable Christian constant witness and influence cultural transformation. Participants' responses to questions relating to chaplaincy vindicates the proposal in this study for chaplaincy involvement to help Christianity transform chieftaincy. According to Table 7.1 (Appendix 1), six organising themes emerged from analysing interview transcripts. These organising themes supported by twelve basic themes are used to discuss the global theme: role of chaplaincy in transforming the IoC.

The figure below illustrates the thematic network where codes provide the phrases in Figure 8.1 as basic themes, leading to organizing themes in circles, on which the role of chaplaincy in transforming the IoC shown in the rectangle was anchored[1]

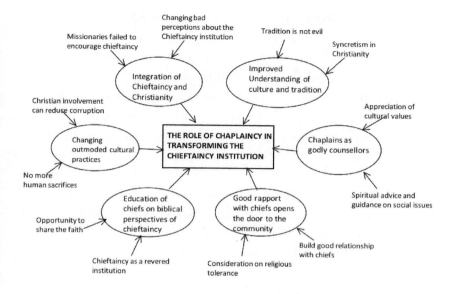

Figure 8.1: Thematic network for 'The role of chaplaincy in transforming the IoC'.

This network represents an exploration[2] of participants' view of the role of chaplaincy in the context of Christians engaging with the IoC.

8.1.1 Organizing theme: Integration of chieftaincy and Christianity

This organizing theme focuses on the need to integrate chieftaincy and Christianity as characterized by participants. Participants used phrases such as 'Ministers need to get closer to chiefs' in their response to the questionnaire. The participants saw integration as something essential for the cultural identity and social behaviour of the people in order to express their faith in God within Christian values. According to this organizing theme, integration can be possible by addressing the past and present failure of the church, not encouraging believers to participate in chieftaincy and changing the bad perception about the IoC. A participant noted:

Jesus said, you are the light of the world and my thinking is that, Jesus in a way says that the world is already a dark place because of Satan's evil... If I sit back and say as a Christian I cannot be chief because the world is already dark, then why am I the light? A light is meant to influence darkness and draw people from that darkness and let them have a view of the values of life, so... in the context of scripture I would want to think that yes, a child of God [Christian] should desire to be a chief.[3]

The need for integration was acknowledged by all participants who emphasised that Christians' involvement with chieftaincy would address the church's past and present failure to encourage believers' participation and move the church closer to the IoC.

The churches must accept that chieftaincy is also a divine calling which should be promoted and encouraged. Christian royal family members must be encouraged to take up appointments ... unless that happens Christian influence can never be felt in chieftaincy.[4]

I wish that as a pastor, I will counsel the people that after all it is not bad, it is not wrong if a Christian should be a chief there is nothing wrong with it.[5]

The changes that I will want to see are that Christians should move into chieftaincy. Christian royal families should participate in contesting for Chieftaincy. When you become the chief as a Christian, people in the community will see you as a representative of God and they will do the right thing.[6]

Additionally, it was seen as an opportunity for the church to practically contextualize the culture of chieftaincy with Christian principles that would help to change the bad perception about chieftaincy. The change of bad perception of chieftaincy is possible because some of the obsolete customs and cultures are abandoned and there is a way of compromising.[7] The lack of Christian presence makes chiefs seek other forms of spiritual protection. A respondent noted:

> I will want some kind of integration. When the chieftaincy institution is brought into mainstream Christianity, then many chiefs will be inclined to begin to pour out their hearts ... even about Spiritism because we don't feel protected. We think that Christ is there but we can't see so we run to people that we can see who can protect us.[8]

One of the participants expressed his desire to help change this bad perception of chieftaincy by going to Bible school for more training as an evangelist.

> As a chief, I have the desire to preach the gospel and I do it as an evangelist. I would go to Bible school and be trained and hopefully be the first chief in Ghana who has ever done that... I wish that more chiefs would go to church and also be preachers of the gospel.[9]

This notion of changing the bad perception was a central theme in the context of integration of chieftaincy and Christianity. However, integration alone would not guarantee transforming chieftaincy; something else was required as chaplaincy facilitates the process which leads us to the next organizing theme: improved understanding of culture and tradition.

8.1.2 Organizing theme: Improved understanding of culture and tradition

Participants used words and phrases such as 'culture', 'tradition', 'not hostile', and 'not evil' to stress the need for a chaplaincy role to facilitate improved understanding of chieftaincy culture and tradition among Christians. Two basic themes identified in figure 8.1 for this section are 'tradition is not evil' and 'syncretism in Christianity'. Whereas some thought that some chieftaincy cultures and traditions are evil, others were of the view that lack of proper contextualization have led to syncretism of these practices in chieftaincy. Participants also emphasised the need to differentiate culture from ATR and take away elements which are in conflict with Christianity and promote culture which is very good.[10]

> ...if the minister is frequently seen at the chief's palace to provide spiritual guidance to help the chief succeed in his leadership, the church will not be seen as an alien but as part of the culture and tradition of the people which is not evil.[11]

> Once people begin to understand through education that culture and tradition are not evil and there is the need for the chieftaincy institution and Christianity to fuse, chaplaincy ministry will be central in all this because no chief will leave out the role of the pastor.[12]

The basic necessity of tradition and culture in chieftaincy that carries substantial importance in how the institution is portrayed in public cannot be reduced into something that is evil, especially when part of chiefs' roles includes being custodians of the people's culture, noted in chapter two of this study. Additionally, culture and tradition were seen as the functional aspects of chieftaincy that chaplaincy needed to study in order to provide acceptable Christian alternatives. The absence of chaplaincy has contributed to some extent to syncretism in chieftaincy although denominational theological emphasis may also be a contributing factor. One participant remarked: It is not right to provide the sacrifice for the priest to offer on your behalf and say you are not participating in the worship.[13] Other denominations have contributed to this when they accepted traditional sacrifices alongside Christian worship with members of royal families in the past and currently. Chiefs feel more comfortable with those denominations than Pentecostals.[14]

...my life as a Christian has really influenced the chieftaincy institution in my home. Because there are some things, some of the family members will want to do and will want to involve me but they will say because I am Christian..., don't just touch him. Forget him because he is a Christian, if you tell him he will not do it.[15]

As a chief who is Catholic, I do not see anything wrong with the wooden stools that are used as symbols to remember former chiefs. These stools are not images of worship. The first time I was introduced to the Stool-room and was asked to pray, I took the schnapps and prayed to God through Christ who has brought me to chieftaincy for leadership and development of the community.[16]

The effect of different church tradition interpretation as noted in the above quote was raised among participants where one was of the view that Pentecostals have lost the opportunity to effect any changes.[17] I disagree, and state that our absence will not only deny those who are willing to change but also a betrayal to our commitment to mission. Accordingly, chaplaincy presence in chieftaincy would help Christians have better knowledge of chieftaincy culture, tradition and reduce if not eliminate syncretism. An improved understanding of culture and tradition would offer chaplains the opportunity of being godly counsellors to chiefs.

8.1.3 Organizing theme: Chaplains as godly counsellors

In considering the role of chaplains as godly counsellors, the participants used words and phrases such as: 'not shun tradition', 'appreciation', 'cultural values', 'spiritual advice', 'guidance', and 'social issues'. These words led to identifying the two basic themes: appreciation of cultural values and spiritual advice and guidance on social issues as illustrated in figure 8.1 of this chapter. Participants were of the view that better understanding of culture and tradition would help chaplains appreciate chieftaincy cultural values that would enhance their role of providing spiritual advice and guidance on social issues in the context of Christian godliness. Hence, the need for chaplains becoming godly counsellors to chiefs. In chapter five of this study, the traditional priest is seen to occupy a vital role in chieftaincy. Nevertheless, the Christian chaplain who appreciates chieftaincy cultural values would be offered the privilege of counselling the chief, according to participants interviewed as referenced below. In responding to the question on the need for ministers to visit palaces and engage with chiefs consistently whether they are Christians or not, all participants were in the affirmative.

> I will very much like to see ministers establish a sustained contact with chiefs to pray and advise them. Interestingly, no chief in Ghana would object to that and say do not pray for me. They will rather ask for it. If you go, they are so open for it.[18]

> I think the pastor should continually be seen at the chief's palace as doing his work, I mean respecting chieftaincy culture, offering the needed spiritual support and advice to the chief. If ministers come to that understanding and become chaplains to the chiefs and also partner with them for the development of the society, that would be a service to humanity that pleases God as well.[19]

In defining godly counselling, participants made reference to Old Testament prophets' role to kings of Israel and other nations. They intimated that some of these kings were not 'righteous' in the sense of keeping faith with Israel's God. Nevertheless, prophetic and priestly services were made available so that the kings were left with a choice to either obey or not.

> The Scriptures say that no chief is put there without God's knowledge [Proverbs 8:15; Daniel 2:21; 1 Timothy 2:1-3]. God installs chiefs and so whether the person is a pagan or not there is already a connection between God and so the minister has the responsibility to visit the palace ....and... advice on issues that affect the people in the community.[20]

Daniel outlived about four or five kings. If they didn't see his worth, the next king who had come would not have sought for him, but all the kings that had come each one of them sought Daniel's counsel. They realized something in Daniel that the king could use his counsel to help rule the people.[21]

The reference to scriptural examples once again reminds us of the scope of the minister's calling that sets no boundaries or limitations and the kind of people mandated to reach. The views of responders expressing chaplains becoming godly counsellors represent an effort of contribution towards transforming the IoC. The established relationship between chaplains and chiefs through godly counsel leads us to the next organizing theme: good rapport with chiefs opens the door to the community.

8.1.4 Organizing theme: Good rapport with chiefs opens the door to the community

This organizing theme focuses on the chaplain's enduring presence at the palace and their being acquainted with proceedings at the IoC offers the opportunity of ministering to the people from a position that is likely to be of acceptance rather than rejection. Chiefs are revered and honoured according to the Ghanaian culture, and so if the chief is seen to accept the ministry of the pastor, the people would most equally accept him. The participants used words and phrases such as; 'relationships', 'consideration', 'religious tolerance', 'open doors', and 'community' to express their views.

According to this organizing theme, building a good relationship with chiefs and being considerate on religious tolerance would create an enabling environment for effective chaplaincy ministry and enhance evangelizing the community. A minister shared his experiences of how the chief of his former place of ministry felt his absence in the community development programmes when he left the place. On the contrary, a visit to Manhyia Palace of the Asante Kingdom showed that the King had more cordial relations with the

Presbyterians than AoG, which in his view was down to the latter's lack of constant visits to the palace.[22] Participants noted that:

> Any time the missionaries go to the community they try to contact the chief and have a good relationship with him because they have seen that the chief rules the people and if they want to get to the people, it can be done through the chief.[23]

> Some of the early missionaries had good relationships with traditional chiefs even though they were not Christians and because of that they were able to convert them to Christianity. Chiefs also approved missionaries' presence and guaranteed their safety as they ministered in the community.[24]

If some missionaries had good relationships with chiefs that led to their conversion, then nationals have no excuse but to seize the opportunity to engage with chiefs.

Religious tolerance was considered as one of the most essential factors needed for peaceful co-existence in a country whose constitution guarantees freedom of religion.[25] Consideration on religious tolerance was perceived as founded on respect, sharing, patience and understanding, which Christian leaders need to exhibit to have the desired results of connecting well with traditional leaders and gaining access to the people. If chaplains are able to build a good relationship with chiefs, they would have the privilege of educating traditional leaders on the biblical perspective of chieftaincy.

8.1.5 Organizing theme: Education of chiefs on biblical perspective of chieftaincy

The education of chiefs on biblical perspectives of chieftaincy[26] was certainly seen as an important factor towards transforming the IoC and participants elaborated on the need for chaplaincy to assume this responsibility. The Biblical perspectives of chieftaincy as shown from the data include first of all, the understanding that God is not

against the role of chieftaincy to provide leadership and governance to the people. Secondly, it is clear that the understanding that
ancestors may be remembered or venerated but should not be
worshiped and viewed as intermediaries to the almighty God.
Thirdly, the understanding that blood sacrifices made during
rituals were fulfilled in the ultimate sacrifice of Christ as such
should be abolished. Finally, identifying redemptive analogies in
festivals so that rituals and ceremonies linked to chieftaincy can be
ennobled to reflect biblical values. In this organizing theme, transformation was conceptualized as something that involves learning,
changing attitudes, identifying and embracing new ideas to make
an institution relevant with changing times. Participants used
words and phrases such as: 'revered', 'educate', 'biblical perspectives', 'sharing the faith', 'opportunity', and 'enlightenment' to
express their views.

These words led to identifying the basic themes: 'chieftaincy as a
revered institution' and 'opportunity to share the faith' illustrated
in Figure 8.1 of this chapter. Chapter two of this study has shown
how chieftaincy is linked to the spirit world in its beliefs and practices in rites and ceremonies that has made the people revered the
IoC. Beliefs in the 'Supreme Being – God', 'deities', and 'spirits'
provides the opportunity for the chaplain to engage chiefs in these
areas and relay biblical values on chieftaincy. Participants noted
that the changing attitude of traditional leaders toward Christianity
by accepting Christian candidates to ascend the thrones, and the
willingness to change obsolete customs and cultures offers the
church an opportunity of sending workers to palaces.[27] Furthermore, Christian chiefs who have resolved to rule with the convic-
tion of their faith are trail blazers in the course of transforming the
IoC. One participant remarked on the influence of a Christian chief:

> Nana Abonhyia is doing very well. In fact, ...he is quite influential
> and is gradually turning the people's hearts back to God. He holds
> a series of all nights with the people once a month, the whole

community and the church of Pentecost... He has also been made, I think, the secretary to the western regional house of chiefs, ...his influence is being felt.[28]

In responding to the question as to whether the church should have a policy document on Christianity and chieftaincy, all participants acknowledged that such a document was long overdue, but not too late and a step in the right direction.

> We should have position papers. We should find people to work out the modality for Christian royal families because God is reaching out to all flesh and not just to one section of people... Traditional leaders should sit together with pastors and brainstorm and see how they can make the chieftaincy institution godly with Christian principles... If we are able to have policies that can guide and help our people, then no one will be afraid to become a chief.[29]

In educating chiefs on biblical perspectives, the opportunity of sharing the faith was considered by all participants as something that should not be overlooked as it is core to the mission of the Church. A participant referred to the ministry of Paul before kings:

> Apostle Paul saw the palace as a ripe mission field. Soldiers who were constantly sent on duty to the palace and had no contact with the outside world had the opportunity of hearing the gospel whilst Paul was in the palace as a prisoner. The impact that ministers would make going there as free people would be greater.[30]

The need to share the faith as part of educating chiefs represents an effort to emphasise the ultimate goal of Christian witness which is having a personal relationship with God through Jesus Christ.[31] It is an attempt to let people make wilful choices as to whom they will serve as they deal with the inward work of grace through the teaching of God's word. It is hoped that in addition to educating chiefs, chaplaincy involvement with chieftaincy will result in changing outmoded cultural practices of the IoC.

8.1.6 Organizing theme: Changing outmoded cultural practices

The ultimate aim of transformation is having evidence of change in one way or another; and so, participants' view of chaplaincy involvement with chieftaincy will help to change outmoded cultural practices as one of the paths towards transforming the IoC. As illustrated in Figure 8.1 of this chapter, 'Christian involvement can reduce corruption' and 'no more human sacrifices' were the basic themes identified in the thematic analysis for this section. Most participants admitted that unfortunately corruption existed in the IoC because a lot of chiefs are self-centred in enriching themselves rather than thinking of developing the community.[32] Hence, the need exists to have Christians becoming chiefs and being assisted with chaplaincy ministry.

> I want to see pastors and Christians get more involved in chieftaincy because we need to push the Kingdom of God into the society through the chieftaincy.... Unless we enter in there we cannot change what we perceive as evil.[33]

> I think that Christians should be more involved in chieftaincy and those who for one reason or the other, God has put them in royal families, who have the chance to become chiefs should not shun it. The only important thing is that they should ensure that in taking up this important chieftaincy role that they do it the Christian way.[34]

All participants who called for Christian involvement in chieftaincy stressed the need to uphold Christian virtues in their roles as traditional leaders. One participant remarked:

> As a chief, I have been guided by Christian principles and my desire to satisfy Christ has influenced my dealings with the people.

Initially, they thought I was going to be like former chiefs who sold land and properties to enrich themselves but saw that I came with good intentions to help bring development to the community. My Christian belief is driving me towards being careful with money even as a lecturer and consultant.[35]

One notable influence of Christianity on chieftaincy to which participants referred was the abolishing of human sacrifices that was held in the past.

Yes, Christianity has removed a lot of negatives from the chieftaincy institution. For instance, in the past when the Asantehene died, they would have killed people but now, the legalities would not permit but they could have still done it quietly but Christianity will not permit. Those things are immoral. And also there are many things that many chiefs will not do because of their Christianity.[36]

The many other things Christian chiefs will not do due to their faith form the reasons why chaplaincy involvement in chieftaincy is needed, which leads us to the next section.

8.2 Global Theme: Calls for Chaplaincy Involvement in Chieftaincy

Participants echoed the need for chaplaincy involvement in some specific services to chieftaincy. The thematic analysis identified 'installation of Christian chiefs', 'meeting chiefs' spiritual needs' and 'partnership with chiefs for developments' as the organizing themes for this section. The figure below illustrates the thematic network[37] where codes provide the phrases in *Figure 8.2* as basic themes, leading to organizing themes in circles, on which the global theme: 'Calls for chaplaincy involvement in chieftaincy' in the triangle was anchored.

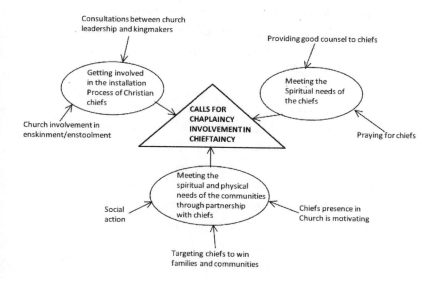

Figure 8.2: Thematic network for 'Calls for chaplaincy involvement in chieftaincy'

8.2.1 Organizing theme: Getting involved in the installation process of Christian chiefs

The participants' call for chaplaincy to have active participation during installation of a chief was based on their understanding that such roles would not only act as some of the visible signs of chief-taincy transformation, but also as credible identification of the chief's faith and support shown from the Christian community. They used words and phrases such as: - 'consultations', 'leader-ship', 'church involvement', 'enskinment/enstoolment', 'support', and 'priestly service' to express their views. All participants talked about the importance of the church having installation services for Christian chiefs in consultation with traditional leaders and kingmakers.[38]

In fact, it will be a good opportunity and will need consultation with kingmakers to explain things so that it allays their fears because the person is a Christian. It will be good if church leadership are present at the ceremony praying or laying their hands on the new chief and set him apart for the ministry to which God is putting on him.[39]

It would be most hypocritical of the church to abandon a Christian who is chosen by the traditional leaders as the new chief. This is rather the most appropriate time for the church to surround themselves around this individual and give the best of counsel and prayer and try to find out how we will work together in your coronation. The church needs to work alongside the kingmakers and play a role to make this function glorify God.[40]

Some of the Christian leaders recounted instances where Christian chiefs invited them to preach at their installation functions to which no one objected as it was peacefully done. One participant noted 'I preached the word of God during the ceremony of enskinning the new chief and after prayer wished him well as the new traditional ruler'[41]

The response from the interviews revealed that it was elected Christian chiefs who took the initiative and invited church participation at these ceremonies. A Christian chief's response to a follow up question on chaplaincy involvement with chieftaincy stated:

I think the memory that will stay with me forever is when the kingmakers with consent from family members pronounced me as a chief, I decided to make the inauguration just to show that chieftaincy is not from Satan but from God... so I decided that in my installation I would make it a biblical one. I called pastors, ministers everywhere; Presbyterian church [and] Pentecostals churches Pastors. There were about 3000 people who came for my inauguration and instead of the old-time sacrifices and what nots, I was kneeling down in front of 3000 people and these many consortiums of God's men and women pastors laid their hands on me in a park with so many chiefs watching and they praying for me to anoint me as God's child. I will never forget that.[42]

This suggests that there is the desire for church involvement in chieftaincy ceremonies and an opportunity for chaplaincy ministry not just for the installation service but constantly providing services that chiefs would need, identified in the analysis as the next organizing theme: 'Meeting the spiritual needs of the chiefs'.

8.2.2 Organizing theme: Meeting the spiritual needs of the chiefs

One of the primary reasons why respondents called for chaplaincy involvement in chieftaincy was due to the need to meet the spiritual needs of chiefs. It was obvious from their response to the questionnaire that the chaplaincy role of praying for chiefs and providing good counsel were services that chiefs should not be denied due to their beliefs. How much more appropriate it would be to provide these spiritual services to Christian chiefs. This role which has already been articulated in the previous section and considered here emphasises the level of importance that participants attach to it and the opportunity available to pursue it. This opportunity is reflected in the perception that 'most traditional rulers have seen the light and they realize that there is more glory in serving Jesus Christ'[43] than serving idols, a desire which chaplaincy should facilitate.

> ...there is a need for a pastor to always be closer to the chief to advise in a God-fearing manner and then he will also be there to pray for the development and the guidance of God for the chief and his jurisdiction and that is very, very important and it is mandatory.[44]

Participants referred to biblical examples of prophets' roles to kings to support their calls for chaplaincy involvement with chiefs to enable them to pray and provide good counsel to chieftaincy.

Definitely, in the Bible we saw somebody like Isaiah who was a chaplain to several Kings and even whether Christians are chiefs or not you still need people who will give them Godly counsel like Nathan advising David. So,... I wish that almost every chieftaincy should have a Christian chaplain who the king or the chief can confide in.[45]

The kings that Daniel and others were advising were ungodly people but the wisdom God gave them made those chiefs listen to them and it went well with them. ... so, for that one, a pastor should be involved whether the chief is a Christian or not, that is not your problem, you get involved and respect him for the fact that he is the chief or the king of the place.[46]

According to the response of those interviewed, the results of chaplaincy's constant presence at the palace to provide spiritual service to chieftaincy was seen as something that would eventually allow the church to meet the spiritual and physical needs of the communities through partnership with chiefs.

8.2.3 Organizing theme: Meeting the needs of communities through partnership with chiefs

All the participants acknowledged the importance of the church meeting the spiritual and physical needs of the communities through partnership with chiefs. Throughout the interviews, it was emphasised that the church should impact chiefs, their families and the people through the provision of spiritual and social care. The use of phrases: 'target chiefs', 'chiefs' presence in church', 'partnership with chiefs' and 'social action' were thus frequently quoted by respondents during the interviews. One Christian leader for instance noted that when the church went to evangelize a village, the chief welcomed them and said it was good they came because the church brings developments to people. He added, 'chiefs want to partner with church leaders so that their communities would develop and their people's lives would improve.'[47]

In response to the question on what it means to have a chief as a member of the church. All participants indicated that it brought growth and enhanced the public image of the church.

> The congregation increased because the chief himself is a Christian. Anywhere we are meeting, the Bulpela chief is there, so his presence there helped make the church strong. After I left, the church established a primary school and also a clinic and so the community got a lot of help from the church and the chief who is also a Christian.[48]

> It makes us accepted; it tells us that the society has accepted us. If a chief or an elder of the palace is one of us, then we can be proud of our church because we have a royal who is part of us.[49]

A Christian leader noted that his grandfather who was a Christian chief ruled for a long time and was a source of inspiration to other chiefs among the Konkombas and Saboba area. His Christian faith influenced him to protect the church and never allowed idols and fetishes in the village during his reign as chief.[50] A traditional leader also remarked that his pastor has seen that his role as a chief has not tarnished the image of the church but rather 'brought glory to God and the local church because of the testimonies that many hear of my Christian influence'.[51]

The emphasis on the church targeting chiefs to win families and communities as well as engage in social action reminds Christians of the need to be missional in fulfilling church's mission. One traditional leader commented that apart from the spiritual needs, the church can build schools and hospitals if possible, and provide scholarship schemes to help educate poor but bright students.[52]

> Chaplaincy to chiefs is very important. It is an opportunity and a privilege for the minister to get to know the chief and by so doing he can convert the chief and some of the elders to Christianity.

Ministers should not say they have nothing to do with chiefs because they are not Christians.[53]

It is evident from the above that chaplaincy ministry to chieftaincy should be considered one of the missional outreaches within the Ghanaian context where chieftaincy is still relevant. The network analysis of this section explored the themes drawn from responses of participants, who indicated that there was the need for chaplaincy involvement in chieftaincy.

8.3 Discussion and Interpretation of Data

The findings presented in this thesis point to the fact that chaplaincy would offer a valuable missional strategy for Pentecostal denominational involvements with the IoC. Christian chaplaincy to chieftaincy, like any other missional intervention can affect the shape of future traditional leadership in Ghana. As indicated in the findings, the role and call for chaplaincy involvement with chieftaincy was central in the understanding of how Christianity can impact the IoC. Here the emphasis was that responding to the calls for chaplaincy involvement with chieftaincy in order to facilitate transformation was a missional obligation that participants hope Christianity can offer. And the main contention is that while the opportunity to engage is evident, the church should be intentional with its outreach to chieftaincy.

8.3.1 Cultural conversion and transformation

A number of authors[54] have explored the new face of Christianity in Africa and how culture and chieftaincy may be transformed within Christianity. Indeed, Opuni-Frimpong argues that Akan traditional leaders can easily relate with leadership ethics and values if royal consciousness is explored in Christian leadership formation. That is why he sided with Busia with which I agree, that the Church 'must seek ways of ennobling the Akan culture, instead of distancing ourselves from our own.'[55] In explaining the conversion of culture which in this case is linked to chieftaincy, Walls states that conversion of culture is not about substitution or replacement of existing structures, but about the transforming and turning of those structures to new directions.[56] I agree with Walls' view on conversion of culture, in that it can be applicable in addressing issues relating to chieftaincy culture and Christianity. For instance, cultural forms and symbols of prayer may be used but directed to Jesus Christ instead of the ancestors.[57] Pentecostals in Ghana need to consider Walls' view on cultural conversion and redirect existing chieftaincy structures and practices to Christ, towards the path of transformation.

The church in Ghana should consider 'hybridity' when dealing with traditional rituals and ceremonies vis-à-vis Christians' ceremonial services for traditional leadership to facilitate cultural transformation. Shaw showed in his reflection on hybridity that the system worked well when introduced in the health service where Anglo and indigenous health practitioners satisfactorily offered their services together at a hospital. Shaw found out that curing rituals offered to patients did not compete with modern medical practices but was necessary to affect a more complete cure.[58] Criticism of Shaw's reflection on hybridity at the health services is that the conditions are not the same in the context of Christianity and the IoC where faith and belief systems are taken into consideration in both institutions. There is less conflict when one institution leans more on spirituality than the other. For instance, state institutions such as the House of Parliament allow traditional priests and Christian ministers to offer prayers at public events, showing the image of a combination of time-honoured customs and modern political institutions in Ghana.[59]

In a situation where there are two opposing spiritual institutions, hybridity would have conflicting issues to deal with. In this case, the solution as raised by other scholars which the researcher supports, is the conversion of an indigenous worldview and its belief and value systems.[60] Though Opuni-Frimpong admits that previous attempts to indigenize worldview conversion had been incomplete and often superficial,[61] leading to syncretism. This can be addressed with proper practical theological interventions and continued education. Nevertheless, what is good about Shaw's reflection on hybridity and marks its usefulness is just like the *O'odham ma:kai* or Papago diagnostician and the Anglo doctor co-operated in discharging their duties for a common objective of securing complete healing for patients. Traditional and Christian rituals in chieftaincy should not be in competition but rather complementary to offer their services to members who belong to both institutions. For instance, the process of identifying, nominating and appointing a chief is the sole responsibility of traditional elders guided by certain cultural norms. The chaplain's role as a prophet or agent of change may challenge unjust and ungodly traits in the process for cultural transformation but cannot and should not appear to influence the process. The chaplain as a spiritual representative and a person of peace should be neutral in the selection process. However, when the elders have duly appointed a Christian royal candidate as a chief, calls for chaplaincy involvement in the installation process is where a public coronation church service may be held for the new chief due to his faith. Participants were of the view that such a service right from the beginning of the new chief is one possible way of Christianity involvement in chieftaincy ceremonies to facilitate cultural transformation.[62]

Those engaged in chaplaincy ministry have shown how the ministry facilitates transformation in institutions with the services that members offer.[63] Chaplains as entrepreneurs in managing Multifaith Spaces adapt themselves to the organisations that they serve by adding value to it.[64] This skill is relevant for chaplaincy to the IoC as the chief's faith may either be ATR or Islam or both. I stated in chapter two that the lack of Christian engagement with chieftaincy has made Islam a viable alternative faith for chiefs through the services of Imams. It is a situation that the chaplain needs to acknowledge and be able to manage in the spirit of patience and tolerance. When the non-Christian chief sees the value of a chaplain, the objective of ministry is fulfilled. Newitt states that the role and skills of a chaplain, which broadly includes Pastoral and spiritual care, leading worship and education/training enables chaplains to walk alongside people with a view of offering the hope of transformation.[65] Similarly, Paget comments that in a world of multicultural institutions, the chaplain's role as an institutional advocate assists the organization to clarify appropriate action for suitable outcomes and right behaviour among members.[66] It could be argued that the roles of chaplaincy noted by these writers that help facilitate transformations of other institutions can be applicable to chieftaincy as well.

Furthermore, some African Christian initiatives[67] that have increased in recent times in evangelical revival offer the opportunity for chaplaincy involvement with chieftaincy. Walls goes on to say that these African initiatives that could be termed as 'a new African asceticism' which emphasise prayer and fasting, 'share with the prophet-healing churches a quest for the demonstrable presence of the Holy Spirit and direct address to the problems and frustrations of modern African urban life.'[68] Although Pentecostals consider some of these African initiatives as 'spiritual churches' with much syncretism in their practices, their emphasis on the Holy Spirit to address problems is significant to chaplaincy role with chieftaincy. Moreover, Slater notes that the benefit of chaplaincy allows the church to minister within the different social structures that the people inhabit.[69] Therefore, highlighting the importance of chaplaincy involvement with chieftaincy as a social structure to facilitate transforming the institution in fulfilling the church's mission.

8.3.2 Calls for intentional missional involvement with chieftaincy

Over the past two decades, there has been increasing calls for Christians to engage with chiefs which support the second global theme of the thematic analysis of interviewees' response in this chapter. According to Quayesi-Amakye, the CoP leadership sees how the church's witnessing space in its cultural environment increases with "Christianised" chieftaincy.[70] That is why Onyinah, who was chairman of the CoP leadership, encouraged the training of members on how to become chiefs and still maintain their Christian identity. He prays for the Spirit to grant illumination about Christian presence in chieftaincy and believes that future generations will justify this cause.[71] The call for Pentecostal chaplaincy role in chieftaincy is further supported by the lack of major Pentecostal denominational involvement as noted in chapter six of this study which also acknowledged the establishment of Christian chieftaincy groups that need the services of chaplaincies. Moreover, Asamoah-Gyadu and Quayesi-Amakye note that some Pentecostal ministers have served as "prophets" or "chaplains" to past and present political leaders in Ghana.[72] Therefore, highlighting the possibility of ministers also serving as chaplains to chiefs who are the political traditional leaders of the communities.

The Old Testament has several examples of God's servants ministering to Kings and at palaces. Jacqueline Grey in a paper to explore the concept of mission as expressed through the themes of holiness and incarnation in Isaiah 1-39, outlined the prophetic role of Isaiah to the kings of Israel and the nations of the world.[73] Grey stated that Isaiah spoke about the need for Israel and her kings to live holy lives to reflect God's mission to other nations and warned the kings of Israel not get into alliance with rulers of their neighbouring nations but place their trust in God.[74] A reflection on Grey's paper and its implications to Pentecostal ecclesiology in the context of Christianity and chieftaincy suggests that chaplains as prophets and priests should carry God's message to the IoC and must be aware of the tendency of being drawn to political correctness with God's mission in pluralist cultures.

In contrast, Yankah sees the role of chaplaincy and Christianity to chieftaincy to have dire consequences. According to Yankah, unbelievers would see Christian chiefs' attempts to purify the culture to

be hypocritical and dishonest as they participate in some ceremonies of enstoolment such as entering the stool room. He explains
that for the unbelievers, chiefs' confinement to the stool-room
means honouring ancestral spirits and deities, whilst some Christians may see that as compromise to the Christian chiefs' faith that
could undermine loyalty and trust.[75] However, with education and
enlightenment, Yankah's concerns raised above are eroding as
noted in previous chapters of this study. Nevertheless, for places
where these concerns are still raised, the introduction of chaplaincy
would facilitate education and understanding between Christianity
and chieftaincy as proposed in this study.

8.3.3 Chaplaincy ministry to chieftaincy

The primary focus of this thesis was to explore how chaplaincy
would enable Pentecostals to engage with the chieftaincy institution in Ghana. The historical account of the developments of major
Pentecostal denominations in chapter six showed lack of ministry
engagement of Pentecostals with chieftaincy. This is further
supported by the evidence from the empirical data that raised theological concerns of Pentecostals engaging with chieftaincy.
However, due to the rise of Christians becoming chiefs and even
the establishments of Christian chiefs' associations as shown in
chapter 6.2, the proposal of chaplaincy to chieftaincy in chapter five
offers Pentecostals the opportunity to missionally engage with
chieftaincy. I argued in this study that the ability for chaplaincy to
provide spiritual service outside structures considered 'sacred' is
the reason why it is suitable for the IoC. Therefore, the missional
model of chaplaincy requires that a chaplain to the IoC shall be:

- A credentialed minister of the gospel of Jesus Christ whose
  missionary role enables one to uncompromisingly
  evangelize during festivals, ceremonies, and any public
  gatherings relating to chieftaincy. Here, the chaplain is
  guided by the evangelical motivation that souls lost need to
  be saved.

- The chaplain's role as a pastor requires sharing God's love and care for chiefs, their families and members of the IoC. The chaplain provides spiritual services such as prayers, ministering God's Word, advice, moral and material support in acts of kindness to chieftaincy.
- The chaplain as prophet or agent of change challenges the unjust and ungodly existing state of affairs in chieftaincy to facilitate cultural transformation. As a social activist, the chaplain encourages leaders/chiefs to embrace justice, love mercy and despise distorting all that is right.[76]
- The chaplain's incarnational/sacramental role is inspired by Christ's example and sees their service as expressing God's presence in the place of ministry. The ministry of presence reassures Christian chiefs of spiritual support and Christian witness to nonChristian chiefs. This role is relevant for ministry in multifaith societies such as the IoC.
- The chaplain's historical-parish role requires the physical presence of chaplaincy ministry to a specific locality. The levels of chieftaincy should be taken into consideration and assign senior ministers to chiefs of higher status. Guided by the principles, practices and ministry of the credentialed and endorsed Pentecostal denomination, this role enables the chaplain to theologically reflect on some chiefly cultural practices that need ennobling and redirection to Christ.[77]

The proposal is further strengthened in the outcome of the data analysis shown in chapters seven and eight where the thematic analysis identified three global themes namely: perception of the IoC, role of chaplaincy in transforming the IoC and calls for chaplaincy involvement in chieftaincy. In a message entitled 'Africa and Her People', Garlock[78] lamented on how Africans have been segregated, discriminated against and considered outcast from society. Nevertheless, they are God's creation who deserve to hear the message of redemption.[79] In this case, Pentecostals cannot continue to perceive chieftaincy as a dark institution and left alone as outcasts to perish in practices that they have not been given any alternatives that would enable any transformation. Rather, Pentecostals have the responsibility of making every effort to provide redemptive opportunities for chieftaincy and its culture. In the light of these pieces of evidence, it is possible that the proposal of chaplaincy as a missional model would enable Pentecostal denominational involvement with the IoC.

8.4 Summary

The objective of this chapter was to continue the thematic analysis of the empirical data which identified two global themes: the role of chaplaincy in transforming the IoC and calls for chaplaincy involvement in chieftaincy. The findings in this chapter offer solutions to address the previous chapter's differences in perceptions of the IoC. Both traditional and Christian leaders agreed that it was necessary to have constant dialogue between the two institutions rather than staying apart.

Although the call for Christian involvements in chieftaincy is on the increase in recent times,[80] there are still some who reject such moves, claiming that it is hypocritical on the part of Christians to be involved with chieftaincy.[81] This rather brings us to the reason why it is necessary for Christians to engage and offer credible contextualized alternatives for Christian chiefs. The final chapter will consider some recommendations to this effect.

---

1. Attride-Stirling, 'Thematic', pp. 385-405.
2. Attride-Stirling, 'Thematic', p. 397.
3. ASRCL4, Interview, (Kumasi, 12th February, 2014).
4. NRTL2, Interview, (Tamale, 4th February, 2014).
5. ASRCL6, Interview, (Kumasi, 11th February, 2014).
6. NRCL11, Interview, (Accra, 26th January, 2014).
7. ASRCL1, Interview, (Accra, 26th January, 2014).
8. ASRTL2, Interview, (Kumasi, 13th February, 2014).
9. ASRTL4, Interview, (Kumasi, 17th February, 2014).
10. ASRCL1, Interview, (Accra, 26th January, 2014).

11. NRCL3, Interview, (Tamale, 29th January, 2014).
12. NRTL8, Interview, (Nalerigu, 2nd February, 2014).
13. ASRCL5, Interview, (Kumasi, 13th February 2014).
14. ASRCL6, Interview, (Kumasi, 11th February, 2014).
15. NRCL11, Interview, (Accra, 26th January, 2014).
16. ASRTL2, Interview, (Kumasi, 13th February, 2014).
17. See Chapter 7.2.1.
18. NRCL9, Interview, (Tamale, 7th February, 2014).
19. NRCL2, Interview, (Tamale, 4th February, 2014).
20. NRTL1, Interview, (Tamale, 29th January, 2014).
21. ASRCL4, Interview, (Kumasi, 12th February, 2014).
22. ASRCL3, Interview, (Kumasi, 13th February, 2014).
23. NRCL4, Interview, (Tamale, 31st January, 2014).
24. ASRCL6, Interview, (Kumasi, 11th February, 2014).
25. The Constitution of Ghana, <http://ghana.gov.gh/images/documents/constitution_ghana.pdf> [accessed, 4 November 2017].
26. See Chapter 9.2.1, 9.2.2 and 9.2.3.
27. ASRCL1, Interview, (Accra, 26th January, 2014).
28. NRCL2, Interview, (Tamale, 4th February, 2014).
29. NRCL7, Interview, (Kumbungu, 5th February, 2014).
30. ASRCL4, Interview, (Kumasi, 12th February, 2014).
31. Mtt. 16:26; Mark 8:36; Luke 9:25.
32. NRTL1, Interview, (Tamale, 29th January, 2014).
33. NRCL2, Interview, (Tamale, 4th February, 2014).
34. NRCL9, Interview, (Tamale, 7th February, 2014).
35. ASRTL2, Interview, (Kumasi, 13th February, 2014).
36. ASRTL5, Interview, (Kumasi, 13th February, 2014).
37. Attride-Stirling, 'Thematic', pp. 385-405.
38. NRCL9, Interview, (Tamale, 7th February, 2014).
39. NRCL13, Interview, (Tamale, 29th January, 2014).
40. ASRCL4, Interview, (Kumasi, 12th February, 2014).
41. NRCL7, Interview, (Kumbungu, 5th February, 2014).
42. NRTL1, Interview, (Tamale, 29th January, 2014).
43. NRCL11, Interview, (Accra, 26th January, 2014).
44. NRCL6, Interview, (Tamale, 30th January, 2014).
45. ASRCL1, Interview, (Accra, 26th January, 2014).
46. ASRCL6, Interview, (Kumasi, 11th February, 2014).
47. NRCL4, Interview, (Tamale, 31st January, 2014).
48. NRCL17, Interview, (Wulugu, 1st February, 2014).
49. NRCL22, Interview, (Nalerigu, 2nd February, 2014).
50. ASRCL6, Interview, (Kumasi, 11th February, 2014).
51. ASRTL4, Interview, (Kumasi, 17th February, 2014).
52. ASRTL1, Interview, (Kumasi, 17th February, 2014).
53. ASRCL6, Interview, (Kumasi, 11th February, 2014).
54. Opuni-Frimpong, *Indigenous,* (Accra: SLP, 2012), Asamoah-Gyadu, *Pentecostal Christianity,* (Oxford: RBI, 2013), Allan H. Anderson, *African Reformation: African Initiated Christianity in the 20th Century,* (Trenton, NJ: Africa World Press, Inc., 2001), Safo-Kantanka, *Christian,* (Kumasi: PPL, 1999).

55. Opuni-Frimpong, *Indigenous,* pp. 228-52.
56. Andrew F. Walls, *The Missionary Movement in Christian History: Studies in the Transmission of Faith,* (Maryknoll: Orbis Books, 2000) p. 28.
57. Safo-Kantanka, *Christian,* pp.65-67; Afriyie, 'Christ, our Perfect Sacrifice', pp. 31-33.
58. Shaw, 'Beyond Syncretism', p. 15.
59. Richard Rathborne, *Nkrumah & the Chiefs: The Politics of Chieftaincy in Ghana 1951-60,* (Accra: F Reimmer, 2000), p. xvi.
60. Smith, *Presbyterian,* (Accra: GUP, 1966), Busia, *The Position,* (London: AUP, 1957), Opuni-Frimpong, *Indigenous,* (Accra: SLP, 2012), Safo-Kantanka, *Christian,* (Kumasi: PPL, 1999).
61. Opuni-Frimpong, *Indigenous,* p. 87.
62. See Chapter 8.2.1 NRTL1, Interview, (Tamale 29th January 2014).
63. Paget and McCormack, *Chaplain,* (Valley Forge, PA: Judson Press, 2006); Threlfall-Holmes and Newitt, *Chaplain,* (London: SPKC, 2011); Slater, *Chaplaincy,* (London: SCM Press, 2015); Swift, Cobb and Todd (eds.), *Chaplaincy Studies,* (Farnham, Surrey: APL, 2015).
64. Chris Hewson and Andrew Crompton, 'Managing Multifaith', in Swift, Cobb and Todd, (eds.), *Chaplaincy Studies,* pp. 123-36.
65. Mark Newitt, 'The role and skills of a chaplain', in Threlfall-Holmes and Newitt, *Chaplain,* pp.103-05.
66. Paget and McCormack, *Chaplain,* pp. 24-25.
67. Walls, *Missionary,* p. 92.
68. Walls, *Missionary,* p. 93.
69. Slater, *Chaplaincy,* pp. 65-82.
70. Quayesi-Amakye, *Christology,* p. 220.
71. Quayesi-Amakye, *Christology,* pp. 227-31.
72. Kwabena Asamoah-Gyadu, 'African Pentecostal/Charismatic Christianity: An Overview', <https://www.lausanneworldpulse.com/themedarticles-php/464/08-2006> [accessed 9 December 2017]; Quayesi-Amakye, *Christology,* p. 234.
73. Jacqueline N. Grey, 'Holiness and Incarnation in Isaiah 1-39: the implications of Isaiah's Mission for a Pentecostal Ecclesiology', *European Pentecostal Theological Association Conference,* (Elim Conference Centre, Malvern, UK: EPTA Conference, 3-6th July, 2017), unpublished.
74. Grey, 'Holiness and Incarnation', (2017).
75. K. Yankah, *Crossroads at Ankobea,* (Accra: Asempa Publishers, 1986), pp. 51-53.
76. Mic. 3:1, 8-9 and 6:8.
77. Threlfall-Holmes and Newitt, *Chaplain,* pp. 116-122; Rryan, 'Theology and models of chaplaincy', in Caperon, Todd and Walters, *Chaplaincy,* pp. 79-93; Paget and McCormark, *Chaplain,* pp. 14-34; Walls, *Missionary Movement,* p. 28.
78. H. B. Garlock, 'Africa and Her People', *The Pentecostal Evangel, No. 1778,* (Springfield, MO: June 5, 1948), pp. 2-3 pdf, Garlock was USA Assemblies of God Missionary to Ghana and West Africa. As field secretary for Africa, he travelled across 24 African countries and visited over 100 mission stations.
79. Garlock, 'Africa', *Pentecostal Evangel,* p. 3.

80. Safo-Kantanka, *Christian*, (Kumasi: PPL, 1999), Dankwa, *Chieftaincy*, (Accra: KAF, 2004), Opuni-Frimpong, *Indigenous*, (Accra: SLP, 2012), Quayesi-Amakye, Christology, (Amsterdam: Rodopi B. V., 2013).
81. Yankah, *Croosroads*, (Accra: AP, 1986), Brobbey, *The Law*, (Accra: Wrenco Ltd, 2008).

NINE

Summary With Recommendations and Conclusion

9.0 Introduction

By combining a historical account with a qualitative research approach this dissertation has sought to explore how chaplaincy ministry would enable Pentecostal denominational involvement with the IoC in Ghana. The focus of this chapter is to summarize the key conclusions by examining the main themes of the research that were first presented as objectives in chapter one. The chapter will therefore bring in applicable conclusions, highlighting policy recommendations and action points to help in the efficient implementation of chaplaincy ministries amongst Pentecostal denominations in Ghana and to show that the study has a practical value to stakeholders. Therefore, herein lies a conclusion for the way forward for Pentecostal Christianity and the IoC in Ghana, as well as noting the key areas that need to be addressed by future researchers.

9.1 Summary of Key Conclusions

This section provides the key summary and conclusions based on the research objectives stated in chapter one.

9.1.1 Cultures of chieftainship that have limited Missionaries and Christian leaders' missional engagement with chieftaincy

In chapter three I narrated chiefly rituals and responsibilities just as sustained contact with missionaries and Christianity increased. It examines what missionaries and Christian leaders were criticising about the IoC and their reasons. Discerning that the IoC was central with the political role of chiefs lending itself with the missionaries' first contact, the initial converts should have realised the importance of relating to chiefs.[1] Having lost that momentum due to what I have termed the 'demonising' of rituals associated with tribal spirituality, Pentecostalism in particular will have to now reassert itself to make its pastors available to chiefs. Some chiefs protected and guaranteed missionaries' safety as they lived and ministered with the people,[2] whilst others were hostile to initial contacts with Christianity.[3] The study showed that some chiefs were converted to Christianity, attended church and some Pentecostal missionaries also made attempts to understand chieftaincy culture in order to minister effectively. However, the perception that chieftaincy was linked to traditional religion and ancestral worship where chiefs rely on traditional priests affected the way Christians related with the IoC.

Despite the growth of Christianity in the country and the valuable role played in changing certain aspects of chieftaincy cultural practices, the visible presence of Christianity is lacking in the Palaces, most especially from Pentecostal denominations. However, the changing perception of attitudes towards understanding and cooperation from both institutions calls for an intentional missional engagement of Christians with chieftaincy so as to provide contextual cultural alternatives for the increasing number of royals who are Christians.

9.1.2 Chaplaincy as a missional model for chieftaincy

In chapter five, it was argued that chaplaincy ministry developed as a result of people needing spiritual care whatever their faith, and especially when in crisis situations.[4] It emerged that mainline churches in Ghana used chaplaincy to engage with other institutions but not chieftaincy. These churches that have formal chaplaincy services with other institutions are not Pentecostals in practice. It was discovered that one of the prominent Kings of the Ashantis – King Prempeh became a Christian whilst in prison through the ministry of a chaplain.[5] However, this same chaplaincy ministry that existed in other institutions did not extend their services to the IoC.

Chapter five also explored the role of the African traditional priest to chieftaincy and proposed chaplaincy as a missional model for Christianity to engage with the IoC. It accounted for the theory, practice and theology of chaplaincy and its ability to function in multi-faith institutions. It assessed the purpose and potential of chaplaincy where the role of the minister would provide spiritual care for the chief and elders so as to enable the church to exert some physical presence with the IoC in a more practical way. The empirical research results have demonstrated the change of attitude that is presently coming to the fore for Pentecostals to be involved with the IoC. This is a significant paradigm shift from 30 years ago, let alone pre-independence days.

9.1.3 Pentecostals' minimal ministry with the institution of Chieftaincy

In chapter six, the thesis set out information showing the developments and growth of Pentecostal denominations in Ghana since the 1930s. In brief, it was found that these Pentecostal denominations lacked intentional missional engagement with chieftaincy. It was discovered that this lack of intentional missional engagement with the IoC was due to the perception of Christians that chieftaincy culture and practices were evil, due to its link to traditional religion of the people. This negative perception influenced the way Christians related with chieftaincy, especially among Pentecostals who advised members to avoid chieftaincy. In contrast, due to changes in perception in recent times, some Christian and traditional leaders from the data were of the view that lack of understanding had led to the negative perception of chieftaincy.[6]

The evidence showed that this changing perception has led to an increase in numbers of Christians becoming chiefs and the establishments of Christian chiefs' associations noted in chapter six. The creation of these associations across the country is a further proof that chaplaincy as a missional model to chieftaincy would have ministry opportunities in engaging traditional leaders with the gospel. In contrast to the formation of Christian chiefs' associations, some Christian leaders were of the view that the church had already lost the opportunity to engage with chieftaincy.[7]

9.1.4 Theological concerns for Christians being involved with chieftaincy

The evidence showed that Pentecostals have concerns over how Christians can effectively function as chiefs without being pressured to adhere to culture and practices that would undermine their faith.[8] Nevertheless, it was discovered that all participants wanted a situation where Christians can be involved in chieftaincy. Similar views have been supported by calls on the church to bridge the gap between Christianity and the IoC from key scholars.[9]

It was also found that 'non-Pentecostal' churches, which have engaged with chieftaincy already, in some cases embraced syncretism due to their initial approach to contextualization with chieftaincy culture and practices.[10] The concern of syncretism has over the years contributed to Pentecostals being kept apart from chieftaincy.[11] Additionally, the research showed that Pentecostals needed to review their theology and missiological approach to the IoC to facilitate the transformation and impact expected.[12] In the same way, Onyinah suggests that Christians need to actively participate in traditional leadership of the people to facilitate cultural reformation.[13]

It can be argued that theological concerns can only be addressed if the church provides contextually acceptable alternatives to chieftaincy rituals, sacrifices and ceremonies that have since prevented Christian participation. The possibility of syncretism should not keep Pentecostals and chieftaincy apart. Chaplaincy can provide an advisory role as spiritual mentors to Christians who are either in the process of becoming chiefs or already chiefs. Chaplaincy would be appropriate to provide the opportunity for ministry as well as addressing theological concerns that Pentecostals have with the IoC.

9.1.5 Chieftaincy's potential for cultural transformation

The influence of Christianity on Ghanaian traditional leadership that led to some chieftaincy cultural transformation can be traced back to the early years of missionary activities explored in chapter two. Here, it was found that chiefs who converted to Christianity such as King Prempeh of the Ashanti kingdom abolished inhumane chieftaincy cultural practices observed over the years, which subsequent chiefs who are not necessarily Christians have maintained until now. However, the data analysis in chapters seven and eight showed that there was still the need for chieftaincy cultural transformation to meet acceptable standards for Christianity as well as current social demands. It was discovered through empirical research that chaplaincy can play a role in transforming the IoC. It was found that education would improve understanding of biblical values and cultural tradition between the institutions. Additionally, the role of chaplains with chieftaincy as godly counsellors would improve relationships and help change outmoded cultural practices.

Furthermore, chapter eight reported on calls for chaplaincy involvement in chieftaincy in the installation process of Christian traditional leaders. The palace chaplains who have built good relationships with the chiefs can lead consultations between church leadership and kingmakers to facilitate such ceremonies, resulting in chieftaincy cultural transformation. It was also suggested that chaplains' presence in palaces would enable them to meet the spiritual needs of chiefs, their families, the community and also in partnership with traditional leaders to meet the physical needs of the community.

9.2 Fulfilling the Objective and Answering the Research Question.

In fulfilment of the objective of this study and answering the research question - *'How would chaplaincy enable Pentecostal denominational involvement with the institution of chieftaincy?'* - the data and literature reveal that Pentecostals do not have intentional missional engagement with the IoC, and thus chaplaincy ability to function outside church structures and in multifaith societies[14] would facilitate such engagement. The missional model of chaplaincy in this research provides ministry opportunities with the IoC and therefore, needs Pentecostal denominational leadership support to effectively facilitate its implementation.[15] Theologically, this research was able to make some sense with issues that Pentecostal were criticising the IoC by relating it to God's mission to the world and redemptive analogies in chieftaincy.[16] Biblically, Christian chiefs saw their role as God ordained, related with Old Testament kingship and called on the church to actively engage with the IoC (e.g. NRTL1, ASRTL2 and NRTL8). The establishment of Christian chiefs associations enable members to maintain their relationship with God while calling on the church to actively engage with the IoC.[17]

Based on the literature, data analysis in chapters seven, eight and the conclusions drawn above, this section now highlights some of the key recommendations that need to be implemented to enhance chaplaincy involvement with the IoC in Ghana. Pentecostal denominations would thus consider the following key aspects:

9.2.1 The need for Biblical alternatives as seen in the data

Firstly, it is recommended that Pentecostals should consider Biblically based alternatives appropriate for the IoC because most of the respondents, especially the traditional leaders, did not see the church provide solutions to address any theological concerns. Such Biblical alternatives should include:

- Identifying redemptive analogies in festivals for continual celebrations in thanksgiving to God
- Ennoble chieftaincy rituals observed in burials, enstoolment/enskinment or coronation to reflect Christ
- Forms of prayer may vary but should be offered through Jesus Christ who is our great ancestor, mediator and high priest
- Stools, skins and other objects may be used as symbols and ancestors may be remembered and celebrated but a change in worldview and belief must be stressed that these objects do not contain the spirits of the ancestors, have no influence over the living and should not be worshiped
- Establish prayer rooms and intercessors in place of shrines and altars of idols.

The evidence from the study showed that Church members were rather told of how chieftaincy was associated with traditional religion and for that reason, should avoid any form of participation.[18] Pentecostals should recognize the fact that chieftaincy is part of the customs, culture and traditional governance of the people.[19] In this regard an understanding of the biblical context of ascertaining types of leadership to determine the feasibility of contextualization with existing frameworks taken as resources rather than challenges. It can be argued that, from a missional point of view there should be alternatives for strong cultural practices and structures instead of antagonism.

A good example of positive use of existing culture is the redemptive analogies of *Odwira* festival of the Akans and Old Testament festivals of priests' consecration, the day of atonement and the feast of the first fruits.[20] Similarly, Marfo writes on the significance of altars and sacrifices as important elements in the worship of God in the life of the patriarchs.[21] Marfo also states that although Ghanaian traditional rituals and sacrifices have similarities with Old Testament sacrifices in the use of animals and blood, they differ in the belief.[22] It can be argued that the differences in belief that Marfo identified and evidenced in this research, further offers the Church the need to constantly engage with the people with biblical truths for redemption. In this case, the church in Ghana has the advantage of using what traditional leaders are familiar with and lead them to the Christian way of doing things.[23]

Safo-Kantanka suggests and I agree that Paul's attitude and practices in his evangelism provides us with a model to follow in dealing with Christians' involvement with chieftaincy.[24] In the context of evangelism Paul expressed his motivation to be with different groups, in defending the truth Paul was prepared to make some concessions at the Jerusalem Council, Paul accepted the circumcision of Timothy but Titus was not compelled to be circumcised, Paul observed the purification rite in Jerusalem and yet held convictions over and gave instruction about food offered to idols.[25] Similarly, Paul's ability to adapt to win people of different backgrounds to Christ challenges the church in Ghana to bridge gaps that exist between Christianity and the IoC. In this case, if Jews adapted to purification rites, ceremonies and festivals, and the church in the West such as the British Monarchy has adapted to coronation of kings and queens, what guidance can the church in Ghana give Christians chiefs who have rites, ceremonies and festivals to observe?

Therefore, it is recommended that the church should seriously review its missiology in order to contextually adapt to the Ghanaian society. Such missiological reviews should be handled by mature theologians of the denomination who would discuss policy changes within the context of their ecclesiastical tradition. If the scriptures admonish the church to pray for kings and all those in authority,[26] how advantageous it will be if these people in authority are Christians.

9.2.2 Developing a theology of chieftaincy

Secondly, it is recommended that the church in Ghana should develop a theology of chieftaincy using mature theologians of its denomination in consultation with traditional leaders. The research showed there are differences in culture and practices between the north and south of the country, and so one prescription cannot fit all. Nevertheless, basic Christian principles should guide any leadership role. A theology of chieftaincy should include:

- Acknowledging the rich cultural heritage within the IoC for Christians to ennoble in order to reflect Christ.
- Christian royal candidates for chieftaincy must inform church leaders their intention to accept traditional leadership for advice and spiritual support. They must be convinced that God has called them to serve in that capacity. They must make their intentions to rule with their faith clear to traditional leaders right from the beginning.
- The Lordship of Jesus Christ and the power of the Holy Spirit made available for committed Christians must be emphasized to address the constant fear of evil forces, demons, witches and curses.
- A demand for a high standard of leadership roles expressed in righteousness, justice, mercy, self-sacrifice, and love for the people.

In the theology of chieftaincy, God's standard of righteousness should only be a guide for Christian traditional leaders but not enforced on members of the IoC who are not Christians. Paul states that the righteousness of God is revealed through faith in Jesus Christ to all and on all who believe, and that by His grace through the redemption that is Jesus Christ, we are justified freely.[27] When traditional leaders understand Christian candidates believe in God's standard of righteousness, it is sufficient to not enforce other forms of sacrifices that would compromise Christianity. The message to support this view is that Christians do not need to offer sacrifices to the ancestors anymore because Christ, who is our great ancestor, has offered the once-for-all sacrifice to God by his death on the cross and resurrection.[28]

Following righteousness is the chief's responsibility of upholding justice, treating all cases before him without any hint of discrimination, fear or undue influence.[29] The Christian chief should show mercy when needed and guided by love not fear nor asserting aggressive authority throughout his reign. He should be willing to sacrifice some material gain for the welfare of his people. There was the perception that some become chiefs for the material benefits.[30] It is also recommended that this document on the theology of chieftaincy should contain God's covenant relationship with the chief as well as the chief's covenant relations with the people and their culture. In dealing with cultural hindrances, Dankwa III comments on the issues of mysticism and outmoded customs of chieftaincy that:

> Before we can decide that a particular traditional act or rite is anti-Christian, we must be sure that the roots of such rites are well grounded in knowledge and understanding and that we have overcome the problem of meaning that usually surrounds the particular rite, to enable us either to improve upon it or condemn it as outmoded and unfit for Christian use.[31]

Therefore, an outlined policy of the chief's covenant relation with the people's culture will help address some of the issues concerning outmoded or condemned rites. My position is that the theology of chieftainship is for Christian chiefs and should not be enforced on the IoC. It should be applied to all levels of the IoC leadership roles that Christian candidates are qualified and appointed to serve.

9.2.3 A theology of anointing for leadership – Kings

Thirdly, it is recommended that the Pentecostal denominations in Ghana acknowledge the leadership role of chiefs and kings in the society and develop a theology of anointing for the IoC. One of the key findings of the study was the need for the church to actively participate in the proceedings leading to the appointment of a chief. Therefore, a theology of anointing for leadership/kings would enable the church to organize a public coronation service for appointed Christian chiefs and with a chaplain should outline guidelines for Christians considering accepting appointments with the IoC. The Old Testament gives us a pattern of how kings were anointed.[32] These were physical ritual ceremonies to confirm God's choice on a person for a particular task. Isaiah spoke of a spiritual anointing on God's servant which was fulfilled in Jesus Christ.[33] Similarly, Joel prophesied the outpouring of God's Spirit on all people for service.[34] In the New Testament, Luke shows how Jesus emphasized the need to seek this spiritual anointing that he later referred to as *the Promise of the Father*, fulfilled on *the Day of Pentecost*.[35] One of the cardinal teachings of Pentecostals is the need for believers' to seek the baptism of the Holy Spirit for Christian living and service to the Lord.[36]

In addition, Pentecostals have developed systems of recognizing God's call to different areas of Christian service in leadership roles. These roles are publicly recognized in ceremonies where candidates are anointed and prayed for. Such should be applied to chieftaincy as a call to leadership. The following serves as a guide:

- It should state what spiritual and physical support the church can offer members seeking to serve in traditional leadership roles.
- The document should include how ceremonial services for newly appointed chiefs would be conducted for public coronations. The Officiating ministers for such occasions should correspond to the level of traditional leadership in question. For instance, Regional Superintendents to officiate service for community chiefs and General Superintendent or his representative to handle services relating to divisional and paramount chiefs.
- Forms and symbols of anointing such as 'anointing oil' may be determined by each Pentecostal denomination with laying of hands and prayers of consecration by church leaders.
- The consecration service should include a charge on the elected chief to uphold the values of his faith in the discharge of chiefly duties.
- A pronouncement of God's blessings, prosperity and peace on the chief's reign, the people, land and neighbours.

It is important that Pentecostals should not just critique and question chieftaincy, but to support it as a leadership role for traditional governance and community development. The proposal of 'hybridity'[37] stated in the previous chapter would enable the church to provide public coronation for Christian chiefs as one of the necessary sides of the coin when dealing with traditional rituals and ceremonies vis-à-vis Christians' ceremonial services for traditional leadership. Whilst the legitimate authority to appoint chieftainship is the sole responsibility of Kingmakers of each traditional council, the church has the spiritual responsibility to anoint and show public support for the Christian who assumes the role of traditional leadership.

9.2.4 The role of Chaplains as prophets and priests to chiefs

Fourthly, one of the primary objectives of this study was the proposal of chaplaincy as a missional model for Pentecostal denominational involvement with the IoC. It is evident from the literature and data gathered that such a proposal is necessary. For that reason, it is recommended that chaplains should consider their role as prophets and priests to the IoC. The priestly service is reflected in the pastoral, incarnational or sacramental and historical-parish roles of the proposed missional model of chaplaincy; whilst the prophetic service is seen in the missionary and the prophetic or agent of change roles. In the Old Testament, prophets carried God's message to leaders to instruct, rebuke and warn.[38] The prophetic is classified as one of the ministry gifts that Jesus Christ has given to the Church.[39] God calls both Israel and the church into being a priesthood and holy nation.[40] The Priestly role in both the Old and New Testament is also given to those specifically called to perform religious duties. Due to ATR, the prophetic and priestly services are familiar to chiefs and these terms could be considered as the preferred way of providing religious support for Christians with the IoC. Chaplains, conscious of their role, would help Chiefs uphold the integrity of their calling within and beyond the related denomination that they represent as servants of God. As a guide, these roles may be supported by having a code of ethics for chaplains serving with the IoC suitable for institutional chaplaincy[41] and adapted as follows:

- A promise to abide and hold in the trust the direction and practices of the church
- A promise to follow the vision and requirements needed to maintain credentials with the church
- A promise to serve in a pluralistic environment like the IoC, recognizing the rights of other faiths and providing Christian ministry to people entrusted to my care
- A promise to build healthy relations with colleagues and

maintain a disciplined ministry for personal and professional development

- A promise to hold in confidence all privilege and confidential communications
- A promise not to discriminate in the discharge of my duties, not to be involved in chiefly matters outside the remit of my duties but to be a person of peace.
- A promise not to violate others unethically, but to love God and promote the integrity of the ministry.

It is recommended that chaplains should sense the need of being called to this role and be aware of the dangers of manipulations and spiritual encounters. It is further recommended that there should be a manual for chaplaincy with the IoC as it is done with other institutions that have chaplaincy ministries. This document should outline chaplains' ethical relationships with traditional leadership, guidance on ceremonies, rituals, festivals and other public events held at the palace with Christian involvement. Such a document should reflect the ecclesiological tradition of the denomination, taking into consideration the different cultural traditions of chieftaincy in the country. This dissertation prescribes a manual suitable for the church in Ghana.

It is recommended that training for chaplaincy with the IoC be taught at the Bible Seminaries. According to Frimpong-Manso, the training of workers became very necessary because missionaries were handicapped in communication with the local people and encountered cultural barriers as they ministered. 'Therefore, local people were trained to fulfil those roles in the local cultural context of the people.'[42] Though some customs of the people among whom Pastors minister, such as child-naming, funeral celebration, contracting traditional marriages, chieftaincy issues and how to visit the chief's palace are not studied at the Bible Colleges.[43] Hence, there is the need to review the theological disciplines taught at Bible colleges in Ghana.

9.3 Future Direction and Conclusion

This research project focused on Pentecostalism and the IoC in two regions in Ghana to ascertain how Pentecostals have engaged with traditional leadership who are historically responsible for governance and custodians of the culture of the people. It proposed chaplaincy as a missional model that would facilitate engagement with chieftaincy to enhance Christian presence in the palace and encouraged members participation in traditional leadership.

Further studies using the same selection criteria in the other regions of the country and the nations in Africa would contribute to the current literature on Christianity and the IoC in particular and missional activities in general and provide additional information for leaders of both institutions to effectively serve their people. There is the need to increase the sample size to include church members and unbelievers in order to provide a fairer reflection on Christianity and chieftaincy. This study relied mostly on those in leadership roles of both institutions and within the methodology of the research project for the doctoral work. Further studies might consider:

1. A comparative study on how chaplaincy to the institution of Chieftaincy is perceived and practiced by Pentecostals and other Christians in Ghana. There is also the need to explore the role of female chaplains and Queen mothers to ensure how women could be appropriately placed to contribute towards the development and growth of Christian presence with chieftaincy.
2. A study on chaplaincy from other para-church organisations and from the Muslim Community with the IoC.
3. A comparative study on Christian chiefs' leadership perspectives versus traditional leadership.
4. A case study on a Christian chief whose leadership has

greatly impacted the community and enhanced Christian witness in the IoC.

5. An in-depth study on chieftaincy culture, rituals, sacrifices, ceremonies, festivals and ethical decision-making for Christian chiefs.

The studies presented thus far provide evidence from the literature and data analysis that can be concluded that there is the need for Christianity to engage with the IoC in Ghana. The perceived gap that exists between both institutions has narrowed in recent times due to Christian influence and modern civilisation. Irrespective of how wide or narrow the gap may be, it is important that this gap be bridged to allow the involvement of Pentecostal Christian royal families in traditional leadership. For this reason, the proposal of chaplaincy as a missional model for the IoC is necessary to have Pentecostal Christian presence at the palace and encompass traditional leadership in the frame of God's mission. When church leaders in Ghana embrace their responsibility to provide theological solutions to challenges facing members, it will be a step in the right direction to address some of the mistakes that have marred the efforts of the African church till now.

1. Dankwa, *Chieftaincy*, (Accra: KAF, 2004), Opuni-Frimpong, *Indigenous*, (Accra: SLP, 2012), Frimpong-Manso, 'Origins', (Glyndwr University, 2014).
2. Frimpong-Manso, 'Origins', (Gyndwr University, 2014).
3. Muller, *Religion*, (Zurich: LVG & Co., 2013).
4. Paget and McCormack, *Chaplain*, p. 4.
5. Boahen, Acheampong, et al., *History*, pp. 28 and 29.
6. See Chapters seven and eight.
7. ASRCL5, Interview, (Kumasi, 13th February, 2014).
8. See Chapter 7.3.
9. Safo-Kantanka, *Christian*, (Kumasi: PPL, 1999), Opuni-Frimpong, *Indigenous*, (Accra: SLP, 2012), Quaysie-Amakye, *Christology*, (Amsterdam: Rodopi, 2013), Dankwa, *Chieftaincy*, (Accra: KAF, 2004).
10. ASRCL5, Interview, (Kumasi, 13th February 2014), NRCL5, Interview, (Tamale, 7th February 2014).
11. NRCL2, Interview, (Tamale, 4th February 2014), ASRCL5, Interview, (Kumasi, 13th February 2014).

12. Dankwa III, *Chieftaincy*, (Accra: KAF, 2004), Quayesi-Amakye, *Christology*, p. 221, Frimpong-Manso, 'Origins', (Glyndwr University: 2014).
13. Quayesi-Amakye, *Christology*, p. 221.
14. Caperon, Todd, and Walters, *Chaplaincy*, (2018); Threlfall-Holmes and Newitt, *Chaplain*, (20110; Slater, *Chaplaincy Ministry*, (2015).
15. See Chapters 5.3, 5.4 and 6.4.
16. Bosch, *Transforming Mission*, (2016); Safo-kantanka, *Christian*, (1993); See Chapter 3.6.
17. See Chapters 6.3 and 8.2.
18. Smith, *Presbyterian*, pp. 100, 255 and 273.
19. Dankwa, *Chieftaincy*, p. 1.
20. Sarfo-Kantanka, *Christian*, pp. 22-25.
21. Marfo, *Christian*, pp. 8-22.
22. Marfo, *Christian*, pp. 37-44.
23. Acts 17:22, 23.
24. Safo-Kantanka, *Christian*, pp. 61-64.
25. 1 Cor. 3:19-23; Acts 15; 16:1-5; Gal. 2:3; Acts 21 and 1 Cor. 8.
26. 1 Tim. 2:1-4.
27. Rom. 3:21-26.
28. Safo-Kantanka, *Christian*, p. 61.
29. Mic. 3:1, 9.
30. ASRTL2, Interview, (Kumasi, 13th February 2014).
31. Dankwa, *Chieftaincy*, pp. 86, 110.
32. 1 Sam. 10:1, 16:13; 2 Sam. 2:4 and 5:3.
33. Isa. 61:1-2; Luke 3:22, 4:18-21.
34. Joel 2:28-29.
35. Luke 24:49; Acts 1:4-8; 2:14.
36. Anderson, *Pentecostalism*, (Cambridge: CUP, 2014); Anderson, *To the Ends*, (Oxford: OUP, 2013); Kalu, *African Pentecostalism*, (Oxford: OUP, 2008); Larbi, *Pentecostalism*, (Accra: CPCS, 2001) AoGG, 'AoG Statement of Fundamental Truths', https://www.agghana.org/fundamental-truth/ [accessed, 13th March, 2020].
37. Shaw, 'Beyond Syncretism', p. 6.
38. Isa. 1-39.
39. Eph. 4:11.
40. Exod. 19:6; 1 Pet. 2:9.
41. EFCA, *Chaplains Handbook*, (Commission: 2013), https://www.efca.org [accessed 15 July 2019].
42. Frimpong-Manso, 'Theological', p. 162-75.
43. Frimpong-Manso, 'Theological', p. 162.

Bibliography

Books

Adotei, I. K., and Awedoba, A. K., (eds.), *Chieftaincy in Ghana: Culture, Governance and Development*, (Accra: Ghana, Sub-Saharan Publishers, 2009).

Amenumey, D. E. K., *Ghana A Concise History from Pre-Colonial Times to the 20th Century*, (Accra: Woeli Publishing Services, 2011).

Amoateng-Boahen, G., *Integral Pastoral Care in Ghana*, (Amazon, GB: Xlibris, <www.Xlibris.com> 2016).

Anderson, A. H., African Reformation: African Initiated Christianity in the 20th Century, (Trenton, NJ: Africa World Press, Inc., 2001).

_____, To the Ends of the Earth: Pentecostalism and the Transformation of World Christianity, (Oxford: Oxford University Press, 2013).

_____, *An Introduction to Pentecostalism*, 2nd ed. (Cambridge: Cambridge University Press, 2014).

Anderson, A., Bergunder, M., Droogers, A., and van der

Laan, C., (eds.), *Studying Global Pentecostalism: Theories and Methods*, (Los Angeles CA: University of California Press, 2010).

Arhin, K., *Traditional Rule in Ghana: Past and Present*, (Accra: Sedco Publishing Limited, 1985).

Asamoa-Gyadu, J. K., *Contemporary Pentecostal Christianity*, (Oxford: Regnum Books International, 2013).

Asante, E., 'The relationship between the chieftaincy institution and Christianity in Ghana', in Adotei, I. K., and Awedoba, A. K., (eds.), *Chieftaincy in Ghana: Culture, Governance and Development*, (Accra, Ghana: Sub-Saharan Publishers, 2006).

Baker, P., *Peoples, Languages, and Religion in Northern Ghana – A Preliminary Report*, (Accra, Ghana: Evangelism Committee and Asempa Publishers, 1986).

Barnett, M., and Martin, R., (eds.), *Discovering the Mission of God*, (Downers Grove, Illinois: IVP Academic, 2012).

Bazeley, P., & Jackson, K., *Qualitative data analysis with NVivo. 2nd ed.* (London: SAGE, 2013).

Bediako, K., Jesus in Africa: The Christian Gospel in African History and Experience, (Carlisle: Paternoster Publishing, 2000).

Birikorang, E., 'Annual Report by the Regional Superintendent', *Assemblies of God Ghana: Greater Accra West Region*, (Accra: AoGG, February 2020).

Boahen, A. A., Akyeampong, E., Lawler, N., McCaskie, T. C., & Wilks, I., (eds.), *'The History of Ashanti Kings and the whole country itself' and other Writings by Otumfuo, Nana Agyeman Prempeh I*, (Oxford: Oxford University Press, 2014).

Bosch, D. J., Transforming Mission: Paradigm Shifts in Theology of Mission, New ed. (Maryknoll, NY: Orbis Books, 1991).

Bosch, D. J., (ed.), Transforming Mission: Paradigm Shifts in Theology of Mission, (Maryknoll, NY: Orbis Books, 2016).

Boyce, W., *Statistics of Protestant Missionary Society 1872-1873*, (London: W. Nicholas 1874).

Brobbey, S. A., *The Law of Chieftaincy in Ghana*, (Accra: Advanced Legal Publications, 2008).

Brown, C. G., *The death of Christian Britain, 2nd ed.* (London: Routledge, 2009)

Buah, F. K., *West Africa since AD1000*, (Hong Kong: Macmillan Publishers, 1977).

Busia, K. A., *The Position of the Chief in Modern Political System of Ashanti*, (Oxford: Oxford University Press for the International African Institute, 1951).

Caperon J., Todd, A., and Walters J., (eds.), *A Christian Theology of Chaplaincy*, (London: Jessica Kingsley Publishers, 2018).

Charmaz, K., Constructing Grounded Theory: A Practical Guide through Qualitative Analysis, (London: Sage, 2006).

Corbin, J., and Strauss, A., *A Basics of Qualitative Research*, 3rd ed. (Los Angeles: Sage, 2008).

Cox, J. L., A Guide to the Phenomenology of Religion: Key Figures, Formative Influences and Subsequent Debates (London: T&T Clark, 2006).

Cox, J. L., An Introduction to Phenomenology of Religion, (London: Bloomsbury, 2009).

Creswell, J. W., Qualitative inquiry and research design: choosing among five approaches, 3rd ed. (Thousand Oaks, CA: Sage, 2013).

Dankwa III, O. A., *The Institution of Chieftaincy in Ghana – the future*, (Accra: Konrad Adenauer Foundation, 2004).

Dantzig, A. V., *Forts and Castles of Ghana*, (Accra: Sedco Publishing, 1980).

Debruner, W. H., *A History of Christianity in Ghana*, (Accra: Waterville Publishing House, 1967).

Denscombe, M., *The Good Research Guide: For Small Scale*

Research Projects, (Buckingham, Philadelphia: Open University Press, 1998).

Dickson, K. B., and Benneh, G., *A New Geography of Ghana,* Revised edn (Harlow, Essex: Longman Group UK Limited, 1995).

Ela, J., Brown, J. P., *My faith as an African,* (Eugene, OR: Wipf and Stock Publishers, 2009).

Flett, J. G., *The Witness of God,* (Grand Rapids, Michigan: William B. Eerdmans Publishing Company, 2010).

Flick, U., *An Introduction to Qualitative Research,* 3rd ed. (London: Sage, 2006).

Foli, R., Christianity in Ghana: A Comparative Church Growth Study, (Accra: Trust Publications, 2006).

____, *Towards Church Growth in Ghana,* (Accra: Trust Publishers, 1996).

Gadzekpo, S. K., *History of Ghana,* (Accra: EPP Books Services, 2005).

Gehman, R. J., *African Traditional Religion in Biblical Perspective,* (Nairobi: East African Educational Publishers Limited, 1989).

Ghana Statistical Service, *Population and Housing Census 2010,* (Accra, Ghana: Sankofa Press Limited, 2012).

Gifford, P., *Ghana's New Christianity: Pentecostalism in a Globalizing Economy,* (Bloomington & Indianapolis: Indian University Press, 2004).

Gillham, B., *Research Interviewing: The Range of Techniques,* (Maidenhead: Open University Press, 2005).

Giorgi, A., The Descriptive Phenomenological Method in Psychology: A Modified Husserlian Approach, (Pittsburgh, PA: Duquesne University Press, 2009).

Glaser, B. and Strauss A., The Discovery of Grounded Theory: Strategies for Qualitative Research, (New York: Aldine, 1967).

Glasser, A. S., *Kingdom and Mission,* (Pasadena, CA: Fuller Theological School of Mission, 1989).

Graham, E., Walton, H., & Ward, F., *Theological Reflection Methods* 2nd ed. London: SCM Press, 2019).

Groves, C. P., *The Planting of Christianity in Africa*, Vol. 1 (London: Lutterworth, 1954).

Gutierrez, Sr. N., 'Cultural Competencies', in Roberts S. B., (ed.), *Professional Spiritual & Pastoral Care: A Practical Clergy and Chaplain's Handbook,* (Woodstock, Vermont: Skylight Paths Publishing, 2016), pp. 407-20.

Gyekye, K., Tradition and Modernity – Philosophical reflections on the African Experience, (New York: Oxford University Press, 1997).

Hackman, M. Z., & Johnson, C. E., *Leadership: A communication perspective*, (Long Grove, IL: Waveland Press, 2000).

Hewson, C., and Crompton, A., 'Managing Multifaith', in Swift, C., Cobb, M., and Todd, A., (eds.), *A Handbook of Chaplaincy Studies: Understanding Spiritual Care in Public Places*, (Farnham, Surrey: Ashgate, 2015).

Hiebert, P. G., *Anthropological Insights for Missionaries*, (Grand Rapids, Michigan: Baker Book House, 1985).

Hittleman, D. R., & Simon, A. J., *Interpreting educational research: An introduction for consumers of research*, (Upper Saddle River, NJ: Prentice Hall, 1997).

Holloway, I., and Wheeler, S., *Qualitative Research in Nursing and Healthcare*, [3rd edn] (Oxford, UK: Blackwell Publishing Company, 2002).

Huppenbauer, D., 4th edn *Von Kyebi nach* (Kumasi: Basel, 1905).

Isichei, E., *A History of Christianity in Africa: From Antiquity to the Present*, (London: Society for Promoting Christian Knowledge, 1995).

Johnstone, P., Mandryk, J., and Johnstone, R., (eds.), *Operation World: 21st Century Edition*, (Milton Keynes: Authentic Media, 2005).

Kalu, O., *African Pentecostalism: An Introduction*, (New York: Oxford University Press, 2008).

Kpobi, D. N. A., 'African Chaplains in Seventeenth Century West Africa' in Ogbu Kalu, *African Christianity: an African story*, (Trenton, NJ: African World Press, 2007), pp. 140-171 pdf.

Kraft, C. H., *Christianity in Culture*, (Maryknoll, NY: Orbis Books, 2002).

Kristensen, W. B., 1960. *The Meaning of Religion: Lectures in the Phenomenology of Religion*, trans. John B. Carman. (The Hague: Martinus Nijhoff, 1960).

Kumar, R., *Research Methodology*, (London: Sage Publications Inc. 1999).

Kwadwo, O., *An Outline of Asante History*, (Kumasi: CITA press Ltd., 2009).

Kvale, S., and Brinkmann, S., Interviews: Learning the Craft of Qualitative Research Interviewing, 2nd ed. (London: SAGE, 2009).

Langdridge, D., Phenomenological psychology: theory, research and method, (Harlow: Pearson Prentice Hall, 2007).

Larbi, E. K., Pentecostalism: The Eddies of Ghanaian Christianity, (Accra: CPCS, 2001).

Lentz, C., and Nugent, P., (eds.), *Ethnicity in Ghana. The Limits of Invention*, (London: Macmillan Press, 2000).

Liamputtong, P., *Qualitative Research Methods*, (Oxford: Oxford University Press, 2013).

Lincoln, Y., and Guba, E., *Naturalistic inquiry*, (Newbury Park, CA: Sage, 1985).

Luzbetak, L. J., The Church and Culture: New Perspectives in Missiological Anthropology, 2nd ed. (New York: Orbis Books, 1989).

Marfo, E. K., *The Christian Faith & Traditional Rituals*, (Kumasi: Ed-Jay Services Ltd, 2009).

Mbiti, J. S., *Introduction to African Religion*, 2nd ed. (Oxford: Heinemann Educational Publishers, 1991).

Merriam, S. B., *Qualitative Research: A Guide to Design and Implementation*, (San Francisco, CA: John Wiley and Sons, 2009).

Moreau, A. S., *Contextualization in World Missions*, (Grand Rapids, MI: Kregel Publications, 2012).

Moustakas, C., *Phenomenological Research Methods*, (London: SAGE Publications, 1994).

Muller, L., *Religion and Chieftaincy in Ghana*, (Zweigniederlassung Zürich: Lit Verlag GmbH & Co. KG Wien, 2013).

Nelson, J. M., 2009 'Phenomenological approaches to religion and spirituality', In Nelson J. M., (ed.), *Psychology, Religion, and Spirituality*, (Springer, New York, NY: 2009), pp. 103-142.

Newbigin, L., *One Body, One Gospel, One World: The Christian Mission Today*, (London: International Missionary Council, 1958).

Newitt, M., 'The role and skills of a chaplain', in Threlfall-Holmes, M., and Newitt, M. (eds.), *Being a Chaplain*, (London: SPCK, 2011).

Nukunya, G. K, *Tradition and Change in Ghana: An Introduction to Sociology*, 2nd edn (Accra: Ghana University Press, 2003).

O'Donovan, W., *Biblical Christianity in Modern Africa*, (Carlisle, UK: Paternoster Press, 2000).

Opuni-Frimpong, K., Indigenous Knowledge & Christian Missions: Perspectives of Akan Leadership Formation on Christian Leadership Development, (Accra: SonLife Press, 2012).

Paget, N. K., and McCormack, J. R., *The Work of the Chaplain*, (Valley Forge, PA: Judson Press, 2015).

Paterson, M., 'Supervision, Support and Safe Practice', in Swift, C., Cobb, M., and Todd, A., (eds.), *A Handbook of*

Chaplaincy Studies, (Farnham, Surrey UK: Ashgate, 2015), pp. 149-59.

Patton, M. Q., *How to Use Qualitative Methods in Evaluation*, (Newbury Park, CA: Sage Publications Inc., 1987).

Patton, M. Q., Qualitative research and evaluation methods: integrating theory and Practice, 4th ed. (London: SAGE, 2015).

Peel, J. D. Y., 'History, culture and comparative method: a West African puzzle', in Holy, L., (ed.), *Comparative Anthropology*, (Oxford: Basil Blackwell, 1987), pp. 88-118.

Priddy M., General (ed.), *Introducing the Missional Church*, (Grand Rapids, Michigan: Baker Books, 2009).

Otumfuo Opoku Ware Jubilee Foundation, *A Guide to Manhyia Palace Museum*, (Kumasi: Gyabious Printing Press, 2003)

Quayesi-Amakye, J., Christology and Evil in Ghana: Towards a Pentecostal Public Theology, (Amsterdam: Rodopi B. V., 2013).

Rathborne, R., Nkrumah & the Chiefs: The Politics of Chieftaincy in Ghana 1951-60, (Accra: F Reimmer, 2000).

Reppenhagen, M., and Guder, D. L., 'The Continuing Transformation of Mission: David J. Bosch's Living Legacy 1991-2011', in Bosch, D. J., *Transforming Mission: Paradigm Shifts in Theology of Mission*, 20th Anniversary ed. (Maryknoll, NY: Orbis Books, 2011), pp. 4-11 and 533-56.

Rheenen, G. V., *Communicating Christ in Animistic Contexts*, (Pasadena, CA: William Carey Library, 1991).

_____, *Contextualization and Syncretism: Navigating Cultural Currents*, (Pasadena, CA: Evangelical Missiological Society, 2006).

Richards, L., Handling Qualitative Data: A Practical Guide, 3rd ed. (London: SAGE, 2015).

Roxburgh, A. J., and Boren, M. S., (ed.), *Introducing the Missional Church: What It Is, Why It Matters, How to*

Become One, (Grand Rapids, Michigan: Baker Books, 2009).

Ryan, B., A Very Modern Ministry: Chaplaincy in the UK, (London: Theos, 2015).

Ryan, B., 'Theology and models of chaplaincy', in Caperon, J., Todd, A., and Walters, J., *A Christian Theology of Chaplaincy,* (London: Jessica Kingsley Publishers, 2018), pp. 79-100.

Safo-Kantanka, O., *Can a Christian become a Chief?* (Kumasi: Payless Publications Ltd. 1999).

Sarpong, P. K., *Libation,* (Accra: Anansesem Publication, 1996).

_____, *The Sacred stools of the Akan,* (Accra: Ghana Publishing Corporation, 1971).

Silverman, D., *Qualitative Research: Issues in Theory, Methods and Practice,* 3rd ed. (Los Angeles, CA: Sage Publications, 2011).

Slater, V., Chaplaincy Ministry and the Mission of the Church, (London: SCM Press, 2015).

Smith, J. A., Flowers, P., Larkin, M., Interpretative phenomenological analysis: Theory, Method, and Research, (Los Angeles: SAGE, 2009).

Smith, N., *The Presbyterian Church of Ghana – 1935-1960,* (Accra: Ghana University Press, 1966).

Stogdill, R. M., & Bass, B. M., Stogdill's handbook of leadership: A survey of theory and research, (New York: Free Press, 1981).

Swift, C., Hospital Chaplaincy in the Twenty-First Century, 2nd ed. (Farnham: Ashgate, 2014)

Swift, C., Cobb, M., and Todd, A., (eds.), A Handbook of Chaplaincy Studies: Understanding Spiritual Care in Public Places, (Farnham, Surrey: Ashgate, 2015).

Tengan, E., The Land as Being and Cosmos: The Institution of the Earth Cult among the Sisala of north-western Ghana, (Frankfurt Am Main, NY: Peter Lang, 1991).

_____, (ed.), Christianity and Cultural History in Northern Ghana, (Oxford: P.I.E. Peter Lang, 2013).

Threlfall-Holmes, M., and Newitt, M. (eds.), *Being a Chaplain*, (London: SPCK, 2011).

Tienou, T., The Theological Task of the Church in Africa: Theological Perspectives in Africa No. 1, 2nd ed. (Achimota, Accra: Africa Christian Press, 1990).

Todd, A., Slater, V., & Dunlop, S., *The Church of England's involvement in Chaplaincy*, (The Cardiff Centre for Chaplaincy Studies & The Oxford Centre for Ecclesiology and Practical Theology, 2014)

Turaki, Y., *Christianity and African Gods: A Method in Theology*, (Potchefstroomese: S. A. Christain Higher Education Press, 1999).

Vespa, D. C., *To Africa by God's Design*, (East Lakeland, FL: n. p., 2015).

Walls, A. F., The Missionary Movement in Christian History: Studies in the Transmission of Faith, (Maryknoll: Orbis Books, 2000).

Walters, J., and Bradley, C., 'Chaplaincy and Evangelism', in Caperon, J., Todd, A., and Walters, J., (eds.), *A Christian Theology of Chaplaincy*, (London: JKP, 2018), pp. 143-57.

Wilks, I., Forests of Gold. Essays on the Akan and the Kingdom of Asante, (Athens: OH, 1993).

Williamson, S. G., and Bardsley, J., *The Gold Coast: What of the Church?* (London: Edinburgh House Press, 1953).

Woodhead, L., 'Introduction', In Woodhead L., and Catto, R., (eds), *Religion and Change in Modern Britain*, (Abingdon: Routledge, 2012a), pp. 1-33.

Yankah, K., *Crossroads at Ankobea*, (Accra: Asempa Publishers, 1986).

Journals

Addo-Fening, R., 'From Traditionalist to Christian Evangelist and Teacher – The Religious Itinerary and Legacy of Emmanuel Yaw Boakye (1834-1914)', *Journal of African Christian Thought,* Vol. 7, No. 1, (Akropong-Akwapem: Akrofi-Christaller Institute of Theology, Mission and Culture, June 2004), pp. 3-13.

Afriyie, E., 'Christ our Perfect Sacrifice: The Odwira Festival and Christianity in Contemporary Ghana', *Journal of African Christian Thought,* Vol. 17, No. 1, Akropong-Akwapem: Akrofi-Christaller Institute of Theology, Mission and Culture, June 2014), pp. 26-33.

Amanor, K. J. D., 'Pentecostal and Charismatic Churches in Ghana and African Culture: Confrontation or Compromise?' *Journal of Pentecostal Theology* 18 (2009) 123-40.

Anamzoya, A. S., 'Neither fish nor fowl': an analysis of status ambiguity of Houses of Chiefs in Ghana', *The Journal of Legal Pluralism and Unofficial Law,* 46.2, (2014), pp. 218-34 DOI: 10.1080/07329113.2014.902652 [accessed 12 February 2017].

Anderson, A. H., and Hollenweger, W. J., (eds.), *Pentecostals after a Century: Global Perspectives and a Movement in Transition,* (JPTSup, 15; Sheffield: Sheffield Academic Press, 1999), p. 190.

A Guide to Manhyia Palace Museum, (Kumasi: Otumfuo Opoku Ware Jubilee Foundation, 2003).

Attride-Stirling, J., 'Thematic networks: An analytical tool for qualitative research', *Qualitative Research,* 1, (2001), 385-405.

Ballard, P., 'Locating Chaplaincy: A Theological Note', *Crucible: The Christian Journal of Social Ethics,* July-September 2009, pp. 18-24.

Banks, J. A., 'The Lives and Values of Researchers: Implications for Educating Citizens in a Multicultural Society', *Educational Researcher*, 27 (1998), pp. 4-17 < http://www.jstor.org/stable/1176055 > [accessed 12 August 2019].

Bediako, K., 'Gospel and Culture: Some Insights for Our Time from the Experience of the Earliest Church', *Journal of African Thought*, 2.2. (1999), pp. 8-17.

Boafo-Arthur, K., 'Chieftaincy in Ghana: Challenges and Prospects in the 21st Century', *African and Asian Studies*, vol. 2, no. 2, pp. 126-53, http://www.brill.com> [accessed 7 January 2017].

Braun, V., & Clarke, V., 'Using thematic analysis in psychology', *Qualitative Research in Psychology*, 3, (2006), 77-101.

Burgess, R., 'Pentecostalism and Democracy in Nigeria: Electoral Politics, Prophetic Practices and Cultural Reformation', *Nova Religio*, Vol. 18, Issue: 3, pp. 38-62.

Crompton, A., 'The architecture of Multifaith spaces: God leaves the building', *The Journal of Architecture* (2013), 18:4, 474-96, DOI: 10.1080/13602365.2013.821149 [accessed 1 June 2017].

Davis, D. C., '"Then the White man Came with His Whitish Ideas...": The British and the Evolution of Traditional Government in Mamprugu', *The International Journal of African Historical Studies*, Vol. 20, No. 4 (1987), pp. 627-46.

Drucker-Brown S., 'The Court and the Cola Nut: Wooing and Witnessing in Northern Ghana', *The Journal of the Royal Anthropological Institute*, Vol. 1 No. 1 (March, 995), <http://about.jstor.org/terms> [accessed 7 January 2017].

_____, 'Mamprusi installation ritual and centralisation: a convection Model', *The Journal of Royal Anthropological Institute (MAN) 24, No. 3*, (University of Cambridge, 1989).

_____, 'Horse, dog, and donkey: the making of a Mamprusi king', *The Journal of Royal Anthropological Institute, (MAN)* 27, No.1, (1992).

_____, 'The Grandchildren's Play at the Mamprusi King's Funeral: Ritual Rebellion Revisited in Northern Ghana', *The Journal of the Royal Anthropological Institute,* Vol. 5, No. 2 (June 1999), pp.181-92 <http://www.jstor.org/stable/2660692> [accessed: 7 January 2017].

Dwyer, S. C., and Buckle, J. L., 'The Space Between: On Being an Insider-Outsider in Qualitative Research', *International Journal of Qualitative Methods,* 8 (2009), pp. 54-63.

Feeley-Harnik, G., 'Issues in Divine Kingship', *Annual Review of Anthropology,* Vol. 14 (1985), pp. 273-313.

Fereday, J., & Muir-Cochrane, E., 'Demonstrating rigor using thematic analysis: A hybrid approach of inductive and deductive coding and theme development', *International Journal of Qualitative Methods,* 5, pp. 1-11.

Foli, R., *Christianity in Ghana: A Comparative Church Growth Study,* (Accra: Trust Publications, 2006).

Frimpong-Manso, P., 'Theological Education of Assemblies of God Ghana', in *Journal of the European Pentecostal Theological Association,* 33.2 (2013), p. 162-75.

Garlock, H. B., 'Africa and Her People', *The Pentecostal Evangel,* No. 1778, (Springfield, MO: June 5, 1948).

Gilbert, M., 'The Christian Executioner: Christianity and Chieftaincy as Rivals', *Journal of Religion in Africa,* Vol. 25 (Nov. 1995), pp. 347-86.

Gilbert, M., and Jenkins, P., 'The King, His Soul and the Pastor: Three Views of a Conflict in Akropong 1906-7', *Journal of Religion in Africa,* Vol. 38 (2008), pp. 359-415.

Hiebert, P. G., 'Transforming Worldviews', *Mission Focus: Annual Review,* Vol. 10, (2002), <www.anabaptistwiki.org> [accessed 20 February 2017].

Iqbal, N., Radulescu, A., Bains, A., Aleem, S., 'An Interpretative Phenomenological Analysis of a Religious

Conversion', *Journal of Religion and Health,* 58: (2019), pp. 426–43.

Kleist, N., 'Modern Chiefs: Tradition, Development and Return among Traditional Authorities in Ghana', *African Affairs,* Vol. 110, No. 441 (2011), pp. 629-47.

Kowalski, R. D., 'What Made Them Think They Could? Ten Early Assemblies of God Female Missionaries', *Assemblies of God Heritage: Celebrating 100 Years of the Assemblies of God, Vol. 34,* (Springfield, MO: Gospel Publishing House, 2014).

Kpobi, D. N. A., 'African Chaplains in Seventeenth Century West Africa', in *African Christianity,* pdf, pp. 140-71, https://repository.up.ac.za/bitstream/handle/2263/21579/007_Chapter6> [accessed 21 January 2017].

Lehmann, H. S., 'The Ghana Story', *Assemblies of God Ghana 1931-1981,* (Accra: AOG Printing Press, 1981).

MacGaffey, W., 'Death of a king, death of a kingdom? Social pluralism and succession to high office in Dagbon, northern Ghana', *Journal of Modern African Studies,* 44, 1 (Cambridge: Cambridge University Press, 2006), pp. 79-99.

Mason, M., 'Sample size and saturation in PhD studies using qualitative interviews', *Forum: Qualitative Social Research,* 11(3) Art. 8 (September 2010), <http://nbn-resolving.de/urn:nbn:de:0114-fqs100387> [accessed 3 January 2019].

Meyer, B., 'Make a Complete Break with the Past' Memory and Post-Colonial Modernity in Ghanaian Pentecostal Discourse', *Journal of Religion in Africa,* Vol. 28 (Aug. 1998), pp. 316-49.

Meyer, B., 'Translating the Devil: Religion and Modernity among the Ewe of Southeastern Ghana', *Ghana Studies Review,* (2001).

Mullings, B., 'Insider or Outsider, Both or Neither: Some

Dilemmas of Interviewing in a Cross-cultural Setting', *Geoforum*, 30 (1999), pp. 337-50.

Natogma, E. A., 'Leadership Styles in Assemblies of God Bible Colleges in West Africa: A Study of Perspectives of Alumni, Academic Deans and Presidents', *PhD Thesis*, (Ann Arbor, MI: ProQuest LLC, 2008).

Nelson, M., 'Phenomenological approaches to religion and spirituality', In J. M. Nelson, (ed.), *Psychology, Religion, and Spirituality*, (Springer, New York, NY: 2009), pp. 103-42.

Nketia, J. H. K., 'Christianity and African Culture: Remodelling Tradition', *Journal of African Thought*, Vol. 13, No. 1, (Akropong- Akwapem: Akrofi-Christaller Institute of Theology, Mission and Culture, (June 2010), pp. 10-18.

Obeng, P., 'Re-Membering Through Oath: Installation of African Kings and Queens', *Journal of Black Studies*, Vol. 28, No. 3 (Jan. 1998), pp. 334-56.

Omenyo, C. N., 'Agenda for a Discussion of African Initiatives in Christianity: The West African/Ghanaian Case' in *Missiology: An International Review*, Vol XXXIX, no. 3, July, ATLAS, pdf [accessed 5 June 2014].

Peel, D. J. Y., 'History, Culture and Comparative Method,' in *Comparative Anthropology*, ed. by L. Holy, (Oxford: Oxford University Press, 1987).

Ray, D. I., & van Rouveroy van Nieuwal, E.A.B., 'The New Relevance of Traditional Authorities in Africa', *The Journal of Legal Pluralism and Unofficial Law*, (1996), 28:37-38, 1-38, DOI: 10.1080/07329113.1996.10756473 [accessed 17 January 2017].

Shaw, R. D., 'Beyond Syncretism: A Dynamic Approach to Hybridity', *International Bulletin of Mission Research, 2018 Vol. 42(1)*, <https://uk.sagepub.com> pdf [accessed 6 February 2018].

Slater, V., 'The fresh significance of chaplaincy for the Mission and Ministry of the Church of England: Three case studies in community contexts', *Thesis*, (Anglia Ruskin University, 2013).

Stetzer, E., 'A Brief History of 'Missional': Moving from Concept and Conversation to Leaving it out', *The Exchange: Missiology*, Feb. 23, 2015, <http://www.christianitytoday.com> [accessed 11 August 2016].

Swift, C., 'How should Health Care Chaplaincy negotiate its Professional Identity?' in Ward, F., Hampton, C., and Woodward, J., (eds.), *Contact: The interdisciplinary Journal of Pastoral Studies*, 144, (Oxford: Contact, 2004), pp. 4-13.

Todd, A., 'Chaplaincy Leading Church in(to) the Public Square', *Crucible: The Christian Journal of Social Ethics*, October-December 2011, pp. 7-15.

Ubink, J., 'Traditional Authority Revisited: Popular Perceptions of Chiefs and Chieftaincy in Peri-Urban Kumasi, Ghana', *The Journal of Legal Pluralism and Unofficial Law*, 39:55, (2007), pp. 123-61, DOI: 10.1080/07329113.2007.10756610 [accessed 12 February 2017].

White, P., 'A missional study of Ghanaian Pentecostal churches' leadership and leadership formation', *HTS Teologiese Studies/Theological Studies*, 71(3), Art. #2865, (2015), <http://dx.doi.org/10.4102/hts.v71i3.2865> [accessed 2 March 2016].

Peter White, P., and Niemandt, C. J. P., 'Ghanaian Pentecostal Churches' Mission Approaches', Journal of Pentecostal Theology, 24, (2015), pp. 241-69.

William, H., Trey & KJ's, 'The Hauns in Africa', <http://haunsinafrica.com/2014/11/10/bugum-fire-festival/> [accessed 29 January 2017].

Internet

Akuaku III, Dzetse Nene A. K., 'Clergy and Traditional
    Rulers need to work together', *Ghana News Agency*, 12th
    April 2013, <http://www.ghanaweb.com> [accessed 15
    October 2014].

Arts Ghana, 'Damba as a festival and dance form', Admin,
    July 11, 2014, <http://artsghana.org/damba-as-a-
    festival-and-dance-form/> [accessed 30 January 2017].

Anderson, A.H., 'Contextualization in Pentecostalism: A
    Multicultural Perspective', *Academia*, https://www.
    academia.edu pdf, [accessed 28 February 2020].

Asamoah-Gyadu, K., 'African Pentecostal/Charismatic
    Christianity: An Overview', <https://www.
    lausanneworldpulse.com/themedarticles-php/464/08-
    2006> [accessed 9 December 2017].

Assemblies of God, Ghana, 'Vision 3000', <http://www.
    agghana.org/v3000/vision-3000.html> [accessed 1
    February 2017].

Assemblies of God, Ghana, 'AoG Statement of Fundamental
    Truths', https://www.agghana.org/fundamental-truth/
    [accessed, 13th March 2020].

Canada: Immigration and Refugee Board of
    Canada, 'Ghana: Information on the number of
    paramount chiefs and wing chiefs including the names
    and the authority they wield', 1 May 1993, https://www.
    refworld.org/docid/3ae6acdd5c.html> [accessed 27
    November 2017].

Central Intelligence Agency, 'The World Factbook',
    <https://www.cia.gov/library/publications/resources/
    the-world-factbook/geos/gh.html> [accessed 28
    December 2018].

Christ Apostolic Church International, <http://cacihq.org>
    [accessed 26 October 2015].

Evangelical Free Church of America, *Chaplains Handbook*, (Chaplains Commission: 2013), https://www.efca.org [accessed 15 July 2019].

Eshun, D., 'A study of social ministry of some Charismatic Churches in Ghana: A case study of the provision of educational and healthcare services by four selected churches', *Thesis*, (MPhil), (Accra: University of Ghana, 2013), pdf <http://ugspace.ug.edu.gh> [accessed 17 November 2017].

Festivals in Ghana, <http://www.ghanagrio.com/ festivals/> [accessed 29 October 2016].

Ghana News Agency, 'Religion', 12th April 2013, http:// www.ghanaweb.com/GhanaHomePage/religion> [accessed, 7 November 2014].

Ghana News Agency, 'Religion', 2nd January 2013, http:// www.ghanaweb.com/GhanaHomePage/religion> [accessed, 3 January 2013].

Ghana Religions, <https://www.indexmundi.com/ghana/ religions.html> [accessed 28 December 2018].

Ghana Rural Integrated Development (GRID) and Northern Empowerment Association (NEA), <https://grid-nea. org/about> [accessed 12 April 2017].

Google Images, 'Northern Ghana Chiefs', https://www. google.co.uk/search?q=northern+ghana+chiefs&client> [accessed 20 December 2016].

Google images, 'Political Map of Ghana', https://www. google.com/search?q=political+map+of+ghana> [accessed, 12 February 2018].

Ikenye, N.J. B., 'Chaplaincy: African Theory and Practice of Clinical Pastoral Care and Cure of the Soul', (Nairobi, Kenya: St Paul's University, 2011), https://www. academia.edu [accessed 25 September 2019].

Kornu, M. A. Rev., 'Christians can be Chiefs', *Catholic Diocese of Ho*, (Accra: GNA, 23rd June 2013), <http://www. ghanaweb.com> [accessed 17 March 2014].

Mensah, B., '2011 Christian Chiefs Conference', *GRID & NEA Sustainable Development in Ghana*, May 2011, p. 3, <https://grid-nea.org/wp-content/uploads/2011/05/GRID-Newsletter-May-2011.pdf> [accessed 12 April 2014].

Opuni-Frimpong, K., 'Let's take the Gospel to the Palace', *Ghana News Agency*, (Accra: Christian Council of Ghana) <http://www.ghanaweb.com> [accessed 21 January 2014].

Osei Tutu II, Asantehene Otumfuo, 'The Role of Modern Traditional Chiefs in Development in Africa', an address delivered at the 2nd *Bonn Conference on International Development Policy*, World Conference Centre, Bonn, Germany, 27th-28th August 2009, <http://manhyiaonline.org> [accessed 2 November 2014].

The Apostolic Church Ghana, <http://www.theapostolicchurch.org.gh> [accessed 12 September 2014].

The Church of Pentecost, Ghana, <http://www.thecophq.org> [accessed 3 November 2016].

The Constitution of Ghana, <http://ghana.gov.gh/images/documents/constitution_ghana.pdf> [accessed, 4 November 2017].

The General Council of the Assemblies of God, Ghana, 'Assemblies of God Statement of Fundamental Truths', <http://www.agghana.org/gchq/fundamental-truths.html> [accessed, 11 August 2016].

The St. George Church – Police Depot was recently elevated to a Parish in April 2016. <http://accracatholic.org/st-george-church> [accessed 24 July 2016].

Webster, D., 'Christian Chiefs Conference 2014', *GRID & NEA Sustainable Development in Ghana*, GRID Newsletter May 2014, p. 2 <https://grid-nea.org/wp-content/uploads/2014/05/GRID-Newsletter-May-2014.pdf> [accessed 12 April 2017].

Unpublished Sources

Aryeetey, E. A., 'A Paper on the Abokobi Chieftaincy Institution' to Commemorate the 10th Anniversary Celebrations of the Installation of Nii Samuel Adjetey Mohenu as Chief of Abokobi (Presbyterian Women's Centre, Abokobi, 4th August 2007).

Awedoba, A. K., et. Al, 'Traditional Leadership Rules and Ceremonies in the Upper Region of Ghana', (Tamale: n.d.).

Brobbey, J., Interviewed at Manhyia Palace Museum, (Kumasi: 14th February 2014).

Dickinson, J. R., District Commissioner, Eastern Province, Kumasi, 21st August 1931.

Fiennes, E., Lt. Col. Bart, Governor, Registered No. D 367/20, Government House, Seychelles, 2nd February 1921.

Frimpong-Manso P., 'The origins, growth, developments and influence of Assemblies of God, Ghana', *PhD Thesis,* (Glyndwr University, 2014).

Fuller, F. C., Chief Commissioner, Ashanti, to The Revd. Samuel Kwafo, Basel Mission, Mampong 11th December 1915.

Grey, J. N., 'Holiness and Incarnation in Isaiah 1-39: the implications of Isaiah's Mission for a Pentecostal Ecclesiology', in a paper presented at European Pentecostal Theological Association Conference, (Elim Conference Centre, Malvern, UK: EPTA Conference, 3-6th July 2017).

Heard, J., 'Re-evangelizing Britain? An Ethnographical Analysis and Theological valuation of the Alpha Course', *PhD Thesis,* (London: King's College, 2008).

Kwafo, S., to Juase, D. C., Mampong, Ahanti: Basel Mission, 11th September 1915.

Prempeh, E. (Ex-King of Ashanti) Le Rocher, Ashanti Camp,

Seychelles, 13th December 1920.

Walter Edward Davidson, Governor, 'Correspondence copy No. 449/1911', Government House, Seychelles, to His Excellency, the Governor, Gold Coast, 3rd March 1911.

Watterworth, W. G., Acting General Superintendent, Wesleyan Methodist Missionary Society, Gold Coast District, West Africa, 20th July 1931.

Waterworth, W. G., to Arthur J. Philbrick, Wesleyan Mission Society, Coomassie, West Africa, 11th September 1914.

Yamusa, P. D., *A History of Assemblies of God, Ghana*, (Kumbungu: n.d.).

Yidana, G. N., 'Pentecostalism in Northern Ghana, Origins, Growth & Potentials', *MTh. Thesis*, (Mattersey Hall: University of Wales Bangor, 2006).

Scriptural Index

General Index

Appendices

Appendix 1: Thematic Analysis

Table 7.1: Thematic analysis

Thematic Analysis

1. Codes	2. Basic Themes	3. Organizing Themes	4. Global Themes
Corruption	Christians to avoid chieftaincy	7.2.1 Chieftaincy as a dark institution	7.2 Perceptions of the institution of chieftaincy
Satanic influences	The dangers of getting involved Negative perceptions		
Taboos		7.2.2 Lack of education	
Rituals/sacrifices			
Shun chieftaincy	God's power required		
Idol worshiping	to succeed		
Compromise	Temptation to compromise God's standards	7.2.3 Divine protection required to succeed	
Persecution			
Fear of death	Chiefs play pastoral role		
Fervent prayers			
God's protection			
Leaders	Chiefs decide the course of the community	7.2.4 Chiefs as heads of the communities	
Influencers			
Role models			
Chiefs are adored			

Ministers to get closer to chiefs	Missionaries failed to encourage chieftaincy	8.1.1 Integration of chieftaincy and Christianity	8.1 Role of Chieftaincy in transforming the institution of chieftaincy
Not hostile	Tradition is not evil	8.1.2 Improved understanding of culture and tradition	
		8.1.3 Chaplains as godly counsellors	
Not shun tradition	Appreciation of cultural values	8.1.4 Good rapport with chiefs opens the door to the community	
Understanding tradition	Build good relationship with chiefs	8.1.5 Education of chiefs on biblical perspectives of chieftaincy	
Romans Catholics as an example	Chieftaincy as a revered institution	8.1.6 Changing outmoded cultural practices	
Encourage Christians to get involved	Christians involvement can reduce corruption		
Cultural values	Syncretism in Christianity		
Culture not fetish			
No more human sacrifices			
Communities appreciate chiefs			
Chiefs are gatekeepers			

Church approval and educate chiefs	Church leadership meet kingmakers	8.2.1 Getting involved in the installation process of Christian chiefs	8.2 Calls for chaplaincy involvement in chieftaincy
Prayer support from church	Church involvement in enskinment / enstoolment		
God installs chiefs			
Chieftaincy belongs to Christians			
Pastors to install chiefs			
Doing it the Christian way			
Installation process demonized			
Target chiefs			
	Changing bad perceptions about the institution of chieftaincy	8.2.2 Meeting the spiritual needs of chiefs	
Praying for chiefs	Chiefs presence in church is motivating		
Share the love of Christ	A chief's salvation affects the family and community		
Schools and hospitals	Meeting the physical needs of the community	8.2.3 Meeting the needs of the community through partnership with chiefs	
Social action			
Advisors	Providing good counsel to chiefs		

Appendix 2: Letter of invitation to Christian and traditional leaders, consent form and questionnaire

Letter of Invitation to Participants – Christian Leaders

Name:

Address:

Date:

Dear Name

Christianity and the Chieftaincy Institution in Ghana

This letter is an invitation for you to consider participating in a study I am conducting on Christianity and Chieftaincy as part of my Doctorate degree in the Department of Theology and Religious Studies at the University of Chester under the Supervision of Dr Anne Dyer.

The study aims to find out the influence that Christianity has made on the Chieftaincy Institution in Ghana. It is my hope that the information on the findings of this study will assist church leaders in the formulation of future mission strategies and theological views amongst Pentecostal denominations. It will also help to find out ways in providing pastoral care to the chieftaincy institution.

You are a very important person; a church leader of your denomination and I will like to find out your views on this study. The research will be conducted in the Northern, Ashanti and Volta regions of Ghana. If you decide to take part in the study, I will visit you at a time convenient to you for an hour of interview. You might also be asked to participate in a regional discussion with other leaders on the subject.

I have included some detailed information about the study with this letter, together with a consent form for your consideration.

Thank you.

Yours Sincerely,

Gabriel Yidana

Letter of Invitation to Participants - Traditional Leaders

Name:

Address:

Date:

Dear Name

Christianity and the Institution of Chieftaincy in Ghana

This letter is an invitation for you to consider participating in a study I am conducting on Christianity and Chieftaincy as part of my Doctorate degree in the Department of Theology and Religious Studies at the University of Chester under the Supervision of Dr Anne Dyer.

The study aims to find out the influence that Christianity has made on the Chieftaincy Institution in Ghana. It is my hope that the information on the findings of this study will assist church leaders in the formulation of future mission strategies and theological views amongst Pentecostal denominations. It will also enhance a mutual understanding and cooperation amongst Christianity and chieftaincy for peaceful co-existence and national development in serving the people under their care.

You are a very important person; a prominent leader and chief of your community and I will like to find out your views on this study. The research will be conducted in the Northern, Ashanti and Volta regions of Ghana. If you decide to take part in the study, I will visit you at a time convenient to you for an hour of interview. You might also be asked to participate in a regional discussion with other leaders on the subject.

I have included some detailed information about the study with this letter, together with a consent form for your consideration.

Thank you.

Yours Sincerely,

Gabriel Yidana

Consent Form

Title of Project: Christianity and the Chieftaincy Institution in Ghana

Name of Researcher: Gabriel Yidana

Please initial box

1. I confirm that I have read and understood the participant information sheet, dated ...., for the above study and have had the opportunity to ask questions.
2. I understand that my participation is voluntary and that I am free to withdraw at any time, without giving any reason and without my care or legal rights being affected.
3. I agree to take part in the above study.

Name of Participant:

Date:

Signature:

Name of Person taking consent (if different from researcher):

Date:

Signature:

Researcher:

Date:

Signature:

Questionnaires for Christian and Traditional Leaders

Section A. Demographic Information

Q1. Questionnaire Number:

Date:

Venue:

Q2 Region:

(a) Northern

(b) Ashanti

Q3. Community / Tribe:

Q4 Stakeholder type:

(a) Chief

(b) Traditional Elder

(c) Minister

(d) Church lay leader

Q5 Gender:

(a) Male

(b) Female

Section B. Stakeholders Interviews

B1 General Questions

Q6. What is the importance of a chief in the spiritual development of a community?

Q7. What is the importance of a chief in the socio-economic development of a community?

Q8. Why should Christians be involved in chieftaincy?

- As a chief

- As Elders

- As advisors / chaplains

Q9. How do you think early Pentecostal Missionaries perceived African Traditional Religion (ATR)?

Q10. What were some of the Missionaries' engagements with chiefs?

Q11. How do you think Missionaries influenced attitudes of Christians towards ATR and the involvement of Christians in chieftaincy?

Q12. How do you think the Roman Catholics view ATR and the institution of chieftaincy?

Q13. How do you think Protestants and Evangelicals view ATR and the institution of chieftaincy?

Q14. How do you think Pentecostals view ATR and the institution of chieftaincy?

Q15. How satisfied are you with the current level of involvement of Christianity with the institution of chieftaincy? (a) Highly satisfied (b) Satisfied (c) Not satisfied

Q16. What changes would you want to see?

Q17. How has the church influenced the institution of chieftaincy?

B2. Questions for Chiefs and Traditional Elders

B2.1 Questions for Non-Christian chiefs

Q18. How long have you been a chief?

Q19. Was your father a chief before you?

Q20. How long has your family ruled this area?

Q21. What system is used to appoint chiefs?

Q22. What led you to being appointed in your current role as a chief?

Q23. Are there any great memories that you could share with me concerning this appointment?

Q24. What is your view about chiefs being Christians?

Q25. How would you like Christian candidates to chieftaincy handle ceremonial rites that are in conflict with Christianity?

Q26. Has there been any chief who has been a Christian before you?

Q27. How would you describe his period of reign?

B2.2 Questions for chiefs who were converted to Christianity

Q28. How long have you been a chief?

Q29. Was your father a chief before you?

Q30. How long has your family ruled this area?

Q31. What system is used to appoint a chief

Q32. What led you to being appointed to your current role as a chief?

Q33. Are there any great memories that you could share with me concerning this appointment?

Q34. How did you become a Christian?

Q35. Has your faith as a Christian been of any significance?

Q36. What are some of the challenges you face in expressing your faith as a chief before your peers, subjects and others who are not Christians?

Q37. How would you like Christian candidates to chieftaincy handle ceremonial rites that are in conflict with Christianity?

Q38. Has the church been of any support to you and can you elaborate on ways in which the church has supported you?

Q39. How would you ensure that the church plays an active role in the ceremony preceding the enthroning of a Christian candidate as a chief?

Q40. Has there been any chief who has been a Christian before you?

Q41. How would you describe his period of reign?

Q42. How has the church influenced the chieftaincy institution?

B2.3 Questions for Christians who became chiefs

Q43. How long have you been a chief?

Q44. Was your father a chief before you?

Q45. How long has your family ruled?

Q46. What system is used to appoint a chief?

Q47. What led you to being appointed to your current role as a chief?

Q48. Are there any great memories that you could share with me concerning this appointment?

Q49. How did you handle ceremonial rites that were in conflict with your Christian faith?

Q50. Has your faith as a Christian been of any significance?

Q51. What are some of the challenges you face in expressing your faith as a chief before your peers, subjects, and others who are not Christians?

Q52. Has the church been of any support to you and can you elaborate on ways in which the church has supported you?

Q53. How would you ensure that the church plays an active role in the ceremony preceding the enthroning of a Christian candidate as a chief?

Q54. Has there been any chief who has been a Christian before you?

Q55. How would you describe his period of reign?

Q56. How has Christianity influenced the chieftaincy institution?

B.2.4 Questions for Traditional Elders

Q57. How long have you held your current role of leadership in your community?

Q58. Have you served under a Christian chief before?

Q59. What is the system used in appointing a chief in your community?

Q60. What is your role in the appointment of a chief?

Q61. What are your responsibilities to the chief?

Q62. Which of your responsibilities do conflict with the faith of a Christian chief?

Q63. How would you like these conflicts to be resolved?

Q64. What are your concerns of a Christian becoming a chief?

Q65. How has Christianity influenced the chieftaincy institution?

B3. Questions for Church Ministers and Elders

B3.1 Questions for Ministers

Q66. How long have you been in ministry?

Q67. How do you relate with chiefs in your community?

Q68. Has there been a chief who has been a Christian before and at present in your church?

Q69. What is your general perception of the chieftaincy institution and Christianity?

Q70. What are the theological concerns, if any, do you have for a Christian becoming a chief?

Q71. How can these concerns be resolved?

Q72. Would you advocate that the church plays an active role in the ceremony preceding the enthroning of a Christian candidate as a chief?

Q73. What in your view would conflict traditional and cultural demands to the previous question?

Q74. How can these challenges to the previous question be resolved?

Q75. How has Christianity influenced the chieftaincy institution?

Q76. How has chieftaincy culture influenced church leadership?

B3.2 Questions for Church Lay Leaders/Deacons

Q77. How long have you been a lay leader in church?

Q78. What is your general perception of the chieftaincy institution and Christianity?

Q79. How would you like the church to be involved in the ceremony preceding the enthroning of a Christian candidate as a chief?

Q80. What is the significance of a chief being a member of the church you attend?

Q81. What kind of support should the church give to Christian chiefs?

Q82. How has the culture of chieftaincy influenced the role of church leaders?

Q83. How has Christianity influenced the chieftaincy institution?

Appendix 3: The CoP Conference for Christian Royals

THE CHURCH OF PENTECOST - GENERAL HEADQUARTERS

OFFICE OF THE CHAIRMAN
P.O. Box 2194, Accra-Ghana
Tel: (+233)-0302-772193; Res: 0302-222861
Fax: (+233)-0302-774721; (Mob) 054-0826525
E-mail: chairman@thecophq.org

OUR REF: COP/CO/VOL.30/1142/13

YOUR REF:

November 28, 2013

All Area HeadS
The Church of Pentecost
Ghana

Dear Sir,

CONFERENCE FOR CHRISTIAN ROYALS - 2014

I am directed by the Chairman to inform you that the Church is organising a Conference for Christian Royals (Chiefs and Queens) from February 17 – 20, 2014 at the Pentecost Conference Centre, Gomoa Fetteh.

The list of chiefs and queens in the Church submitted to the Chairman's office in 2011 is being updated.

He should be grateful therefore, if you could submit the names of chiefs and queens in your Area using the attached format by December 31, 2013.

Yours faithfully,

SAMUEL OTU APPIAH (PS.)
PERSONAL ASST. TO CHAIRMAN

For: Chairman

Document announcing the first royal conference of the Church of Pentecost. Document obtained from one of the participants' interviewed: NRCL2, Interview, (Tamale, 4th February 2014).

Appendix 4: Minister of chieftaincy and traditional affairs address at the first conference of Christian traditional rulers

REPUBLIC OF GHANA

MINISTRY OF CHIEFTAINCY
AND TRADITIONAL AFFAIRS
P. O. BOX 1627
STATE HOUSE
ACCRA

www.mcta.gov.gh

ADDRESS BY THE MINISTER FOR CHIEFTANCY AND TRADITIONAL AFFAIRS, (HON. DR. H. S. DAANAA) AT THE CONFERENCE HELD AT GOMOA FETTEH (KASOA), ON FRIDAY 13TH JUNE 2014 ORGANISED BY THE CHURCH OF PENTECOST FOR CHRISTIAN TRADITIONAL RULERS.

THEME: "IMPACTING GENERATIONS: THE CHURCH'S MISSION TO THE PALACE".

Members of the Executive Council of the Church of Pentecost, All Christian Traditional Rulers present, Nananom, Fellow participants, Distinguished Guests Friends from the Media, Clergymen, Ladies and Gentlemen, it is a great pleasure for me to be invited as Sector Minister to participate in this memorable ceremony.

Looking carefully at the various contributions made by both the Church and the Palace (Traditional Rule)to the peace and development of our society, we can conclude that they share a common goal that is to say, uplifting the betterment of community life thought out the length and breadth of the country.

As Minister for Chieftaincy and Traditional Affairs, I am well aware that, the responsibility of my Ministry covers the full range of Chieftaincy Administration. Against his background, the importance of this conference cannot be over emphasized. It is a development that marks a healthy beginning of collaboration between Clergy and Traditional Rule in Ghana. Indeed, we must not at all forget the wise saying that the voice of the people is the voice of God. So as to speed up the process of development of our dear country Ghana, the message is simple: let us all work together (Church and Palace alike) to serve the good people of Ghana.

Last but not the least, my appeal to all of you who have participated in this Historic Conference is to take advantage of the opportunity afforded us all to worship and pray to the Almighty God to continue to bless abundantly our Clergy, our Chiefs and our Government, and to give all the strength they need to be able to carry this Country higher and higher the ladder of success.

I congratulate you all for taking this bold and noble step forward. While thanking the Church of Pentecost for a good job done, I will like to end by saying: may Lord bless us all and make Ghana great and strong. Amen.

**The Church of Pentecost, Ghana, <http://www.thecophq.org>
[accessed 3 November 2016].**

Appendix 5: Quotes of some participants at the 2017 Northern Christian Chiefs' Conference (Carpenter, Brong Ahafo Region)

GRID Newsletter Spring 2017 p. 3

2017 Northern Christian Chiefs' Conference

NEA once again hosted the annual conference for Northern Christian Chiefs. Participants spent three full days together, learning about leadership, community development, and peace building from a Christian perspective. They shared stories about situations they faced as community leaders, giving and receiving advice from one another. A number of them offered their thoughts on the importance of the Northern Ghana Christian Chiefs' Association (NGCCA) and its annual conference in their role as community leaders:

66 I thought this would be a meeting of old folks resting, eating, and having fun, but I was mistaken. I didn't know the program was going to be full of relevant activities. Next time I will prepare well! I have met many Christian chiefs and spent quality time with God. Here we use our own words to speak our hearts out to the Lord. When I go back to my community, I will be fair in dealing with my people.

66 This has been a big door that God opened to help me in ruling as Paramount Chief. I am learning to be humble and sincere as a leader and to love my people.

66 This association has helped me stop pagan practices in my chiefdom. People in my community have seen a drastic change in their lives. I am very glad; as I think back to when this association started, I now see present some colleagues who I never expected to be a part of this. Being a Christian chief is good because there is liberty in Christ. I am free of entanglements.

66 I have used the experience gained from the Chiefs' Association and Conference to organize my people to improve teamwork and encourage one another.

66 I have learned a lot from this Association and from NEA. I was inspired by the turkeys that I saw raised on NEA's Project site and embarked on turkey rearing when I returned to my home town. I now have 40 turkeys. I have also learned to solve problems amicably in my community. I am learning to be firm and just in my decisions in ways that do not extort money from the poor.

GRID & NEA, GRID Update: News from Northern Ghana, Spring 2017, <https://grid-nea.org/wp-content/uploads/2017/03/GRID-Newsletter-Mar-2017-vFin.pdf> p. 3 [accessed 12 April 2017].

Appendix 6: Images of Christian leaders at a festival and chiefs at church services

Anglican and Roman Catholic Priests at *Akwasidei* festival

The researcher at the *Akwasidei* festival

Chiefs among worshipers at church services.

Images taken from *Akwasidae* festival, (Kumasi: 2014), AoGG and Anglican church services (Accra and Kumasi) and Lehmann, 'Story', p. 2.

"The Tamale chief came to church every Sunday", 1934.

About the Book

This book sets out to understand why there has been relatively little constructive missional engagement between Christianity and chieftaincy, and what advantages there might be for Pentecostalism to adopt chaplaincy to chieftaincy as an effective ministry and form of mission. It does so within a historical account and empirical research framework (in the form of 50 participant interviews) that identifies key themes that characterise prevailing attitudes, placing these in theological context. It is based on my experience as a minister and the experiences of Christian and traditional leaders who have generously given their time in responding to my doctoral research on this subject.

As I begin to explore this question, I remember my early years of joining the teaching staff of Northern Ghana Bible Institute from the mid 1990s where the principal, Rev James Abdulai bemoaned the absence of theological literature that reflected the Ghanaian cultural context. Historically, there is a long tradition of chaplaincy ministry developed over the years to serve the spiritual needs of people in different contexts. Although chaplaincy may mean different things to different people, I have used it here to reflect its ability to offer spiritual services to people outside the traditional setting of sacred religious sites like church buildings used for places of worship. Hence, the corridor and traditional setting of chieftaincy could be a place where Christian chaplaincy ministry may strive.

This book therefore aims to provide a historical narrative of chieftaincy, its responsibilities and associated cultural practices. It sets out to provide a missiological case for Christian witness to traditional leadership, some conceptual clarity for ministry opportunities in chieftaincy and practical suggestions for the development and support of Christians serving in the institution of chieftaincy. My intention is that this book will be useful for church leaders to develop intentional missional policies to engage with traditional leadership. I also hope that it will be helpful to students and those involved in researching practice. It is intended for lay and ordained people in church ministry, theological and ministerial educators, leaders in mission and ministry and Christian traditional leaders. It, of course, may not prove to be an easy read, but the evidence presented here may provide a basis for ongoing discussion on Christian ministry to chieftaincy.

About the Author

Rev Dr Gabriel N Yidana is a Ghanaian ordained minister of the Assemblies of God living in England, UK. He has been in full-time ministry for over 28years. The first fifteen years were ministry in Ghana as a Pastor and Bible College teacher. He is currently the Senior Minister of Good Shepherd Church (AoG, GB) at Leeds, West Yorkshire and teaches church history, missiology, theology and leadership at the Leeds, Manchester and London campuses of ForMission College, UK. His theological qualification includes a Diploma in Biblical Studies from the premier Assemblies of God Bible College at Kumbungu near Tamale - Ghana (NGBI), a BTh from West African Advanced School of Theology (WAAST) in Lomé -Togo, MTh from Mattersey Hall (University of Wales, Bangor, UK) and a doctorate in Pentecostal History & Missiology from University of Chester, UK. He is a conference speaker, mentor and member of some theological associations in Europe and Africa. He is married to Joana and blessed with four children.

Printed in Great Britain
by Amazon